SUPERHERO THOUGHT EXPERIMENTS

SUPERHERO THOUGHT EXPERIMENTS

Comic Book Philosophy

CHRIS GAVALER
AND
NATHANIEL GOLDBERG

UNIVERSITY OF IOWA PRESS, IOWA CITY

University of Iowa Press, Iowa City 52242
Copyright © 2019 by the University of Iowa Press
www.uipress.uiowa.edu

ISBN 978-1-60938-655-9 (pbk)
ISBN 978-1-60938-656-6 (ebk)

Printed in the United States of America

Design by April Leidig

Printed on acid-free paper

Cataloging-in-Publication data is on file
with the Library of Congress.

To the memories of our mothers—

Judy Gavaler

1939–2018

Doris Briggs

1947–2017

CONTENTS

ACKNOWLEDGMENTS

We'd like to thank Mark LeBar, Tracy Lupher, and Howard Pickett for comments on various chapters, and Robert Arp, Peter Coogan, Matt Smith, and especially Rachael Miller for comments on the entire book. We'd also like to thank Washington and Lee University for Lenfest summer and sabbatical funding. We'd like to thank, as well, Ranjit Arab, Meredith T. Stabel, and everyone else at the University of Iowa Press, Michael P. Patton and several anonymous referees, and Christi Stanforth, for suggestions and support. Finally, we'd like to thank our families for putting up not just with the superheroes, not just with the philosophy, but also for this time with both.

Several chapters draw from previously published coauthored work. Chapter 1 draws from "Time to Choose," in *Batman, Superman, and Philosophy*, ed. Nicolas Michaud (Open Court, 2016), 143–52. Chapter 3 draws from "Marvels of Scepticism," *Foundation: The International Review of Science Fiction* 126 (2017): 21–34. Chapter 4 draws from "Dr. Doom's Philosophy of Time," *Journal of Graphic Novels and Comics* 8 (2017): 321–40. Chapter 6 draws from "Alan Moore, Donald Davidson, and the Mind of Swampmen," *Journal of Popular Culture* 50 (2017): 239–58. And chapter 8 draws from "Economy of the Comic Book Author's Soul," *International Journal of Comic Art* 18 (2016): 331–54.

Finally, a note on ellipses within quotations. Bracketed ellipses, like "[. . .]," represent words that we've omitted. Unbracketed ellipses, like ". . . ," occur in the original.

W hat if an evil genius is tricking you into believing that the world around you is real when it really isn't?

What if on an alternate Earth everything is identical but for one almost undetectable detail?

What if trying to travel to the past transported you to a different universe instead?

What if a mad scientist removed your brain and is keeping it alive in a vat of nutrients?

What if lightning struck a dead tree in a swamp and transformed it into The Swampman?

Any of these fantastical plots could be the premise of a superhero comic book. Stan Lee sometimes gave artists at Marvel little more to work with—just a note on a piece of paper or a plot point mentioned on the way to his desk. Jack Kirby or Steve Ditko would work out the details.

Except none of those scenarios comes from comics. They're all thought experiments written by highly regarded philosophers: René Descartes (1641), Hilary Putnam (1973), David Lewis (1976), Hilary Putnam (1981), and Donald Davidson (1986), respectively. We discuss each of them in this book. Fantastical tales are a staple of philosophy, just as they are for comics. Philosopher Peg Tittle includes 126 of them in her 2005 *What If . . . Collected Thought Experiments in Philosophy*. But superhero comics were well ahead of her. Marvel published its first *What If?* in 1977, and DC published a range called "Imaginary Tales" in the 1950s and included two "Just Suppose" tales in one of its first 1936 titles.

Philosophers could fill volumes too. David Chalmers writes about zombies, Laurence BonJour about clairvoyants, and Frank Jackson about a scientifically all-knowing woman who's never seen color. The list of potential "What if?"s seems endless:

What if your body slowly transformed into rock, but no one around you noticed?

What if a god were stripped of his memories and forced to live as a crippled human?

What if a time traveler returned to his childhood and told his past self about the future?

What if you could save the world but had to sacrifice millions of people first?

What if you and all the universe were just the thoughts of a small child?

Except these scenarios don't come from academic philosophy. They're all from superhero comics: *The Fantastic Four* (1961), *The Mighty Thor* (1968), *The Defenders* (1975), *Watchmen* (1987), and *Heroes Reborn: The Return* (1997). We discuss each of these in this book. And they are no more fantastical than scenarios philosophers have been dreaming up for centuries. Not just *What If?* and "Imaginary Tales," but arguably all superhero comics contain thought experiments. So philosophy's most amazing thought experiments could be adapted into a limited series of illustrated superhero comics titled *Thought Experiments*. But the reverse is true too. We could adapt themes from superhero comics into a philosophy book entitled *Superhero Thought Experiments*. Because writers and artists of Marvel and DC can be read as philosophers and their works as comic book philosophy, we could subtitle the philosophy book *Comic Book Philosophy*. That's of course what we did.

Each chapter of *Superhero Thought Experiments: Comic Book Philosophy* presents philosophical thought experiments derived from superhero comics. We then select tools from philosophers—Kant's Categorical Imperative, Descartes's evil genius, Dennett's intentional stance, and others—to help solve the puzzles that those thought experiments pose by helping to understand the thought experiments themselves. Our goal is to use superhero comics to illustrate philosophy, and in turn to use philosophy to analyze superhero comics. Hopefully, you'll learn a lot about both.

Philosophers who identify as analytic—which the majority of English-speaking philosophers do—spend a great deal of time analyzing concepts and defining terms. Though literary critics' attempts at analysis and definition tend to be limited to literary concerns—including, in recent years, comics—that's where philosophy and literary criticism happily collide. For the authors of this book, the collision took place in front of Washington and Lee University's English department photocopier. Nathaniel Goldberg had descended from the philosophy floor because their machine was on the fritz. Chris Gavaler, himself in the English department, was doing some copying of his own. Nathaniel struck up a conversation about Chris's superhero blog. Superheroes are not the most typical focus for literary criticism, but Nathaniel assured Chris that philosophers write about weird things too. In fact, Nathaniel is an expert on Donald Davidson's Swampman, a thought experiment that Chris noticed resembled Alan Moore's own Swamp Thing. A conference paper in Iceland soon followed and now this book. In the process, Nathaniel learned MLA citation norms and Chris learned what is now one of his favorite phrases, "necessary and sufficient," as in "What are the necessary and sufficient conditions of being a comic?"

Chris answers this question in his recent essay "Refining the Comics Form," where he defines a "comic" as

> a static, spatial field with recurrent elements perceived as conceptually discrete images in juxtaposition with other conceptually discrete images, in which the images are pictorial, abstract, typographic, and/or linguistic, but not linguistic and typographic only. (19)

If you prefer a shorter answer, we recommend Scott McCloud's pioneering 1993 definition: "juxtaposed pictorial and other images in deliberate sequence, intended to convey information and/or produce an aesthetic response in the viewer" (*Understanding Comics* 9). And if you prefer a *really* short answer, Will Eisner gets it done in two words: "sequential art" (*Comics and Sequential Art* 1). That said, many comics scholars, including Chris and several philosophers, take issue with McCloud and Eisner for a range of reasons. What about one-panel "comics" like *The Far Side* and *The Family Circle*? What about the moving images juxtaposed in film and TV? What about physical panels displayed on a gallery wall? What about juxtaposed images in mediums that predate the twentieth century and so the term "comics"? While these questions are good ones, they and others like them are not the focus of this book. This volume includes "Superhero" in its title, and the superhero genre squats near the center of the definitional zone. Our reading list includes only multipanel works printed on paper, bound in units of typically twenty-two pages, and published after 1937.

"Superhero," as naming both a genre and a character type, also presents a range of definitions, which variously includes and excludes marginal cases such as Buffy the Vampire Slayer, Harry Potter, and Nick Fury of Avengers fame. Peter Coogan, in *Superhero: The Secret Origin of a Genre*, offers one of the more thorough descriptions of the superhero character type:

> A heroic character with a selfless, pro-social mission; with superpowers—extraordinary abilities, advanced technology, or highly developed physical, mental, or mystical skills; who has a superhero identity embodied in a codename and iconic costume, which typically express his biography, character, powers, or origin (transformation from ordinary person to superhero); and who is generically distinct, i.e. can be distinguished from characters of related genres (fantasy, science fiction, detective, etc.) by a preponderance of generic conventions. Often superheroes have dual identities, the ordinary one of which is usually a closely guarded secret. (30)

Chris takes a different, "no-common-denominator approach" in *On the Origin of Superheroes*, arguing instead that the category "superhero" has no single necessary or sufficient condition but only a list of potential ones, with different characters demonstrating different combinations with potentially no overlap (3). In similar spirit to Chris, twentieth-century philosopher Ludwig Wittgenstein might argue that examples of different superheroes share a "family resemblance" (*Philosophical Investigations* 32). Just as there may be no single necessary or sufficient physical condition of all members of a family, individual members do share some with at least some others, and through a series of overlaps, the family can be picked out as a whole. No matter, though, since instead of exploring border cases to test and refine definitions, we will again stake our analysis at the genre's and medium's centers. Most if not all of the characters discussed in this book fall comfortably within Coogan's definition.

Defining "philosophy" presents challenges, too. Ask people what they think of when they hear the word, and you'll get all sorts of answers. Usually "philosophy" means something like opinion or perhaps contemplated thought. "That's my philosophy on," one might begin, and then follow with "dealing with my boss," "shoveling snow," or "giving a pill to a cat." "Philosophy" can also mean a principle for living life. "My philosophy is to treat others as I'd want them to treat me." Of course, sometimes "philosophy" means the academic discipline, or—related to what is sometimes studied in that discipline—a worldview or way of approaching reality. But it can also mean navel-gazing in the sense of impractical thinking rather than practical doing.

Ask professional philosophers what *they* think of, and that's also unlikely to get you any single answer. Twentieth-century philosopher Wilfrid Sellars wrote,

> The aim of philosophy, abstractly formulated, is to understand how things in the broadest possible sense of the term hang together in the broadest possible sense of the term. Under "things in the broadest possible sense" I include such radically different items as not only "cabbages and kings," but numbers and duties, possibilities and finger snaps, aesthetic experience and death. (1)

Besides cabbages and kings (and all these others), Sellars might have included comics and superheroes. Even so, the aim of something doesn't necessarily provide us with a definition. Besides, depending on how we understand "things" and "hanging together," Sellars need not be talking exclusively about philosophy. Many scientifically minded people think that all "things" are ultimately physical things. And how do physical objects hang together if not by being governed by physical laws? In that case it looks as though physics counts as philosophy. While the two weren't always distinct, philosophy wasn't always distinct from what today are other disciplines, either. For much of Western history, "philosophy" was the name given to academic knowledge generally. The word itself derives from two ancient Greek words, *philos* and *sophia*, together meaning "love of wisdom."

That "philosophy" derives from ancient Greek shouldn't be surprising. Ancient Greek philosophers Plato and Aristotle are largely responsible for the Western philosophical tradition. Twentieth-century mathematician-turned-philosopher Alfred North Whitehead wrote: "The safest general characterization of the European philosophical tradition is that it consists of a series of footnotes to Plato" (39). Plato authored what today seems most clearly philosophy. In semifictionalized dialogs, his hero, Socrates, asks not "What if?" questions but "What is?" ones: "What is virtue?" (*The Meno*), or "What is justice?" (*The Republic*), or "What is love?" (*The Symposium*). Aristotle was Plato's most famous student, and though Aristotle called himself a "philosopher," he's also the father of modern science. Isaac Newton likewise called himself a "philosopher." When Shakespeare's Hamlet tells Horatio, "There are more things in heaven and earth, Horatio, / Than are dreamt of in your philosophy" (1.5.166–67), Hamlet means what we refer to as "science." Even today, the PhD, the highest degree in most academic disciplines from anthropology to zoology, is an abbreviation for *philosophiae doctor*, Latin for "teacher of philosophy."

Though "philosophy" once meant science and academic knowledge generally, philosophers did eventually specialize. Natural philosophers, like Newton, became natural scientists. While there still are moral philosophers around—we usually call them "ethicists"—moral philosophy used to include the social sciences. Those have spun off as anthropology, economics, political science, sociology, and allied fields. Mathematical philosophy itself was divided between the more mathematical natural sciences, like physics, and just plain math.

Yet what Plato was himself doing by asking those "What is?" questions never spun off. Because Plato's method of investigation was conceptual, we might call Plato's project "conceptual analysis." For a lot of philosophers, that's what the discipline is still about. Many in the twentieth century, while agreeing with Plato's theme, preferred it in a linguistic key. Instead of asking, "What is virtue?" they might ask, "What does 'virtue,' the word, mean?" Regardless, both analyzing a concept and defining a word involve investigating necessary and sufficient conditions. And that's why philosophers spend so much time trying to conceive of or define things.

Not all philosophers think this is what philosophers should be doing. Twentieth-century philosopher Willard van Orman Quine argued that there's no such thing as pure conceptual analysis or determinate definitions to begin with. Even so, enough philosophers think that some sort of analyzing concepts and defining words is what philosophy amounts to, and that we accept that as our working definition of "philosophy." That helps explain why philosophers often trade in conceptual or definitional work. One common philosophical tool is to try to conceive of or define situations that are not real but that instead reveal lessons for us. In a word, philosophers "experiment" in thoughts, rather than, as scientists do, in labs. These conceived of or defined situations are *thought experiments*, the "What if?"s.

Generally, thought experiments involve conceiving of or defining a situation where a few key details are changed from how they ordinarily are to test particular philosophical views. What if an evil genius *did* trick you into believing that the world around you were real when it really wasn't? Does imagining that reveal anything interesting about the nature of knowledge? What if your body *were* slowly transformed into rock and no one around you noticed? Does imagining this reveal anything interesting about the nature of personal identity?

The first thought experiment is from an academic philosopher. The second is from a comic book writer. Each could be developed by either sort of person. Plato wrote semifictionalized dialogs, encouraging readers to imagine themselves in particular situations. Most academic philosophers, before and since, write essays, treatises, or technical books—which are arguably less engaging than Plato's work. While typical thought experiments, unlike Plato's, are not presented in fiction, they can be. As philosopher Ross P. Cameron explains, "A typical fiction tends to be much longer than your typical thought experiment and hence can present you with a more detailed scenario" (31). Philosophers Jonathan Jenkins Ichikawa and Benjamin Jarvis even call philosophical thought experiments "mini-fictions," as opposed to the standard-sized ones. Likewise, philosophers Johan de Smedt and Helen de Cruz argue that, though both typical philosophical thought experiments and fiction rely on similar cognitive mechanisms, fiction "allows for a richer exploration of philosophical positions than is possible through ordinary philosophical thought experiments" (59). The exploration is richer not only because it's more developed, but also because readers of fiction are immersed in a way that readers of philosophy usually aren't. Smedt and Cruz continue: "Regardless of whether they are outlandish or realistic, philosophical thought experiments lack features that speculative fiction typically has, including vivid, seemingly irrelevant details that help to transport the reader and encourage low-level, concrete thinking" (64). In short, readers take the scenarios more seriously.

These scholars contrast typical philosophical thought experiments with the longer scenarios in traditional science fiction and fantasy novels, but their points apply even better to comics. Novels employ words to express ideas, while comics employ both words and images, so reading a comic operates on an additional cognitive level. It can be both more immersive and more challenging due to its multimedia form.

Of course, neither science fiction and fantasy novels, nor superhero comics, treat their scenarios explicitly as thought experiments. They don't usually examine the assumptions involved and don't draw broader lessons from them. And they certainly don't consider whether the experiments were done under the appropriate conditions, say, by changing only a few features here and leaving the rest as is. There *are* no appropriate conditions, other than those that make their stories enjoyable. Superhero comics in particular aim first and foremost to entertain. Actual analysis is done better by academic philosophy, just as we'd expect. Combining superhero comics and philosophy could be a powerful way to explore thought experiments because it merges the strengths of each.

But are philosophers interested in comics? The trend of focusing philosophical analysis on common rather than complex topics—more cabbages, fewer kings—keeps growing. Partly that's because philosophers have become increasingly interested in pop culture, but it's also because philosophy is increasingly being practiced by those who aren't academic philosophers. Two book series, the Blackwell Philosophy and Popular Culture series and Open Court's Popular Culture and Philosophy, publish volumes on individual movies and pop-cultural themes—written by philosophers and other philosophically minded people. *New Philosopher*, *Philosophy Now*, and *Think* are popular magazines for philosophy, just as *Discover*, *Popular Science*, and *Scientific American* are popular magazines for science, and in each the professional status of readers and writers varies. *Philosophy Talk*, a radio show hosted by philosophers John Perry and Ken Taylor and syndicated nationally by Public Radio Exchange, invites anyone interested in philosophy to talk about pressing issues. The *New York Times*'s weekly online column "The Stone," written by philosophers and other philosophically minded academics, reaches millions of readers worldwide. Nonacademic philosophy "meetups," with their own website, philosophy.meetup.com, are springing up organically around the world—as are blogs, social media pages, and other online sources, visited by people inside and outside philosophy's academy.

There have also been philosophical publications specifically on comics, including *The Aesthetics of Comics* (2000), *Superheroes and Philosophy: Truth, Justice, and the Socratic Way* (2005), *Comics as Philosophy* (2007), *Manga and Philosophy* (2010), and *The Art of Comics: A Philosophical Approach* (2014). Some include philosophical thought experiments—though not as extensively or uniformly as we do in this book. Some are academic books, written by philosophers for academic audiences. Others are popular books, written by philosophers and those with philosophical interests for general readers. Regardless, there has been some resistance. As comic book writer Warren Ellis observes in the foreword to *The Art of Comics*, comics are as "pervasive as air and yet somehow as shameful as crack" (xiii). His point, which we agree with, is that such shame is misguided. Comics are an art form, and philosophy studies art—and much besides.

Popular or not, all these examples of philosophy share the same standard of success, which Sellars articulates:

To achieve success in philosophy would be, to use a contemporary turn of phrase, to "know one's way around" with respect to all these things, not in that unreflective way in which the centipede of the story knew its way around before it faced the question, "how do I walk?," but in that reflective way which means that no intellectual holds are barred. (1)

Our aim in this book is to show you how to know your way around the philosophical nature of superhero comics—not in an unreflective, centipedal way, but in a reflective one.

We begin with basics and build philosophical complexity. Part I and part II, "Morality" and "Metaphysics" respectively, have to do with topics common in introductory philosophy courses. In them, we read the story content of specific superhero comics as thought experiments. We take the same approach in part III, "Meaning," too, but here our subject matter grows more specialized, delving into the philosophy of language, a subfield probably unfamiliar to undergrads except those majoring in philosophy. Our points of reference grow more specialized also. Many readers with a passing interest in philosophy have heard of Plato, Descartes, and Kant, philosophers central in the first half of this book. We suspect few will be familiar with Davidson, Dennett, and Grice, philosophers central in the second half. Finally, part IV, "Medium," approaches superhero comics differently too. Instead of plumbing story content for thought experiments, we read the comic's form—its mix of words and images by multiple authors—as a kind of thought experiment in itself, analyzing the norms of the medium for its philosophical implications. Where the first three parts might be considered popular philosophy as applied *to* comics, the last concerns the philosophy *of* comics.

Each part also divides into two chapters. The first, "Morality," concerns right and wrong. In chapter 1, "Superconsequences vs. Dark Duties," we focus on the first year of Superman and Batman comics, showing that each superhero represents a different kind of morality. Superman thinks that right and wrong have to do with getting the best consequences, while Batman thinks that they have to do with fulfilling duty. Philosophers often ask similar questions about the nature of morality itself. Are right and wrong relative to one's society, or are they absolute? Does morality rest on subjective inclination or objective fact? In chapter 2, "What Good Are Superheroes?," we consider the nature of superhero morality specifically. We turn to a repeated DC trope—a world similar to ours but where morality plays out differently—to answer the first question. We then turn to the Comics Code Authority, which oversaw the moral content of comics, and other real-world opinions to answer the second.

The nature of morality is the purview of metaethics. The nature of reality is the purview of the philosophical subfield of part II, "Metaphysics." In chapter 3, "Evil Geniuses," we pair seventeenth-century philosopher René Descartes with a series of superhero stories to consider whether reality is "really" real, or whether—as Descartes asked and comics make vivid—all this is but a dream. In chapter 4, "Clobberin' Time," we focus on one particular part of reality: time. We trace Marvel's changing view of time by focusing on stories involving Dr. Doom's time machine, the plot device that established the idea of time travel in Marvel continuity.

While "time" means different things to Marvel at different moments in its publishing history, other words mean different things too. Part III, "Meaning," resolves a philosophical debate between "referential retcons" and "descriptivist reboots," in chapter 5, by looking at the meaning of superhero names in the context of different kinds of story revisions. Retcons are narrative revisions that reinterpret older stories. We have to retcon, or make them retroactively continuous with, newer ones. Reboots are narrative revisions that nullify older stories. Rebooting a story is like rebooting a computer, turning it off and starting an application over again by turning it back on. Do names mean the same things in both contexts? And what happens when retcons and reboots are combined in multiverses? Meaning isn't restricted to names, either. In chapter 6, "Minding the Swamp," we consider how thoughts can have meaning at all. We focus on a series of comic book creatures all having emerged from swamps. By asking whether they have thoughts, we appeal to views that philosopher Donald Davidson proposed on requirements on what makes thought itself meaningful.

While the first three parts look at the story content of superhero comics, the fourth, "Medium," uses philosophy to make sense of what is distinct about comics as an art form. Comics as a medium are themselves thought experiments, we argue, and their readers find themselves inside them. In chapter 7, "Caped Communicators," we consider how comic book creators depict things with images. Sometimes their depictions are conventional. An image of Superman atop a building conventionally depicts Superman atop a building. Sometimes their depictions are conversational, appealing to context. An image of wavy lines emanating from Spider-Man's head conversationally depicts his spider senses "tingling." And sometimes images fail to depict anything at all. Finally, in "True Believers," we ask who the author of a comic ultimately is. We reach two surprising conclusions. First, while typically many people contribute to the creation of any given superhero comic, all those people collectively count as a single, pluralistic author. Second, though that single author is made up of a plurality of parts, as an author she has a single set of beliefs and desires as any other single author would. Reflecting on comic book images and authors reveals that we comic book readers are part of these thought experiments, subject to the distinct nature of comic book form.

We conclude by considering lessons that all these superhero comic book thought experiments have to teach.

PART I

MORALITY

ONE

SUPERCONSEQUENCES
VS. DARK DUTIES

❦

C omic book scholars offer a range of attributes for defining the super-hero character type, including alter egos, code names, and costumes. But the two most central traits are variations on superpowers and goodness. Whether physical strength, intelligence, or some other amazing ability, superheroes must have greater power than the rest of us. And, as Stan Lee first phrased it, with great power there must also come—great responsibil-ity! We discussed in the introduction that, as Peter Coogan put it, superheroes have a "pro-social mission" (30). They must act morally.

But what does "moral" mean? What if different superheroes define the word differently?

Whatever else it means, morality has to do with right and wrong, and ulti-mately codes of conduct. It concerns how people ought to behave toward one another and the world around them. Morality is therefore normative. Rather than describing how people do act, it prescribes how they should act. Because they possess goodness—that is, moral goodness—superheroes do act how they should. Without being moral, a super*hero* wouldn't be a hero at all. She would merely be a superhuman and perhaps even a supervillain.

Because morality is a defining trait of the character type, the focus of our first chapter is ethics, or the study of morality. Philosophers who study ethics examine and evaluate different moral codes and whether particular actions or intentions are morally right or wrong. While the superhero character type acts morally, are individual characters motivated by the same moral code? And what can we say about those codes?

While first-year philosophy students learn about morality in their introductory courses, we turn to first-year superheroes for our first thought experiments. Though superhero comics have evolved vastly since their introduction, two heroes first defined the genre: Superman and Batman. Some might argue that Superman and Batman continue to define the genre, but we would have to ask, *which* Superman and *which* Batman? Like their genre, these characters have undergone major revisions over the decades, with the involvement of hundreds if not thousands of authors in the pages of comic books and novels, in episodes of radio and television shows, in video games, and on the big screen. Though DC has maintained some control through its editorial staff (which itself has been evolving), neither character presents a single, consistent superhero thought experiment or comic book philosophy. Neither presents a single, consistent "What if?"

We therefore limit this first chapter to Superman's and Batman's founding stories, roughly the first year of each comic. For Superman, that's Jerry Siegel and Joe Shuster's *Action Comics* #1 (June 1938) to *Superman* #1 (July 1939). For Batman, it's Bill Finger, Gardner Fox, and Bob Kane's *Detective Comics* #27 (May 1939) to *Batman* #1 (Spring 1940). These year-one incarnations sometimes differ dramatically from how later authors developed them. Superman and Batman are both, for example, surprisingly lethal. Regardless, these early episodes establish the starting points not only for each character but also for comic book superheroes as a genre—so they're an apt starting point for this book.

What if we read these two sets of authors as philosophers and their comics as philosophical treatises? What morality does each advocate through the stories they tell about their heroes? As we're about to see, Superman's and Batman's philosophies have been at odds since their earliest adventures. We take Superman's initial moral code to center around consequences and Batman's initial one around duties. Though they may often act similarly, their core commitments always differ.

Consequences and duties aren't the only such possible commitments in ethics. There is, for example, a third moral code centered around virtue. We put this aside because it's not a central view of either of these founding characters. Yet we don't limit ourselves to Superman and Batman either. Because their moral codes influenced decades of subsequent superheroes, we close by considering a major later case, Alan Moore and Dave Gibbons's acclaimed

Watchmen (1986–87), examining how Dr. Manhattan and Rorschach inherit and alter their predecessors' philosophies.

Superman's Consequences

What if Superman's first year of adventures is read as a thought experiment illustrating one philosophical approach to morality? Superman decided from an early age that "he must turn his titanic strength into channels that would benefit mankind" (Siegel and Shuster, *Superman Chronicles* 1:4). This is a future-focused mission. For Superman, the right thing to do is to benefit people, or bring good to them. That makes him an ethical consequentialist, the most famous in comics.

The most famous real-world consequentialist is nineteenth-century philosopher John Stuart Mill, who believed that an action is morally right if and only if it brings about the greatest good for the greatest number of people. Mill explains in his 1864 *Utilitarianism*:

> Actions are right in proportion as they tend to promote happiness, wrong as they tend to produce the reverse of happiness. By happiness is intended pleasure and the absence of pain; by unhappiness, pain and the privation of pleasure. (7)

Mill means happiness or unhappiness overall. An action is morally right if and only if it brings about the greatest amount of pleasure, and the least amount of pain, for the greatest number of people. Because Mill calls this idea the "greatest happiness principle" or "utility," his kind of consequentialism—which aims at the consequence of overall happiness—is known as "utilitarianism."

Some utilitarians think that when we act we should always appeal directly to the greatest happiness principle. They're called "act" utilitarians. Others think that we can appeal instead to intermediate rules—like don't lie, cheat, or steal—that, over the long run, satisfy the greatest happiness principle. They're called "rule" utilitarians. At times Mill sounds like a rule utilitarian. But because at other times he sounds like an act utilitarian, it's unclear which kind he is. It's likewise unclear which kind Superman is. Is he always thinking about how to make the most people the happiest overall? Or is he following intermediate rules, with the understanding that they lead to the same place? There are plenty of examples in the first year of *Action Comics* of Superman breaking rules—he lies to Lois about his secret identity, he cheats at football by impersonating a star player to upset a rigged game, he steals profits from a crooked stocks company—but only if he achieves a greater good in the process. But he also follows rules at times. Because we can't tell for sure in Mill's or Superman's case, we treat them both as utilitarians generally.

So all utilitarians are consequentialists, even though not all consequentialists are utilitarians. There might be other consequences besides happiness that a consequentialist moral code wants to increase. But Superman and Mill are happy to increase happiness. And they're happy to do it in the aggregate, which means they prioritize society. Mill claims that because people live in societies, the greatest happiness is best achieved if societies are just: "Justice remains the appropriate name for certain social utilities which are vastly more important, and therefore more absolute and imperative, than any others are as a class" (63). For Mill, the elements of justice include things such as security, equality, and fairness—because supporting them tends to promote the greatest happiness. This is where Mill sounds like a rule utilitarian.

Though Superman doesn't talk about utility or the greatest happiness principle, he aims for similar outcomes. And in cases where Superman aims for security, equality, and fairness directly—and so for overall happiness only indirectly—he acts like a rule utilitarian too. Regardless, like all consequentialists, Superman (at least in his first year) thinks that morality has everything to do with positive results. He wants to "champion the oppressed" (Siegel and Shuster, *Superman Chronicles* 1:4) to better their lives. As a consequentialist, he's focused not on punishing past wrongs but on helping as many people as he can.

When Superman faces criminals, he wants to prevent them from harming anyone else, making society more secure over all. He also prefers reformation, because that can lead to the greater good—for both victims and perpetrators. In his third adventure, Superman traps the owner of the Blakely Mine in a cave-in so that he's forced to endure the dangers of his employees' working conditions. Afterward the owner promises that "my mine will be the safest in the country, and my workers the best treated. My experience in the mine brought their problems closer to my understanding" (1:44). The owner sees that justice requires that he and his employees be equally secure. When Superman gives a munitions dealer a taste of military combat, the dealer declares: "When it's your own life that's at stake, your viewpoint changes!" (1:23). This sentiment is echoed by a mayor who was unconcerned with traffic accidents until Superman made him fear for his own life: "You've shown me a viewpoint I never saw before! I swear I'll do all in my power to see that traffic rules are rigidly enforced by the police!" (1:166). Provided that the rules are just—which they are, or Superman wouldn't support them—fairness requires that they be enforced for everyone's safety. In each case, Superman reforms the wrongdoer, which results in the wrongdoer's betterment as well as the betterment of those around him. Superman is motivated by concern for future well-being.

Overall happiness, however, sometimes results in individual unhappiness. As Mill and Superman both acknowledge, individual unhappiness even includes deaths. When wrongdoers can't be reformed, Superman achieves the greatest good by lethally stopping them. When a "camp is being mercilessly riddled by a blood-thirsty aviator" shouting "Die!—like crawling ants!" (1:28), Superman shatters the propeller, allowing the plane "to fall to its doom!" (1:28). Earlier, when Superman "drops toward the ground into the midst of a torturer's inquisition," he tells the torturer that he'll "give you the fate you deserve, you torturing devil!" and "tosses him away." In the next panel, the "torturer vanishes from view behind a grove of distant trees with a pitiful wail" (1:27). Superman doesn't go out of his way to cause criminals pain and suffering—as a utilitarian, he wouldn't—but sometimes causing it is the best way to get the greatest good for the greatest number overall.

Superman also devotes himself to aiding others even when it doesn't involve battling wrongdoers. He donates his services to a circus to prevent the owner from going bankrupt (1:88). He cleans out his own savings to purchase worthless stock from people who had been swindled (1:142). In a special *New York World's Fair* comic, Superman completes the "infantile paralysis exhibit," so the display will raise contributions for those children (1:172). Sometimes his actions are destructive, as when he knocks down a slum to prevent its "poor living conditions" from causing more juvenile delinquents (1:108), but the outcome is still positive. When destroying the cars of traffic violators, Superman does say: "I think I'm going to enjoy this little war!" (1:156). As we'll see in the next section, that sounds like Batman's "warring on all criminals," but Superman remains results-driven. His "little war" is only a means to the end of improving public safety. It's the consequences that count, however they're achieved.

The unimportance of "warring" for its own sake is also apparent in many of the battles Superman fights. Unlike Batman's, Superman's early conflicts are often anticlimactic because the criminals he faces are so easily defeated. His first adversary, a nightclub singer who framed another woman for murder, is unable to fire her gun before Superman grabs it from her and forces her to write her confession, saving the innocent woman from execution (1:199). Likewise, the wife beater he faces next faints before Superman can make good on his promise: "And now you're going to get a lesson you'll never forget!" (1:9). Though the criminal goes unpunished, the lesson is still learned. That positive outcome is all that matters to Superman. His promise to inflict the lesson doesn't.

Batman's Duties

What if we read Batman's first year of adventures as another philosophical thought experiment illustrating an approach to a very different definition of morality? Batman decided to become a superhero at an even earlier age than Superman did. After witnessing his parents' murder, Bruce Wayne declares: "I swear by the spirits of my parents to avenge their deaths by spending the rest of my life warring on all criminals" (Finger, Fox, and Kane, *Batman Chronicles* 63). This is past-focused. For Batman, the right thing to do is to fulfill his duty and uphold that oath to his murdered parents. While Superman could swear an oath too, he would act on it only because of the good that it would bring about. Batman acts on his oath not because of its consequences but because he swore the oath in the first place. That makes Batman an ethical deontologist, the most famous in comics.

The most famous real-world deontologist is eighteenth-century philosopher Immanuel Kant. While Superman's consequentialism is close to Mill's, Batman's deontology isn't quite Kant's. Batman's is focused on revenge, while, as we'll see, Kant intends his to be focused on reason. We'll first consider what makes Kant a deontologist, so that we can then better appreciate Batman's deontological view.

In his 1785 *Groundwork of the Metaphysics of Morals*, Kant maintained: "It is impossible to think of anything at all in the world, or indeed even beyond it, that could be taken to be good without limitation, except a good will" (9). A good will imposes on the subject the duty to will, or intend, to do good things. Kant continued: "A good will is good not because of what it effects, or accomplishes, not because of its fitness to attain some intended end, but good just by its willing, i.e., in itself" (10). Accomplishments and their effects, the consequences so central to Mill, don't determine what's right or wrong. For Kant, being moral means having a good will, which means following our duty to will good things. Whether or not those good things come about is beside the point. Moral worth "does not depend on the actuality of the object of the action." It has nothing to do with whether what we're aiming at by acting is actually achieved. Instead, Kant explains, morality depends "merely on the *principle* of the *willing* according to which [. . .] the action is done" (15). It's the principle, or as Kant puts it elsewhere, the "maxim," behind our action that counts. What makes us good or bad is what we will ourselves to do, not any consequences that follow.

While Batman doesn't have Kant's notion of a good will, he does share Kant's belief that what we will—the maxim according to which we act—matters most, rather than its consequences. To understand Batman and Kant's shared view on this, consider how Kant would think about Batman and his trusty batarang. In his seventh adventure, Batman throws the batarang at the villainous Carl Kruger, but it's deflected by an invisible sheet of glass (Finger, Fox, and Kane, *Batman Chronicles* 67). Though this obviously isn't the result Batman had in mind, according to Kant, Batman is no less moral for failing to stop Kruger. He was just unlucky. In a later incident, Batman does have luck on his side. When fighting the Joker for the first time, "Batman side steps. The killer-clown stumbles forward into the building driving the knife into his own chest!" (189). Though the outcome makes society safer, according to Kant, Batman is no more moral for succeeding in stopping the Joker. He just happened to be lucky this time. The two scenes result in opposite outcomes, but in Kant's view Batman's morality is the same. Good luck, bad luck—these might affect consequences, but for the deontologist they don't affect morality. Kant explains:

> Even if by some particular disfavor of fate, or by the scanty endowment of a stepmotherly nature, this will should entirely lack the capacity to carry through its purpose; if despite its greatest striving it should still accomplish nothing, and only the good will were to remain (not, of course, as a mere wish, but as the summoning of all means that are within our control); then, like a jewel, it would still shine by itself, as something that has its full worth in itself. (10)

Fate in the moment (Kruger's glass wall, the Joker's lethal stumble) or endowment at birth (Superman's strength, Batman's wealth) doesn't affect morality. Batman's good will, like one of the jewels stolen by the Joker, shines no matter what.

Though Batman doesn't talk about a "good will," he would agree with Kant's sentiment. And they'd both be reacting against what twentieth-century philosopher Bernard Williams calls "moral luck." Because luck and morality seem unrelated if not outright contradictory, Williams explains: "When I first introduced the expression moral luck, I expected to suggest an oxymoron" (251). Williams figured that others, rather than taking him seriously, would understand the phrase sarcastically. Morality couldn't be a matter of luck.

Consequentialists might disagree with Williams, but deontologists don't. They maintain that invisible glass and fumbling forward can't make someone moral or immoral, because morality doesn't depend on chance. Since consequences often do depend on chance, deontologists claim that moral evaluation should depend only on factors within our control. And the only thing that's really within our control, in Kant's and Batman's views, is our will. The things we will to do—the maxims according to which we choose to act—are the only things that morally count.

What makes our maxims moral, and thus gives us a duty to follow them, does differ for Batman and Kant. According to Kant, reason tells us that for a code (or, in Kant's terms, a "law") to be a law, it must hold universally. So the *moral* law requires that we "act only according to that maxim through which [we] can at the same time will that it become a universal law" (34). In other words, we should act only in the same way we would permit others to act. This "formula of universal law" is the first version of Kant's Categorical Imperative. It's categorical because, as a law, it holds for everyone. It's an imperative because it tells everyone what to do.

Suppose, to use Kant's example, that we want to know whether lying, or promising falsely, is moral. We should consider the maxim, deciding to promise falsely presumably for some personal gain, and determine whether we could will that everyone act on it. According to Kant, we can't. A promise is a commitment made by one person and accepted by another. Were everyone to promise falsely, then everyone else would eventually become aware that everyone's promise was made falsely—and then no one would accept a promise as a promise anymore. Were we to promise falsely, then we'd be acting on a maxim that only some people could act on, since its universalization would destroy the practice of promising. "Promises" would no longer be accepted and thus wouldn't even count as promises. So we can't universalize the maxim. We'd need to restrict it. But that would make an exception for some, when the moral law must hold for all. Because promising falsely could not be made a universal law, it violates the moral law. It's therefore our duty not to promise falsely.

Kant recognizes that this first version of the Categorical Imperative is unwieldly, so he introduces a second, the "formula of humanity." Because the universalization required by the moral law holds that every person must respect and be respected by the law, Kant argues that the first version of the Categorical Imperative is equivalent to the second: "So act that you use humanity, in your own person as well as in the person of any other, always at the same time as an end, never merely as a means" (41). Morality dictates that we should never treat any human being merely as a means to some other end. We should always treat human beings as ends in themselves. This means that we should respect them as human beings, taking into account their own wills, and not disrespect them by using them merely as a means to realizing our own.

Reconsider the case of promising falsely. Doing so uses people merely as a means because it subjugates their humanity in the service of our own. It dehumanizes them solely for our benefit. We get something that we want by tricking others into believing us when they shouldn't. Because we're using them merely as a means to our ends, promising falsely takes advantage of others and makes an exception of ourselves. Just as there can't be any exceptions in the formula of universal law, there can't be any in applying the formula of humanity.

Batman doesn't endorse anything like the Categorical Imperative. Regardless, he's as much a deontologist as Kant. He's also as much a deontologist as nineteenth- and twentieth-century philosopher William David Ross. In his 1930 *The Right and the Good*, Ross rightly described himself as a deontologist even though he rejected the Categorical Imperative. Ross still thought that we're bound by what we will—and so by the maxims according to which we act—and not in any way by consequences. That's Batman's moral code too. Recall Batman's oath: "I swear by the spirits of my parents to avenge their deaths by spending the rest of my life warring on all criminals." And recall that he abides by it not because of the consequences of doing so, but because he swore the oath itself. If keeping that oath leads him to treat others as merely means to his sworn ends, so be it. By contrast, recall that Superman's moral code doesn't require him to keep his promise to teach a wife beater a lesson. The criminal can learn the lesson in some other way—as long as the consequences are the same—and that's fine by Superman. Because his goal is to benefit others, Superman likely won't use them as a means, though not because he's bound by Kant's Categorical Imperative. Batman's moral code, however, does require him to keep his own promise in the form of his oath. Though doing so often does lead to good consequences overall, for Batman, that's not why he does it. And, on his view, that's not what makes it the right thing to do.

So Batman, like Kant and Ross, is driven by duty rather than consequences. That makes them deontologists. Yet Batman differs from Kant on more than just rejecting the Categorical Imperative. While Kant's deontology is based on reason, Batman's is based on revenge. Rather than a good will, Batman has a dark one. While a good will imposes on the subject the duty to will to do good things, a dark will imposes on the subject the duty to will to do punishing things. When Batman swears to avenge the deaths of his parents, the maxim according to which he acts is vengeance. For the rest of his life, Batman acts according to it—always (dutifully) aiming to fulfill his oath. We might for that reason call Batman a "dark" deontologist.

Regardless of what we call him, Batman is morally bound to war on criminals, "preying upon the criminal parasite, like the winged creature whose name he has adopted" (99). In his first year of adventures, he's never motivated to help the innocent. After the Joker murders his first victim, "Henry Claridge, the millionaire," Batman's new sidekick, Robin, asks: "But Bruce, why don't we take a shot at this Joker guy?" (141). Batman responds: "Not yet, Dick. The time isn't ripe" (142). Batman also doesn't do anything as the Joker claims his second victim, Jay Wilde, stealing the "Ronkers Ruby" in the process (143). For Batman, the right time to strike is independent of any good that might be promoted or evil that might be prevented.

Batman is so focused on his duty rather than its consequences that he appears almost pleased when the Joker escapes: "It seems I've at last met a foe that can give me a good fight!" (147). Even the consequence of catching the Joker is beside the point, though his failure to do so leads to the death of a third victim, Judge Drake. Batman doesn't attempt to save the judge either. He patrols outside Drake's house in the hopes of apprehending the killer *after* the murder, which he eventually does. Similarly, when the Joker returns in a later episode, Batman waits until two more victims are dead, including the police chief, before acting. Batman does prevent the Joker from murdering his next target, Otto Drexel, but only as a side effect of fulfilling his duty to war on criminals. Of course, Batman doesn't go out of his way to cause any of these bad consequences. He's simply oblivious to the plight of innocent people. That's why he's untroubled when the Joker escapes.

In Batman's first year, only one of his actions appears consequentialist. When the Napoleonesque villain Carl Kruger attacks Manhattan in his Dirigible of Doom, "buildings explode, hurling their wreckage upon the crowded streets below" (64). A child shouts: "Help! Mamma, save me! Help!!" After the dirigible leaves, "rescue work begins. Bruce Wayne helps," lifting a steel girder trapping an old man. The situation is more typical of a scene from a Superman comic, but it's "Bruce Wayne," not "Batman," helping others. At this particular moment, Bruce's consequentially motivated aid isn't part of his Batman mission. It's as if the oath applies only to his secret identity. As long as Bruce is helping the needy in the streets, Batman isn't pursuing his deontological duty. When Bruce pursues and battles Kruger as Batman, however, he's his (dark) deontological self again.

Taken as thought experiments exploring ethics, then, in their first years Superman and Batman are moral opposites. Superman strives for the greatest good for the greatest number of people. Along the way, past wrongs might be righted. In that sense, Superman might be thought of as avenging the innocent. But that's beside the point. Though many of his actions are consistent with those of a deontologist, deontology doesn't capture his moral code. Superman has instead devoted "his existence to helping those in need!" (1:196). He's out for the greatest good for the greatest number. By contrast, Batman is duty-bound to vengeance. Though this often results in the greatest good coming about, consequences aren't his concern. Even if Gotham eventually became irredeemable and all its citizens criminals, Batman would still continue his war, though no one would benefit. He's duty-bound to his oath. That the innocent often do benefit from Batman's acts is, for him, beside the point. We can appreciate this from the opposite perspective also. Were Batman a consequentialist, then he might think it moral that his parents were killed. That, after all, led to his becoming a superhero, which likely led to more positive consequences for everyone. Yet there's no way that Batman would ever think his parents' deaths were moral. Batman's just not concerned with consequences. It's all about duty.

Superluck

Once he took his oath, Batman didn't need to depend on anything beyond his own control either. As often as fortune smiles on us, misfortune may frown, and because he's not concerned with consequences Batman's moral code accommodates that. There's something intuitively right about at least that part of Batman's attitude. While being lucky or unlucky is one thing, being moral or immoral does seems like something else. Superman needs to keep in mind how others will act and what effects his actions will have on them, but Batman's deontological reasoning focuses only on himself and society's criminals.

On the other hand, consequentialism's future orientation allows Superman a level of tactical freedom that Batman lacks. No matter what maxims Superman might follow, his actions are moral if and only if they make the world a better place. Consequentialism isn't held hostage by oaths. Every day can be a new day for Superman. Meanwhile, Batman is imprisoned by his past. Whether it's based on vengeance or, in Kant's case, reason, once a duty is established, it guides actions—not for the future's sake but for duty's own. Yet there's something intuitively right about that as well.

Further, though consequentialism does have the benefit of its future orientation, it faces the problem of moral luck, which deontology avoids. Remember Batman and his batarang? Deontology says that whether or not glass blocks his batarang is beside the point. It's Batman's maxim that counts. As a consequentialist, by contrast, Superman must recognize that luck can come into moral play. When Superman is leaping with a mobster in his arms, the mobster attempts to stab him. As a result, "Superman smashes against a nearby building, instead of alighting on it as he had intended," and the mobster falls to his death. Superman explains: "If he hadn't tried to stab me, he'd be alive now.—But the fate received was exactly what he deserved!" (1:185). The outcome is what mattered, even though it was accidental. The mobster deserved to die because in the overall context it led to the greatest good.

Likewise, sometimes Superman succeeds through lucky timing, as when he leaps atop a passing train for no narrative reason and then just happens to overhear an important conversation. Superman thinks aloud: "A crooked coach hiring professional thugs to play football!—Sounds like just the sort of set-up I like to tear down!" (1:48). So he does tear it down. Superman, as a consequentialist, thinks he does the right thing even if what he accomplishes is helped by chance.

When it comes to moral luck, Batman might have the upper hand. It does seem difficult to understand how something outside our control can make us moral. And deontology declares that it can't. While Batman has his share of good and bad luck too, none of it matters morally. Doing the right thing means being willing to fight the good fight, regardless of whether you win or lose, or whether good or bad luck intercedes. That's true regardless of whether you actually even fight. It's willing or acting according to the maxim to fight that counts. For Kant, the will shines by being illuminated by the light of Categorical Imperative. For Batman, it shines by being illuminated by the black light of his dark oath.

Superman also offers an additional thought experiment, one specific to consequentialism. What if an individual could compensate for bad luck and thus always achieve good? The possibility of moral luck seems to be a problem for consequentialism. And it would seem to be a problem for Superman, except for one thing: Superman is no mere consequentialist. Just as we might call Batman a "dark" deontologist, we might call Superman a "super"-consequentialist. Superman is so powerful that he can limit the effects of fortune—or misfortune—on his actions. He's still vulnerable to luck, but his superpowers go a long way to smoothing it over. It's bad luck when Superman is aboard a ship and "braces himself against the rail—and in that second it gives way! He is flung twisting and turning, into the ocean!" (1:21). The thugs think he has drowned, but of course he's back in action and outswimming the ship. When it docks, "Superman subjects the thugs to the severest thrashing of their lives!" (1:22). A moment's bad luck makes no difference to the final outcome. While there is something fishy about moral luck, Superman's superpowers allow him to control for it. He's less subject to fortune or misfortune than the rest of us are.

Despite his duty focus, if you apply consequentialism to Batman, he turns out to be "super" too. Though he can't deflect bullets the way that Superman can, Batman "trains his body to physical perfection" and his intellect to the level of a "master scientist" (63). Add in his seemingly unlimited financial resources, and Batman counters bad luck almost as well as Superman. True, he does suffer more bullet wounds and knockout blows to the back of the head during his first year than Superman does in his, but their creators end each of their adventures the same way: with the superhero victorious. Batman doesn't care about moral luck, because as a deontologist he doesn't believe in it. Yet he's nearly as immune to luck as Superman. So Superman's outcomes aren't what separate him morally from Batman. It's each one's moral code.

Supernets

Another part of a moral code is defining who's morally relevant. Consequentialism casts a broad net: everyone is morally relevant. Aiming to get the greatest good for the greatest number of people, Superman is out to benefit all humankind. His superconsequentialism makes it likely that he can succeed.

By contrast, deontology casts a net only as broad as the duties of the net caster. Kant's Categorical Imperative casts a net over all people. We should never use anyone merely as a means but always at the same time as an ends. Kant himself, however, took only the negative part of the demand—*not* to use anyone merely as a means—to hold absolutely. We're not to infringe on the rights of others, no matter what. Kant calls that a "perfect" duty, one we are obligated to follow completely. Kant did think we also have to follow the positive part of the Categorical Imperative—*to* use them as ends. Yet the extent to which we fulfill that duty is ours to decide. Kant calls it "imperfect," because we're not obligated to follow it completely.

Batman's deontology casts a much narrower net than Kant's, covering only himself and the criminals he's warring on. Though Batman's moral code does establish a positive duty on himself, since he is *to* war on them, it establishes no other positive duty. And it seems to establish no negative duty at all. Batman isn't even under any compulsion to prevent the harm of innocent people. That might be why his writers allow victims to play only small roles in his early stories. Otherwise readers might notice Batman's indifference. When Batman battles a gang of jewel thieves, their intended targets are named—"the Vandersmiths," "the Norton home" (14)—but Kane never draws the individuals.

In Batman's world, victims sometimes aren't even victims. After Batman rescues "Joey" from a gang of thugs torturing him, Joey knocks Batman out and guns down the thugs himself, because they had found out that Joey was double-crossing their mobster employer (114). While Superman might have tried to reform Joey, Batman doesn't even attempt to save him when the boss later stabs him to death (118). Batman has a self-centered duty to fulfill his oath. Unlike the consequentialist Superman, Batman isn't concerned with the well-being of others. And unlike his fellow deontologist Kant, Batman doesn't endorse the Categorical Imperative, either.

As a deontologist generally, Batman's net is likely already narrower than Superman's, for the same reason that Kant's is narrower than Mill's. As a dark deontologist specifically, Batman's net is narrower still. It's so narrow that many might question whether Batman is following a moral code, or is even a superhero, at all. Kant himself would be appalled that Batman is willing to use people merely as a means to fulfilling his oath.

Peaking past Batman's first year of adventures reveals a continuation of this moral ambiguity, especially given his later "Dark Knight" title. While Batman rides to people's rescue, he does so in a sometimes morally suspicious way. Often Batman—especially as later portrayed by Frank Miller in *Batman: The Dark Knight Returns* (1986) and *All Star Batman and Robin* (2005–8)—is better off as nobody's role model. Only because his oath-fulling does usually result in wrongs being righted does Batman fit the definition of being a superhero. By contrast, Superman's status as superhero is never questioned. Peaking past his own first year of adventures we see that, with few exceptions, Superman is consistently portrayed as a positive role model for those around him.

Beyond Superman and Batman

Superman and Batman have appeared in continuous publication since their 1938 and 1939 premieres (a superheroic feat shared only by Wonder Woman, who followed in 1941). Despite their ethical differences, Superman and Batman eventually do fight crime together—appearing side by side for the first time on the cover of the 1941 *World's Best Comics* #1. Admittedly, too, their moral codes evolve—both, for example, avoid killing regardless of consequence or duty. But their characters established two camps for superhero morality that still persist in comics today.

Batman's first writer and cocreator, Bill Finger, developed his character's dark deontology from a hero tradition older than comics, one that includes Alexandre Dumas's 1844 serial novel *The Count of Monte Cristo*, Alfred Burrage's multiple Victorian-era *Spring-Heeled Jack* penny dreadfuls, silent film director Louis Feuillade's 1917 *Judex*, and Lars Anderson's 1936 Domino Lady pulp magazine short stories. While many superheroes might switch between deontology and consequentialism in different adventures, relatively few are strictly deontological, dark or otherwise. Exceptions are notable for their sometimes villainous status. When Gerry Conway and John Romita Sr. introduced the Punisher in *The Amazing Spider-Man* #129 (February 1974), the character's homicidal mission established him as an antihero working outside of superhero moral codes. The character, however, grew popular and received multiple titles of his own. Alan Moore and David Lloyd's 1982–88 *V for Vendetta* features a homicidal, vengeance-seeking superhuman who is overtly linked to Dumas's protagonist and whom Moore himself questions morally: "Is this guy right? Or is he mad?" (Moore, interview by MacDonald). V, like the Count of Monte Cristo and Judex, seeks revenge against specific individuals who wronged him. Though he, like Spring-Heeled Jack, sometimes aids others in the process, he doesn't consider it his moral duty to do so. Batman and the Punisher apply their vengeance mission more broadly, but the way they define their moral duty is the same. Batman falls on the superhero side of the ambiguous divide. His dark deontology is still a moral code, even if it's based on vengeance. Punisher teeters toward villainy.

More often than not, however, superheroes exhibit consequentialist qualities, following the broader approach of Superman. They can still act as if they are doing so ultimately out of duty to help the innocent. But that's because striving to maximize the greatest good for the greatest number achieves the same results. Still, it's the consequences, and not any particular duties, that tend to drive them in many instances. When Stan Lee filled Jack Kirby's talk balloons for *The Fantastic Four* #1 (November 1961), Superman's broad-netted, consequentialist mission to "benefit mankind" generally and for its own sake was already a well-established genre norm. Mr. Fantastic declares, "Together we have more power than any humans have ever possessed," and the Thing interrupts: "You don't have to make a speech, big shot! We understand! We've gotta use that power to help mankind, right?" (*Marvel Firsts: The 1960s* 55). The Thing understands that the consequences of helping people counts more than anything else. It's helping mankind—the greatest good for the greatest number—again.

Perhaps the best example of the deontological vs. consequentialist philosophical debate culminates in Alan Moore and Dave Gibbons's *Watchmen*. Published in 1986–87, arguably the high point of the modern superhero genre, the twelve-episode series is also representative of superhero comics of the previous quarter century. The cast is based on the Charlton Comics "Action Heroes" of the 1960s, which DC acquired in 1983, as Charlton was going out of business. The characters included Captain Atom, an atomic-themed Cold War–era hero created by Joe Gill and Steve Ditko in 1960. Just months later, Marvel introduced their Silver Age–defining Fantastic Four, who, like Captain Atom, received their powers from a space-race disaster. Ditko also created the Question as part of his 1967 *Blue Beetle*, a Golden Age character that Charlton had acquired from Fox Feature Syndicate and rebooted (a phenomenon we discuss in chapter 7).

Moore and Gibbons began drafting a new series for DC, reinterpreting and in some cases killing members of the Charlton cast. DC was pursuing other projects for the characters, so Moore and Gibbons revised them into new counterparts. The blue-armed Captain Atom became the all-blue Dr. Manhattan, and the Question's featureless mask received an inkblot to become

Rorschach's. Moore used them to reveal the superhero character type's pre-existing but largely hidden moral codes and expand them to their implied ends. Where Superman's consequentialism and Batman's deontology are apparent mainly through close analysis, Dr. Manhattan's and Rorschach's parallel philosophies are comparatively overt.

To illustrate Batman and Superman's moral difference, we looked at their first year of stories as a series of related thought experiments. What does consequentialism require, and what does deontology? *Watchmen* proposes a single thought experiment that explores the same contrast. Is saving the entire world from mutually assured nuclear destruction worth sacrificing millions of people? For a consequentialist like Ozymandias—whom Moore and Gibbons based on Pete Morisi's 1966 Thunderbolt—the answer is yes. Ozymandias therefore stages what appears to be an alien attack on New York. Though the attack results in mass death, Ozymandias is able to divert nuclear war by uniting the United States and Soviet Union against a perceived common enemy. While initially working against the scheme, the other heroes, including the Blue Beetle–based Nite Owl and the Nightshade-inspired Silk Spectre, are persuaded by his consequentialist logic.

> SILK SPECTRE: You can't get away with that . . .
>
> OZYMANDIAS: "All the countries are unified and pacified." Can't get away with it? Will you expose me, undoing the peace millions died for? Kill me, risking subsequent investigation? Morally, you're in checkmate, like Blake. Let's compromise.
>
> SILK SPECTRE: Whaat?
>
> DR. MANHATTAN: Logically, I'm afraid he's right. Exposing this plot, we destroy any chance of peace, dooming Earth to worse destruction. On Mars, you demonstrated life's value. If we would preserve life here, we must remain silent.
>
> SILK SPECTRE: Never tell anyone? W-we really have to buy this? Jesus, he was right. All we did was fail to stop him from saving Earth.
>
> NITE OWL: How . . . how can humans make decisions like this? We're damned if we stay quiet, Earth's damned if we don't. We . . . Okay. Okay, count me in. We say nothing. (#12: 20)

Logically, at least according to the consequentialist, everyone should be counted in. Previously, Blake, the nihilistic Comedian—based on Joe Gill and Pat Boyette's 1966 Peacemaker—had agreed. Ozymandias explains: "Though

From *Watchmen* #12.

appalled, exposing my plan would precipitate greater horrors preventing humanity's salvation. Even Blake balked at that responsibility. [...] He knew my plan would succeed, though its scale terrified him" (#11: 25). Ozymandias even murdered Blake to ensure his silence, an action made moral when analyzed by its consequentialist outcome.

Only one character stands apart, both philosophically and even visually. Gibbons depicts the others' philosophical shift toward consequentialism by drawing the scene from a changing perspective that moves each character out of frame. The sequence begins with Ozymandias standing alone in the top row, but then in the middle row of three panels, first Dr. Manhattan, then Silk Spectre, and then Nite Owl vanish as each converts to Ozymandias's figurative and literal viewpoint. The bottom row concludes the sequence with Rorschach standing alone before turning to leave.

> RORSCHACH: Joking, of course.
> NITE OWL: Rorschach . . . ? Rorschach, wait! Where are you going?
>   This is too big to be hard-assed about! We have to compromise . . .
> RORSCHACH: No. Not even in the face of Armageddon. Never
>   compromise. (#12: 20)

Rorschach is the lone deontologist. Because he has sociopathic tendencies, it's not always easy to pin down Rorschach's moral code, or even establish whether he has one. Here, however, Rorschach is channeling not only any old kind of deontology but in fact Kant's own. Unlike Batman, but like Kant would be, Rorschach is repulsed by Ozymandias's using millions of people merely as a means to some other end, even when that end is avoiding complete nuclear annihilation. Though Rorschach shares with Batman a self-imposed duty to battle wrongdoers, as he's facing down Ozymandias Rorschach would agree with Kant that it's wrong to use innocent people. It disrespects them. Even now, in the face of nuclear war, the soon-to-be victims deserve to know the truth. They have to be treated as ends in themselves, consequences be damned.

At this point in the story, Ozymandias recedes into the narrative background, and Dr. Manhattan takes over the consequentialist line, ensuring that Rorschach doesn't ruin Ozymandias's plan.

> DR. MANHATTAN: Where are you going?
> RORSCHACH: Back to Owlship. Back to America. Evil must be punished. People must be told.
> DR. MANHATTAN: Rorschach . . . You know I can't let you do that.
> RORSCHACH: Huhhh. Of course. Must protect [Ozymandias's] new utopia. One more body amongst foundations makes little difference. Well? What are you waiting for? Do it.
> DR. MANHATTAN: Rorschach . . .
> RORSCHACH: Do it! (#12: 22–23)

Dr. Manhattan then executes Rorschach in a telekinetic explosion of body parts. Even though Rorschach faced the consequence of his own death, as a deontologist he knew that it was his duty to act according to his Kantian maxim of never using people as mere means. While in his own adventure Superman also sacrificed the well-being of those whom he couldn't reform, Gibbons foregrounds Rorschach's puddled blood in a full-width panel, highlighting Dr. Manhattan's lethal morality. By contrast, Shuster shrunk Superman's bloodthirsty aviator and torturer as they vanished into the backgrounds of smaller frames, only vaguely implying the same carnage.

Though Dr. Manhattan inherits Superman's ethical philosophy, and though he has physical powers even greater than Superman's, his consequentialism isn't itself super. That's because, unlike Siegel and Shuster with Superman, Moore and Gibbons allow Dr. Manhattan to suffer from moral luck. From Dr. Manhattan's perspective, that mutually assured destruction was avoided is simply a matter of good fortune. He didn't need to do the dirty work but could still reap the reward. Dr. Manhattan even proves his consequentialist credentials by retroactively endorsing their killing. He knows that Ozymandias's actions were the right thing to do—just as he knows that killing Rorschach was. For Dr. Manhattan, maxims be damned. It's the results that count, and as long as the overall happiness of world peace ensues, he did the right thing. By killing his own teammate so gruesomely, he's internalized consequentialism even more than Ozymandias did.

That's why Dr. Manhattan's confrontation with Rorschach is so philosophically powerful. Not only does it end gruesomely for Rorschach, but neither Dr. Manhattan nor Rorschach minds. Dr. Manhattan doesn't mind, because individual deaths are justified if the greatest good overall has been secured. Rorschach doesn't mind, because consequences don't matter at all. He stood his ground, spoke his mind, and acted according to his maxim. Consequences, including his life, are irrelevant.

So, as Mill would want, Dr. Manhattan casts a moral net as wide as Superman's, aiming to bring about the greatest good for the greatest number of people. Killing millions to save billions is on balance an enormous positive in the calculation. Killing one—Rorschach—to save billions is a no-brainer. Given his other narrative conventions, Siegel wouldn't have written a thought-experiment story where Superman had to make that kind of judgment. Presumably, Superman would have been able to avoid nuclear annihilation, spare the millions whom Ozymandias sacrificed, and avoided killing Rorschach too. Still, Superman's motivation to do all that would have been the same as Dr. Manhattan's: to achieve the greatest good for the greatest number. Superman would have simply been more effective, had Siegel written him into the plot of *Watchmen*.

Rorschach, meanwhile, accepts a deontology like Kant's. Rorschach declares not only that "evil must be punished" but also that "people must be told." Consequentialists might agree with the first statement, though they would disagree with deontologists on what counts as evil. Only a deontologist, however, would agree with the second. People must be told because people *deserve* to be told. Not telling people disrespects them *as* people. It dehumanizes them. Dr. Manhattan—not to mention Silk Spectre and Nite Owl—agrees with Ozymandias that people need to be deceived. They can't handle knowing what really happened. Only Rorschach sees them as Kant would: ends in themselves. As a result, he would agree with Kant that it's his duty to tell the truth. To say nothing is to perpetuate a lie. Consequences aren't what matter.

Better that we respect people and let the cards fall where they may, than disrespect them by treating them as pawns.

Perpetuating a lie is close to Kant's example of promising falsely. It therefore violates the second version of the Categorical Imperative as well as the first. Were everyone to perpetuate a lie, then everyone else would eventually become aware that everyone was lying and then no one would believe the lie *as* a lie. Were Dr. Manhattan permitted to perpetuate the lie, then he would be acting according to a maxim that only some people could follow, since its universalization would undercut it. That's to make an exception for some, the superhero elite, when the moral law must hold for all. Because the maxim to perpetuate a lie could not be made a universal law, it violates the moral law. Because Rorschach, as a deontologist, adheres to the moral law, it's his duty not to lie.

When Rorschach says, "Never compromise," he's channeling the categorical nature of morality just as Kant does. The Categorical Imperative *is* categorical, no matter the consequences. While even the nihilistic Comedian and the impotent Nite Owl convert to consequentialism in this most extreme circumstance, Rorschach is willing to sacrifice the lives of everyone on the planet—his own included—rather than violate his moral code. In so doing, he casts a moral net far broader than Batman's. While Batman must war on criminals, all else be damned, Rorschach doesn't want to use innocent people merely as a means. Ozymandias was wrong to sacrifice millions to save billions, and Dr. Manhattan and the others are wrong to remain silent.

Since Moore places the most, and most physically powerful, characters on the side of consequentialism—not superconsequentialism but a kind recognizable by Mill—consequentialism appears triumphant. However, deontology may battle on too, since the closing panel of *Watchmen* depicts Rorschach's truth-revealing diary in the hands of a sympathetically minded publisher. People presumably will be told, as Rorschach insisted they should be. Moore doesn't champion either philosophy, but instead reveals a moral battle still at the heart of the genre a half century after Superman's and Batman's premieres.

TWO

WHAT GOOD ARE SUPERHEROES?

As we just discussed, morality has to do with codes of conduct, while ethics is the study of morality. Ethicists investigate questions like: What would consequentialism and deontology say about the morality of torturing terrorists, using fetal tissue for stem-cell research, or ever telling a lie? And which theory, if either, would be right? Metaethics, by contrast, is the study of the nature of morality itself. Metaethicists investigate questions like: Is morality relative or absolute? Does morality rest on subjective or objective grounds? Academic philosophers have faced those metaethical questions directly by marshaling arguments, raising objections, and giving responses. Superhero comics have faced those same questions indirectly by imagining alternate worlds, relying on fictional and factual authorities, and leaving their readers to ponder the mix. Many readers of superhero comics have been exposed to metaethical questions without even knowing it.

We established in chapter 1 that of the range of qualities for the superhero character type, the most essential are superpowers and some variation on goodness. Whether consequentialists, deontologists, or other ethical adherents, superheroes are meant to be morally good. The *Oxford English Dictionary* describes superheroes as "benevolent." Writers of superhero comics agree. Stan Lee maintains that superheroes use their power "to accomplish a good deed" (115), and Danny Fingeroth says that they possess a "nobility of purpose" (125). Picking up on the preponderance of consequentialist superheroes, Jeph Loeb maintains that superheroes intend "to make a better world" (119). Loeb also calls superhero comics "moral lessons," suggesting that writers "by telling the stories of the heroes in comic books [. . .] are doing a heroic act" (120, 119).

As a result, readers inspired by superheroes "can make the world a much better place" (123).

Whether we're consequentialists, deontologists, or something else, are the terms "good," "right," "benevolent," "noble," and "better"—when applied to superheroes—relative or absolute? Are they subjective or objective? If morality is relative, then right and wrong can differ between cultures or even individuals, with no ultimate standard. If morality is absolute, then while differing cultures or individuals may each believe that its practices are moral, there is an ultimate standard—whether or not anyone ever actually knows what it is. On the other hand, if morality is subjective, then right and wrong depend on who determines it. That's because morality is based on opinion or preference. If morality is objective, then right and wrong are independent of determinations, opinions, or preferences. Morality must instead be discovered.

It might seem that all subjectivists are relativists, but they need not be. Instead of members of a culture, say, determining morality, morality might be based on the preferences of a powerful outside force that imposes it absolutely. In traditions like the ancient Greek, for example, right and wrong are determined by the gods. Because Zeus, the king of the gods, rules absolutely, his subjective moral code is also absolute—even though Zeus decides right and wrong himself rather than discovering it objectively. In monotheistic traditions, the relevant subject is God. The Ten Commandments are moral because God commands them. And though God commands them absolutely, making morality absolute, God's omnipotence doesn't make his morality any more objective in our technical sense. Were it objective, God would be obeying a moral force beyond Godself and therefore wouldn't be its Creator. Monotheism regards God as analogous to a person—an absolutely powerful person, but a person nevertheless—and people are simply subjects. For morality to be objective in our (again, technical) sense, it would have to exist apart from any person and so be discoverable by God, the gods, society, and even superheroes.

To discover the metaethical nature of superhero comics, this chapter turns to both historical and contemporary philosophers. In chapter 1, we met Kant and Mill, philosophers from the eighteenth and nineteenth centuries, respectively. Now we turn to the twentieth century. In their 1992 "Troubles for New Wave Moral Semantics," Terence Horgan and Mark Timmons introduce the thought experiment of Moral Twin Earth, a world just like Earth—each of us even has a "twin" there—except that we and our twins use the word "good" differently. Horgan and Timmons attempt to deduce the nature of morality from how we use moral language to describe this moral Twin Earth. Not everyone agrees that our use of moral language indicates anything about the nature of morality, but enough philosophers do that we employ this strategy to explore the nature of superhero morality specifically.

The notion of Twin Earths—that is, Earth-like worlds populated by twin-like inhabitants—is also a staple of superhero comics. Horgan and Timmons depict their version of Twin Earth as differing from the Earth in only one way. Comic book creators usually depict theirs as differing in many, including differences from our Earth as it actually is and differences from Earth as it is in their superheroes' realities. But the general idea is the same, and so is the philosophical lesson that we're drawing.

This chapter examines three comic book Twin Earth thought experiments: Jerry Siegel and John Forte's *Tales of Bizarro World*, Gardner Fox and Mike Sekowsky's Earth-3, and Grant Morrison and Jim Lee's *Mastermen* world. Like Horgan and Timmons, we attempt to deduce the nature of morality from the moral language used to describe these comic book Twin Earths. Specifically, we investigate whether each description suggests the view that superhero morality is relative or absolute—or left ambiguous.

To explore whether superhero morality is subjective or objective, we turn to Plato. In his dialog the *Euthyphro*, Plato asks whether something is pious because it's loved by the gods, or whether it's loved by the gods because it's pious. The first option makes morality subjective, since the gods—the ultimate subjects—determine piety. Subjective morality can still be absolute, as in the case of Zeus. The second option makes morality objective, since the gods, like the rest of us, have to discover it out there in the objective world.

This chapter applies lessons from Plato to superhero comics' depictions of their own godlike beings; to the analysis of contemporary scholars about the role of society; and to the Comics Code Authority, which governed the moral content of superhero comics directly. By investigating these divinities, critics, and mandates, we investigate whether these different uses of moral language suggest that superhero morality is subjective or objective, or whether in this case too it's left ambiguous.

Before we begin, a methodological point is in order. Academic philosophers often disagree about all sorts of things, including the nature of morality. The comic book authors, scholars, and authorities we consider, too, disagree quite frequently. Sometimes those disagreements fall into neat categories, so we're able to tell where metaethical views lie. Other times the disagreements leave results unsettled. In what follows, we won't always be able to determine things conclusively. Instead we aim to figure out the nature of superhero morality in particular cases—admitting when necessary that even then the answer isn't always clear. That's because philosophical thought experiments are often messy—whether in academic texts or from superhero comics.

Moral Twin Earths

Horgan and Timmons base their Moral Twin Earth on another twentieth-century philosopher's thought experiment. In his 1973 "Meaning and Reference," Hilary Putnam introduces Twin Earth, a world where every person and place on Earth has a molecule-for-molecule duplicate, or "twin." There would, for example, be a Twin Jerry Siegel and a Twin Joe Shuster living in a Twin United States. There is, however, one thing that has no twin: water. On Earth, what we call "water" has the molecular composition H_2O. On Twin Earth, what they call "water" has a more complicated molecular composition abbreviated "XYZ." Coincidentally, H_2O and XYZ taste the same, participate in the same (or nearly the same) chemical interactions, and occur in the same places on their respective worlds. They just have different compositions.

Suppose on our Earth Jerry Siegel asks Joe Shuster: "Could you get me a glass of water?" Jerry's request is fulfilled only if he's given a glass of H_2O. Now suppose that Twin Jerry Siegel asks Twin Joe Shuster: "Could you get me a glass of water?" Twin Jerry's request is fulfilled only if he's given a glass of XYZ. Were Jerry given a glass of XYZ (and he realized it), then he'd say that what he was given wasn't water. According to Jerry, "water" means H_2O. Were Twin Jerry given a glass of H_2O (and he realized it), then he'd say the same but for the opposite reason.

Putnam reads the following philosophical lesson off these facts about scientific language use. What we say or think about things such as water is relative, not just to our culture, but also to our world. Regardless, the possibility of agreeing or disagreeing about what scientific words mean shows that their *meaning* isn't relative. It's absolute. There's got to be an ultimate standard, whether it's known or not. Otherwise Jerry and Twin Jerry wouldn't be in a position to say that they were given something right—or, as it turns out, something wrong. Were everything relative, then Jerry and Twin Jerry would just talk past one another, and genuine agreement or disagreement couldn't occur. Each would merely have his opinion. Neither would be right or wrong, nor have anything significant to say to the other. This doesn't imply that Jerry and Twin Jerry would *agree* on the ultimate standard, of course. As we've seen, they'd disagree. It does, however, mean that the use of their scientific language presupposes that *some* ultimate standard does, in fact, exist.

We're unsure whether Putnam's right about all this, since these are pretty contentious claims. And so much depends on our intuitions about what language does and does not require. Even so, Horgan and Timmons assume that Putnam is right when they apply his tools to investigate moral language. Suppose that when Jerry talks about something being "good," he thinks that it has the best results. As we saw in chapter 1, Jerry would be a consequentialist, like John Stuart Mill, Superman, and Dr. Manhattan. Now suppose that when Moral Twin Jerry talks about something being "good," he thinks that it helps fulfill duties. Moral Twin Jerry would be a deontologist, like Immanuel Kant, Batman, and Rorschach. Were Jerry given something that helps fulfill duties but doesn't have the best results, then he'd say that it wasn't good. Were Moral Twin Jerry given something that has the best results but doesn't help fulfill duties, then he'd say the same but for the opposite reason.

Similar to Putnam, Horgan and Timmons take this to show that what we say or think about things such as goodness is relative, not just to our culture, but also to our world. Also similar to Putnam, they take the possibility of agreeing or disagreeing about what moral words mean, regardless of how we use them, to show that their *meaning* isn't relative either. It's absolute. There's again got to be a (known or unknown) objective standard, or Jerry and Moral Twin Jerry wouldn't be in a position to say that they were given something that was right—or, as it turns out, something that was wrong—either. But Horgan and Timmons argue that there's an important difference between scientific and moral language. In the scientific case, the disagreement is about the meaning of "water." Is it H_2O or XYZ? In the moral case, the disagreement isn't necessarily about the meaning of "good." Jerry and Moral Twin Jerry might actually agree on its meaning, if they could figure it out. Their disagreement is instead about the theory *behind* the meaning. Jerry is a consequentialist, while Moral Twin Jerry is a deontologist. They might *mean* the same thing by "good" but *theorize* about it differently.

We're skeptical about Horgan and Timmons's distinction between meaning and theories behind it, so we're going to bracket the distinction and focus on meaning itself. Though we're also unsure whether Horgan and Timmons are right about morality's being absolute, we're going to adopt their methodology as we consider DC's Moral Twin Earths. If in any of those thought experiments we and our twins can genuinely agree or disagree about what moral terms mean, then those thought experiments suggest that there is a kind of ultimate standard. So meaning is absolute. If we and our moral twins instead talk past one another, then these thought experiments show that there isn't that kind of standard. Meaning is relative. If the results are ambiguous, then they show neither.

Bizarro World and Absolutism

Bizarro World provides DC's first Moral Twin Earth thought experiment. While Earth is home to Superman, Bizarro World is home to Superman's twin, Bizarro:

> Everyone can understand the fear of seeing your beliefs and ideals become twisted and deformed—of seeing everything you stand for reflected darkly back at you. Unfortunately for Superman, and the world itself, he experiences this very thing every single time he faces Bizarro.
>
> An imperfect clone of Superman, Bizarro possesses all of the hero's amazing abilities and none of his moral restraints. He stands for the moral opposite of everything Superman represents, a warped reflection of the Man of Steel's inherent heroism. The uncontrollable villain rampages through the world, causing mass devastation and destruction, his twisted perspective making him as committed to causing violence as Superman is to stopping it. ("Bizarro")

Bizarro was first created by Otto Binder and George Papp for *Superboy* #68 (October 1958) and by Alvin Schwartz and Curt Swan for the separate *Superman* comic strip running in newspapers at the same time. Beginning with issue #285 (June 1961), Jerry Siegel and John Forte's "Tales of the Bizarro World" appeared as a regular feature in *Adventure Comics*. Siegel explains the world's origin in the first episode:

> Some time ago, an amazing duplicator ray formed a grotesque imitation of Superman called Bizarro, and an imperfect imitation of Lois Lane. These creatures can move and talk and have the memories of the real Lois and Superman to a limited degree. In addition, Bizarro has all of Superman's powers! Feared on Earth as monsters, Bizarro No. 1 and his wife,

Bizarro-Lois, fled to another planet. With an imitator machine built by Bizarro, they peopled this world with duplicates of themselves, then rebuilt the planet into a mad Bizarro World. (12)

Most issues also include the "Bizarro Code":

Us do opposite of Earthly things!
Us hate beauty!
Us love ugliness!
Is big crime to make anything perfect on Bizarro World! (13)

In Bizarro theaters, Bizarro audiences cheer against good guys: "Hooray! Bad-guy getting away from sheriff!" (26). When Bizarro kidnaps Jimmy Olsen and brings him to Bizarro World, a Bizarro newspaper employee sees his "depressed expression" and consoles him: "Me glad you sad, because that mean you am happy!" (42). Bizarro firefighters set fires to buildings and add gasoline to spread the flames (43). When a giant gorilla attempts to kill Bizarro, Bizarro responds: "Him lovable, too!" (72). When aliens attack Bizarro World, Bizarro cheerleaders shout: "Hooray, hooray, them am destroying us now!" (81).

So what do these descriptions of Bizarro World say about morality? Is it relative or absolute?

Clearly, Superman and Bizarro have very different moral codes. Superman prevents mass devastation and destruction, while Bizarro causes them. Though they're both concerned with consequences, Superman tries to bring about the greatest good for the greatest number of people, while Bizarro, viewed from Superman's (and our) perspective, tries to bring about the opposite.

Unlike our twins as imaged by Horgan and Timmons, who use their moral terms differently from how we use ours, the people of Bizarro World use their moral and evaluative terms generally the same as we do (though their grammar is less correct). Their "beauty" refers to the same qualities as our "beauty," qualities they hate. Their "ugliness" describes the same thing as our "ugliness," which they love. In response to aliens attacking them, Bizarro cheerleaders mean the same thing by "destroying" as we do, but they cheer it on. To "do opposite of Earthly things" requires Bizarro to adopt our Earthly meanings and then act contrarily toward them.

Regardless, Bizarro's use of terms such as "beauty," "ugliness," and "destroying" suggests that when it comes to superhero morality, Siegel is an absolutist. We would agree with Bizarros about what counts as beauty, ugliness, and destroying. We'd just disagree on the stance to take toward them. When Bizarros cheer that Bizarro World is being destroyed, they apparently mean that this is bad, just as we would. In both worlds, "bad" refers to destruction and harm. Bizarros simply like it. Similarly, when a Bizarro person says she is glad that Jimmy Olsen is sad, she apparently means that he is sad, just as we would. In both worlds, "sad" refers to a depressed mental state. The Bizarro person simply finds this desirable. And to express that, she uses "glad" to describe the same emotional response we mean when we use "glad." Finally, when Bizarros say that they "hate" beauty, they apparently mean that there *is* beauty. They simply react negatively to it. Bizarros generally stand "for the moral opposite of everything Superman represents" and everything we value.

Being able to agree with what Bizarros mean and disagree with their reactions suggests some ultimate standard that we're appealing to. Were morality merely relative, then we'd each merely have our opinions, neither right nor wrong. Superman and Bizarro would be talking past one another. That's not, however, how Siegel describes his thought-experiment scenarios. Superman and Bizarro are depicted as enemies. One way to make sense of this is that they're fighting over some ultimate standard, which suggests superhero moral absolutism.

Earth-3 and Relativism

DC offers a second Moral Twin Earth thought experiment with Earth-3, describing it as a "complete opposite of Earth-0" on their website in 2015:

> From a young age, we're taught the difference between good and evil, and for most of us, those early lessons go on to shape our entire worldview. So imagine what might happen if we were to flip the message. If we were to teach our children that evil was the way of the world. If teachers and philosophers taught their students to "do no good" rather than to "do no harm." If the world leaders and heroes of our planet sought to maintain chaos and corruption rather than peace.
>
> Our world would be starkly different. It would be a nightmare. It would be a place of death and devastation. It would be Earth-3.
>
> A complete opposite of Earth-0 in every way, good and evil are reversed in the ruthless nations of Earth-3. Greed, ambition and conquest are rewarded, especially when they come at the expense of others. Heroes

have no place in a world like this, and so it's a collective of villains that seek to prolong and foster their Earth's way of life. ("Earth-3")

Contrary to the differences between Earth-3 and our own world, called "Earth-0" in DC's New 52 continuity, the way that moral language works here might seem to commit DC to superhero moral absolutism straightaway. The description calls the practices on Earth-3 "evil," where evil is what *we* call "evil." Otherwise it would say: "If we were to teach our children that good was the way of the world," and then define "good" as causing harm. It defines "evil" that way, which is to say, as we do. Again, the possibility of agreement would suggest absolutism. But the description is written only from our perspective. An Earth-3 writer might define "evil" differently. Would we agree or disagree with her or just talk past one another?

The first iteration of Earth-3 was introduced by writer Gardner Fox in *Justice League of America* #29 (August 1964). Fox had scripted the introduction of the DC multiverse with the retconning of Earth-2 in 1961 (which we discuss in chapter 5), and three years later he described "yet another Earth—Earth-3 on the list of possible worlds" (2). While the superheroes of Earth-1 and Earth-2 fight criminals, artist Mike Sekowsky draws their Earth-3 counterparts fighting police:

> But wait, you say! These are not super-heroes but—supervillains! Ah! You're beginning to understand that on Earth-3 some things are drastically different from the way they are on Earth-1 and Earth-2!
>
> On Earth-1 and Earth-2 things are quite similar! Some super-heroes have the same names, although they may not look alike—[...]. But Earth-3! Woww! History repeats itself—in a reversed way! For instance, Columbus did not discover America! Columbus was an American— who discovered Europe! Not only that but colonial England won her freedom from the United States in the Revolutionary War of 1776... And it was actor Abe Lincoln who shot President John Wilkes Booth!
>
> Small wonder, then, that there are no super-heroes on Earth-3! For Earth-3 is a world where every super-being is a criminal—who have banded themselves together to form the Crime Syndicate of America! (3–5)

Metaethical issues don't take center stage until the Syndicate discovers the existence of Earth-1, the home of DC's Silver Age superheroes. Earth-3's Ultra-man, who gains "ultra-vision" from kryptonite, sees "a strange world":

Amazing! I see super-beings on that world—about to battle a master criminal! Fascinated by something so unusual, I spent several hours studying the other Earth and these super-heroes. And—can you imagine?—they were using their powers to stop crimes—instead of committing them . . . (6)

Because we haven't seen any evidence of agreement or disagreement between people from Earth and Earth-3, this too is ambiguous, oscillating between relativism and absolutism. But things settle in favor of relativism when the Syndicate travels to Earth-1 to battle the Justice League. Though weakened by the lack of challenges on their own world, members of the Syndicate are "sure that with our super-powers—we'll triumph!" (7). The Justice League members also have superpowers, but the differences between the two worlds run deeper. The Syndicate expects to win because the Syndicate always wins. It's a quality not of their individual characters but of their world. They just don't realize that that quality is relative to their world—just because it is.

As it turns out, it's a quality of Earth-1 that the Justice League always wins there. The Syndicate never had a chance. When nearly defeated on Earth-1, the Syndicate transports both teams to Earth-3, declaring: "You Justice League members have never been defeated on Earth-One! We Crime Syndicate members have never been beaten on Earth-Three! We brought you here to do battle on our home grounds" (20). Accordingly, the Syndicate, while on Earth-3, "where somehow the advantage is in their favor" (21), defeats the Justice League. They conclude: "All we've proven is that you are better than we are on Earth-One—while we are better than you on Earth-Three!" (21).

The Syndicate might mean "better" in the physical sense. But they should also mean it in the moral sense. Superheroes are do-gooders. The Justice League has to win on Earth-1, because the Justice League exemplifies what it is to do good as a superhero *there*. Likewise, the Syndicate has to win on Earth-3, the Syndicate exemplifies what it is to do good as a superhero *there*. "Better" in the moral sense means different things on each of the different worlds. Unless they specify which world they're talking about, when members of the Justice League or Syndicate use the word they seem to be talking past the other. They're neither agreeing nor disagreeing that something on either world is genuinely better or not. The worlds, and what's better on each, just differ. Neither the Justice League nor the Syndicate declares that it's better overall. They don't agree or disagree on that point either. They're stuck with being better on one world but not another, and any deeper claim about being absolutely better would be meaningless. If the Justice League or Syndicate did say anything about it, it would be mere opinion.

Hoping to find "neutral ground," which would be objective in our sense, "where neither of us has an advantage!" (21), the Syndicate transports both teams to a different world still, Earth-2, the continuing world of DC's Golden Age superheroes. However, even though their "powers are too evenly matched for one to win over the other," the Justice League outwits the Syndicate (#30: 17). After imprisoning the Syndicate between universes, "the triumphant super-heroes depart" (24). That's because the Syndicate mistook Earth-2 as neutral. However, the same relative morality applies to both Earth-1 and Earth-2. Again, there's no agreement or disagreement about who's better overall. Such agreement or disagreement doesn't even make sense, which is why they're world-hopping in the first place. Everything's just relative. It just so happens that Earth-1 and Earth-2 are relative the same way. So where the metaethical thought experiment of Bizarro World suggests that superhero morality is absolute, the metaethical thought of experiment of Earth-3 suggests the opposite.

Overman and Absolutism

In *The Multiversity: Mastermen* #1 (April 2015), Grant Morrison and Jim Lee depict a third Moral Twin Earth thought experiment. What if Superman's rocket landed not in the United States but in Nazi Germany? In this world, Superman becomes "Overman" and leads Hitler to world domination.

Though raised in the values of eugenics and fascism, Overman exhibits tendencies to take "justice" to mean what we mean by it. When Uncle Sam, sixty years later, leads a team of Freedom Fighters against Nazi-ruled Metropolis, the other members of the Nazi Justice League call them "terrorists," but Overman disagrees: "For years we've faced legitimate threats where there was no doubt as to the morality of our actions. [. . .] But this—this is different. These enemies rise from the shame of our past" (unpaginated). Later he adds: "I was sure before, sure we could somehow outrace our past. That mountain of dead . . . But sometimes I just think . . . what if we deserve this?" Reared a fascist, Overman aided the Nazis in achieving world domination. Sometimes this involved helping them push their specifically Nazi agenda. Other times it involved defending them against "legitimate" threats.

Notice how Overman distinguishes the morality of those threats from the morality of the Freedom Fighters they're facing now. These threats were "legitimate" from a non-Nazi perspective. Then their actions possessed "morality," again from a non-Nazi perspective. In other words, even an individual whose moral values were not aligned with the Nazis' might agree that Overman's dealing with those "legitimate" threats was morally justifiable. Yet Overman disagreed. He even felt "shame" for much of what the Nazis, with his help, had previously done. By "legitimate," "morality," and "shame," Overman is using language that Uncle Sam would agree with but that his own Nazi society wouldn't. He's appealing to an ultimate standard of right and wrong. It's against that standard that he's evaluating the Nazis' claims.

When twin Jimmy Olsen interviews Overman, he gives voice to the disagreement between Overman and the citizens of the twin Metropolis:

> You've expressed regret in the past for the ethnic and ideological purges of the Hitler Era. Is there any extent to which you find yourself sympathetic to "Uncle Sam's" rhetoric? I mean we live in a virtual paradise. People are content and life is easy. I have to ask you, what's to regret?

Relative to the Nazi perspective, there's nothing to regret. Yet Overman does regret things. Overman and his countrymen and women aren't talking past one another. They're engaged in a dialog where each side disagrees with the other. Each disagrees about an ultimate standard of morality. That's why twin Jimmy Olsen's interviewing him. Morrison and Lee describe this Twin Earth in a way that suggests superhero moral absolutism.

This thought experiment differs from both the previous superhero Moral Twin Earth ones. Unlike with Bizarro World, Overman isn't comparing himself to a twin in another world, as Bizarro compares himself to Superman. As far as Overman is concerned, there is no twin. Everything stays within one world. Likewise, unlike with Earth-3, Overman isn't traveling to alternate twin worlds, to battle or even just to talk. Overman stays put. His battles are with Uncle Sam, and his talks are with the people around him. The Overman thought experiment is something like what Horgan and Timmons's own thought experiment would be if everyone lived in the same world. Jerry and Moral Twin Jerry might even be neighbors. Here, Overman and Uncle Sam, who shares Superman's morality, are. Overman and his countryfolk genuinely disagree. For Jerry and Twin Jerry, it's about consequentialism and deontology. For Overman and twin Jimmy Olsen, it's about Uncle Sam's and the

Nazis' ideologies. Each member of each pair thinks that the other gets morality wrong, presupposing an absolutist metaethics.

Gods and Ambiguity

So far we've been concerned with answering the first metaethical question as applied to superheroes. Is superhero morality relative or absolute? The use of moral language to describe Bizarro World suggests absolutism, its use to describe Earth-3 relativism, and its use to describe Overman's world absolutism again. Does the use of moral language to describe these worlds also suggest something about our second metaethical question? Is superhero morality subjective or objective? If it's subjective, then whether something is right or wrong depends on the judgment of some authority: society, the gods, or even God. If morality's objective, then whether something is right or wrong is independent of anyone's judgment.

The most famous philosopher to ask this metaethical question did in fact put things in terms of the divine. As Plato phrased it, is something pious because it's loved by the gods, or is it loved by the gods because it's pious? We can generalize the question. Is something moral because it's loved by the gods, or is it loved by the gods because it's moral? In other words, is morality subjective or objective?

According to the *Oxford English Dictionary*, heroes are themselves "favoured by the gods." Since superheroes by definition are do-gooders, doing good would itself be favored by the gods. But the distinction between the two parts of Euthyphro's question is ambiguous. Are superheroes moral because they're favored by the gods (the subjective possibility) or favored by the gods because they're moral (the objective possibility)? There's another ambiguity also. In superhero comics, "the gods" can mean either (a) the plot formulas and outcomes that shape events in a superhero world or (b) the superheroes themselves.

"The gods" in the sense of (a) suggests an all-powerful force that controls events—the way the Syndicate always triumphs on Earth-3, "where somehow the advantage is in their favor." Though the comic book writers are that literal force, within the story world that force is the equivalent of God. In *More Fun Comics* #52 (February 1940), Jerry Siegel and Bernard Baily introduced the first representation of God in DC. "Some higher power, some mysterious voice, told [a murdered police officer] he would go back to Earth and avenge evil," explains *The Spectre* editor Bob Greenberger. In their 1986 *History of the DC Universe: Book One*, Marv Wolfman and George Pérez depict the "single will which brought light to the dark, gave substance to nothingness, and created life from unlife" (unpaginated). But when a scientist investigating "the origin of the Universe" witnesses "the hand of creation reach into the cosmos and pluck that fruit of life," "the Universe exploded" into two universes, and "with the unleashing of the anti-matter universe there came a wave of evil." A second scientist later duplicates the "deadly experiment" and "watched in awe as the hand of creation drew the clouds of chaos together [. . .] until the single will would let him see nothing more."

Despite the depictions of a Creator and an origin myth for evil, however, neither answers Euthyphro's question. The "evil" unleashed in the antimatter universe may be subjective. In other words, it may be evil for superheroes because it's created, and thereby determined, by a godly subject. Or the "evil" may be objective, simply happened upon or discovered by subjects, and therefore simply evil for superheroes. The thought experiment is indeterminate.

Let's focus instead on "the gods" in the sense of (b), by turning to the superheroes themselves. Because superheroes are superhuman and variously godlike and Godlike, Euthyphro's question may be applied to them. Is something moral for superheroes because it's loved by them, or is it loved by superheroes because it's moral for them? Though the character type upholds government-defined morality by routinely aiding law enforcement (even if paradoxically through vigilantism), superheroes don't necessarily accept the legal definitions of "right" and "wrong." Superhero comics scholar Richard Reynolds notes that Superman helps those "victimized by a blind though well-intentioned state" in his first adventure (14). He breaks into the governor's house to prevent the execution of a wrongly convicted woman whom the governor pardons when shown the actual killer's confession (Siegel and Shuster, *Superman Chronicles* 1:5–7). So even when enacting its laws correctly, the legal system can be flawed. That means there must be some ethical standard for superheroes independent of the determinations of the state, so morality would seem objective. Apparently, something is right for superheroes, and that's not because it's loved by the state.

But superheroes could be grounding superhero morality themselves—moving the subjective determiner from the state to them. Maybe Superman rescued the wrongly convicted woman, not because the state was objectively wrong, but because he felt it was subjectively so. Perhaps Superman takes himself to determine morality. Something is moral for Superman if it's loved, not by the gods, but by Superman himself. Like Zeus, who determines morality for his pantheon, in a sense Superman determines it for all superheroes who follow in his genre. But that wouldn't necessarily make morality relative. Superman is himself godlike, the most Zeus-like character in the DC superhero pantheon. Superhero morality could be absolute, even if subjectively so, grounded on Superman's understanding of right and wrong. Reynolds asserts that superheroes champion "a clear understanding of right and wrong" (14), but that could be because it's *their* clear understanding—Superman's or all of theirs, depending on how much Superman enforces his will.

Comic book scholars Hal Blythe and Charlie Sweet argue that a superhero is "morally superior," so that when she acts outside the law "no reader thinks of the illegality" (185). That echoes Reynolds's observation that Superman acts "illegally if he believes national interests are at stake" yet shows "moral loyalty to the state, though not necessarily the letter of its laws" (15, 16). But it's still ambiguous whether a superhero's moral superiority allows her to determine morality or merely to discover it. Something could be morally superior for a superhero because it's loved by the superhero, or it could be loved by the superhero because it's morally superior. In the first case, superhero morality would be subjective. In the second, it would be objective. Comic book narratives leave it ambiguous.

Earth-0 and Ambiguity

So it's unclear whether superhero morality is subjective or objective. But DC universes, like all superhero universes, are fictions crafted in the real world—not Earth-1, Earth-2, or Earth-3 but, as DC sometimes understands ours, Earth-0 or, in an earlier iteration, Earth Prime. The creative "gods" of superhero worlds are the creators of superhero stories, the writers and artists who "favour" their characters. So let's turn our metaethical attention to scholars who explore how real-world writers and artists are influenced to create their stories.

As we discussed earlier, Peter Coogan's superhero definition begins: "A heroic character with a selfless, pro-social mission" (30), adding that "his fight against evil must fit in with existing, professed mores of society" (31). Coogan means *our* society. From the perspective of the real world, superhero creators create their characters with prosocial missions that themselves fit in with professed social mores. Coogan's point might be thought of as making morality socially, and thus subjectively, determined. Something would be moral for superheroes because society loves it. We can't, however, conclude that superhero morality is subjective. Being prosocial could involve supporting a morality that our society discovers. Society professes those superhero mores, not because it determines them, but because it discovers them.

Literary critic Northrop Frye would likely categorize superhero comics as melodramas, which portray "the triumph of moral virtue over villainy, and the consequent idealizing of the moral views assumed to be held by the audience" ("Comic Fictional Modes"). Again, however, we don't know whether the moral views are moral because they're held by the audience, or whether the audience holds them because they're moral. That's again ambiguous, offering no clear answer between subjectivism and objectivism. So it's unclear how this applies to superhero morality.

Literary critic John G. Cawalti does maintain that genre formulas reveal "the collective fantasies shared by large groups of people," specifically "moral fantasies [. . .] constituting an imaginary world" where "things always work out the way we want them to" (7, 16). If superhero morality is based on fantasy, then it's based on opinion or preference rather than anything independent of us. Something is right in a story because we're loving it. We aren't loving it because it's right. That makes superhero morality in particular subjective. Cawalti goes on to define the larger genre principle that superhero stories obey:

> Formula stories affirm existing interests and attitudes by presenting an imaginary world that is aligned with these interests and attitudes [. . .]. By confirming existing definitions of the world, literary formulas help to maintain a culture's ongoing consensus about the nature of reality and morality. (35)

It's ambiguous whether the culture has an ongoing consensus based on ongoing subjective preference or an ongoing objective reality. Given what Cawalti said earlier, however, he would seem to be a superhero moral subjectivist.

Philosopher and literary critic Umberto Eco explores similar themes when he observes that each superhero "is profoundly kind, moral, faithful to human and natural laws, and therefore it is right (and nice) that he uses his power only to the end of good" (22). Yet Eco asks: *What is Good?* He answers: "Superman's civic attitude is perfect, but it is exercised and structured in the sphere of a small, closed community." That's because the "structure of the plot" must "forbid the release of excessive and irretrievable developments," and "the immobilizing metaphysics underlying this kind of conceptual plot [. . .] must be static and evade any development because Superman *must* make virtue consist of many little activities on a small scale" (22). This too leaves ambiguity between subjectivism and objectivism. While Superman doesn't determine what superhero virtue is, it's unclear whether any subject does. Eco does continue that morality generally reflects not the "authors' preferences" but the "concept of 'order' that pervades the cultural model in which the authors live, and where they construct on a small scale 'analogous' models which mirror the larger one" (22). But this is ambiguous as well. While authors construct small-scale models, they might simply be refining the concept of "order" that pervades the large-scale cultural model in which they live. That social model might be ordered based on subjective preference, or it might be ordered based on objective fact. The same ambiguity also applies to superhero morality.

Eco speaks abstractly about how Superman fits our cultural model yet ignores an actual cultural institution that governed the writing of Superman and other comics. The Comics Code Authority, which oversaw the content of comics from 1954 to 2011, mandated until 1988: "In every instance good shall triumph over evil and the criminal punished for his misdeeds" (Interim Report). Yet this doesn't help either. Asking whether something is moral for superheroes because it's loved—or approved—by the Authority (making superhero morality subjective), or whether it's loved by the Authority because it's moral for superheroes (making it objective), is still ambiguous. Internal to a comic book narrative, the second, objective option is correct. Superhero right and wrong are determined not by anything within a story but by the Authority.

External to the narrative, things are even more complicated. The Code never specified what "moral," "good," "criminal," or "misdeeds" means. The Authority appealed to something thought to be already known and accepted. There are two ways that the meaning of these moral terms could already be known or accepted. One is subjective: They're just based on preference, which the Comics Code Authority defers to. The other is objective: The Comics Code Authority, like society at large, discovers what superhero right and wrong are. Society, implicitly in the general case, and explicitly in the Authority case, mandates that comics follow it.

The Authority's 1989 revision of its 1954 Code leaves things just as unclear:

"Heroes should be role models and should reflect the prevailing social attitudes," and "Costumes in a comic book will be considered to be acceptable if they fall within the scope of contemporary styles and fashions." Again, internal to the narrative, morality is objective. The Authority decides it. Again, external to the narrative, prevailing social attitudes and contemporary styles and fashions could be either subjectively or objectively good. Therefore, from a perspective internal *or* external to comic book narratives, superhero morality might be subjective or objective. The actual world, with comic book creators, codes, and society at large, could suggest superhero moral subjectivism or objectivism. Maybe at different times or in different cases it suggests each.

The Goods on Superheroes

So is superhero morality relative or absolute? And is it subjective or objective? Horgan and Timmons's Moral Twin Earth helped us appreciate how Bizarro World suggests that superhero morality is absolute, Earth-3 that it is relative, and the Overman's world that it is absolute. Plato's *Euthyphro* helped us appreciate that DC's divinities, the analysis of literary critics, and the Comics Code Authority's mandate suggest that superhero morality could be either subjective or objective.

Even in these select cases, no clear superhero metaethics emerges. Though superhero comics present their protagonists as "good," "moral," "noble," and "benevolent," what exactly all that means is unclear. The metaethical foundation of the superhero genre is ambiguous. And since the metaethical foundations of the actual world are still being debated, this is exactly what we would expect.

Regardless, superhero comics tweak our moral intuitions. The thought experiments of Bizarro World, Earth-3, and Overman's world get us thinking about moral relativism and absolutism for superheroes—and thus for ourselves too. Various godlike beings, scholars who write about them, and the Comics Code Authority make us ponder moral objectivism and subjectivism for superheroes and so, ultimately, ourselves. As mentioned in the introduction, Wilfrid Sellars remarked that philosophical success is knowing one's reflective way around. Whether or not we converge on a single path, the thought experiments of superhero comics help us know our way around the metaethical nature of morality.

PART II

METAPHYSICS

THREE

EVIL GENIUSES

While metaethics, the focus of chapter 2, is the study of the nature of morality, metaphysics, the focus of this section, is the study of the nature of reality. Metaphysicians ask questions about the fundamental parts of reality, such as space and time, objects and properties, and causes and effects. But they also ask questions about reality as a whole. Is the world around us merely a figment of our imagination? Is what we take to be reality, "our" reality (including space and time and all the rest), really real? And, perhaps more basic of all, do we ourselves really exist?

Metaphysical questions about reality as a whole overlap with epistemological worries stemming from skepticism. Epistemology is the study of knowledge and belief, and the most famous form of skepticism is the view that, for all we know, what we believe about the world might not be true. Philosopher Hilary Putnam proposed this thought experiment in his 1981 *Reason, Truth, and History* to illustrate skepticism:

> A human being (you can imagine this to be yourself) has been subjected to an operation by an evil scientist. The person's brain (your brain) has been removed from the body and placed in a vat of nutrients which keeps the brain alive. The nerve endings have been connected to a super-scientific computer which causes the person whose brain it is to have the illusion that everything is perfectly normal. There seem to be people, objects, the sky, etc., but really all the person (you) is experiencing is the result of electronic impulses travelling from the computer to the nerve endings. (62)

So for all we know, we might be plugged into a computer, living in a virtual reality created by an evil genius. Or, less fantastical than Putnam's scenario, for all we know, we might be lying in bed dreaming right now. We just can't be sure. But if we are plugged in or dreaming or in some other way being deceived, then a lot of what we *think* we know about the world is false. That's an epistemological conclusion. Still, the conclusion follows from what we're assuming about the nature of reality, that it could be a simulation, dream, or deception. That's a metaphysical assumption.

In academic philosophy, the most famous example of skepticism about reality occurs in René Descartes's 1641 *Meditations on First Philosophy*. Descartes's *Meditations* is a series of six essays that ushered in modern philosophy in the Western tradition, and Descartes is taken to be the first modern Western philosopher. In the First Meditation, Descartes raises two related skeptical worries, each in the form of a thought experiment. One is that we are dreaming. The other, and Putnam's inspiration, is that we're victims of a powerful deceiver: "I will suppose not a supremely good God, the source of truth, but rather an evil genius, supremely powerful and clever, who has directed his entire effort at deceiving me" (16). While most translators render Descartes's 1641 Latin "genius malignus" (and 1674 French "mauvais génie") as "evil genius," it can be translated as "malicious demon" as well. Because Descartes contrasts a supremely good God with a supremely powerful but cleverly evil being, some have also equated Descartes's evil genius with a deceiving god.

Neither Putnam's nor Descartes's thought experiment implies that we actually are being deceived. We might or might not be plugged in, dreaming, or otherwise fooled by an evil genius. Our reality might be what we take it to be: a physical world with physical people, places, and things. Or it might be a simulated world, where what look like people, places, and things are phony. Skeptics claim not that we actually are being deceived but that, for all we know, we might be. Their thought experiments make that possibility vivid.

The simulated reality trope of Descartes's evil genius is a staple of science fiction, ranging from the novels of Philip K. Dick, William Gibson, and Kurt Vonnegut to the *Matrix* movie trilogy and the *Star Trek* television and movie franchise. As philosophers Gerald J. Erion and Barry Smith note: "Skeptical hypotheses are especially attractive to two groups of people. First are adolescents. [. . .] Second, and more importantly, are philosophers" (18). Not coincidentally, science fiction is especially popular among both groups too. And superhero comics, perhaps more than any other science fiction subgenre, question whether characters' realities are really real or merely simulations.

This chapter presents a progression of four comic book arcs that amount to four related thought experiments. In them, their writers and artists follow the path first trod by Descartes—and then go farther. If these stories cannot be proven wrong, then the most persuasive element of Descartes's refutation of skepticism fails. If their superhero worlds apply to our own, then these comic book philosophers leave us with less reason to think that our reality is really real than Descartes does.

Waking Up

Echoing Putnam's thought experiment, Alan Moore in his 1982–89 *Marvelman*, retitled *Miracleman* midseries, imagined that the evil scientist Dr. Emil Gargunza kidnapped and subjected several orphans to operations to create superhuman bodies. To keep them under his control, Gargunza has them dream. "You create them," the captions narrate, "and because they are so terrifying and powerful you keep them locked in a world of dreams, studying the play of their minds while their bodies lay sleeping" (*Miracleman* #5: unpaginated). When he later watches the videotapes of his sleeping self, Miracleman asks: "Why didn't we realise what they were doing to our lives?" (#3). Because, fulfilling the role of Descartes's evil genius, Gargunza has "programmed the minds of these near-divine creatures . . . providing them with an utterly manufactured identity which is ours to manipulate at will. To wit: the identity of a children's comic book character" (#3).

By having Gargunza impose dreams on the orphans, Moore combines Descartes's dreaming and evil-genius thought experiments into one. In the First Meditation, Descartes investigates a similar question when focusing on dreaming alone. "How often does my evening slumber persuade me of such ordinary things as these: that I am here, clothed in my dressing gown, seated next to the fire—when in fact I am lying undressed in bed!" (14). Dreaming that things are real doesn't make them real, and because we can't be certain right now that we're not ourselves dreaming, Descartes's thought experiment places doubt in our minds.

Such doubts might be resolved by waking. After dreaming for seven years, Gargunza's orphans stir:

They're over-riding the somatic inducers somehow. [...] One of them
must be reaching out his subconscious mind and over-riding our guid-
ance programme. [...] All the references to dreams ... this "Sleepy-
town" ... their subconscious minds are trying to tell them that what
they're experiencing isn't real. [...] They're trying to wake up [...] trying
to overload on absurdity to shock the brain into wakefulness by crossing
the threshold of disbelief ... (#4)

Still inside the dream world, Miracleman observes: "Something's wrong here.
Something doesn't feel right. It's as if ... it's as if none of this is really happening." Gargunza sees that Miracleman's "subconscious, aware of its true situation, is trying to break down our dreamscape and dragging the others along."
Since the true nature of reality is within Miracleman's grasp, Gargunza needs
"a dream-programme that will explain these lapses in the continuity of his
reality and lull him back into security and sleep" (#5). Gargunza inserts a supervillain with hypnotic powers of sleep into the dreamscape, fooling Miracleman's companion, Young Miracleman: "We might have known! Who else
but the Nabob of Nightmares could come up with a creepy set-up like this?
That explains your weird sensations, M.M.!" Miracleman, however, rejects the
explanation: "No! This is wrong! Don't you see? We're being seduced! They're
trying to stop us from thinking!"

As Miracleman's real body begins to move, Gargunza attempts a final explanation: "And then the Miracleman Family woke up ... and it all had been
a dream." His deception again fools Young Miracleman: "Whew! Hey, M.M.
Kid! I just had the craziest dream." And this time Miracleman too: "Hmmm.
Funny ... so did I. Thank goodness it was only that ... just an insane night-
mare ..." At least for now, with "normal dream patterns re-established completely," Gargunza convinces Miracleman that what he took to be evidence
that he was dreaming was itself a dream. So Moore works into his thought
experiment the idea that its subjects dream that they awake from a dream.
Reality is as Miracleman takes it to be, he thinks, when it really isn't.

After worrying that he was dreaming, Descartes himself maintains: "But
right now, my eyes are certainly wide awake when I gaze upon this sheet of
paper. This head which I am shaking is not heavy with sleep. I extend this
hand consciously and deliberately, and I feel it. Such things would not be so
distinct for someone who is asleep" (14). Unlike Miracleman, though, Descartes concedes: "As if I did not recall having been deceived on other occasions

even by similar thoughts in my dreams!" (14). We sometimes dream that we're not dreaming. We sometimes even dream that we're waking up from dreaming. The last time we thought that we did wake up from a dream, for all we know, we might merely have dreamed that we did.

Other members of the Miracle Family do eventually awake. Miraclewoman, still in a partial hypnotic state, discovers Gargunza's secret laboratory:

> Inside, it was spacious, but deserted. Experiencing creeping déjà vu, gazing at the couches and screens, I grew unaccountably afraid. What had I stumbled upon? The video tapes provided my answer. Watching, my shock, fury, horror and amusement finally crystalized into exhilaration. Knowing the truth, I was free . . . a cartoon figure ripped from her paper universe and given a 3-D world . . . (#12: 10)

Miraclewoman learned the truth. She knew that she exists. Her existence isn't an insignificant metaphysical fact, either. She's real. Whatever other real things there are in the universe, she belongs in their number. This first comic book thought experiment ends with Miraclewoman asserting her own existence.

The series visually depicts a division between real and dreamed worlds by reprinting a ten-page episode of Mick Anglo and artist Don Lawrence's original 1950s Marvelman as the first ten pages of *Miracleman* #1. Page 11 then repeats a single close-up of Marvelman, zooming into an increasingly distorted extreme close-up in a sequence of eight panels emphasizing the character's "paper universe" by revealing its component elements of lines and ink. Moore worked with multiple artists—Garry Leach, Alan Davis, Chuck Beckum, and John Totleben—all of whom contrast with Lawrence, whose 1950s rendering of Marvelman is closer to what comic book scholar Joseph Witek terms the "cartoon mode," which "grows out of caricature, with its basic principles of simplification and exaggeration" (28). Moore's collaborators instead work in the "naturalistic mode," which "derives from the recreation of physical appearances in realistic illustration" (28). The two worlds are visually distinct, each with its own "narrative ethos," which, according to Witek, "makes a very different claim to a very different kind of truth" (28, 32). John Totleben employs both truths in issue #12, rendering Miraclewoman's memories of her dream self with minimal detail and her current self in greater detail. He emphasizes the differences explicitly on facing pages by having the dream version smile with cartoonish features as her current face narrates in a style approaching

From *Miracleman* #12.

photorealism (6–7). Because Miraclewoman, like a reader, recognizes the contrast between them, the deception ends. She's sure of her existence.

Descartes not only separates the skeptical worry about dreaming from the skeptical worry about being controlled by an evil genius like Gargunza, but also treats the latter worry as more serious. Dreams are just a jumble of things that we've experienced while awake. So if we're dreaming, we're not making everything up—just rearranging our waking experiences in fictitious ways. We can imagine on Descartes's behalf another reason that the skeptical worry about an evil genius is more serious. We can wake up from our dreams, but it might not be so easy to escape from an evil genius. Like Moore, Descartes might even maintain that evil geniuses can impose dreams on us. Descartes's second skeptical worry would thus encompass the first.

From *Miracleman* #12.

Regardless, Descartes's solution to that skeptical worry is similar to Miraclewoman's own discovery when she herself learns the truth. Descartes declares that, whether I am being deceived or not, there is one thing I can't be deceived about: that I exist. As he explains in the Second Meditation:

> I have persuaded myself that there is absolutely nothing in the world: no sky, no earth, no minds, no bodies. Is it then the case that I too do not exist? But doubtless I did exist, if I persuaded myself of something. But there is some deceiver or other who is supremely powerful and supremely sly and who is always deliberately deceiving me. Then too there is no doubt that I exist, if he is deceiving me. (18)

If Miraclewoman herself ever entertained the skeptical worry that she was in Gargunza's clutches, it can't then be the case that she too doesn't exist. She was persuaded by Gargunza to believe her dream world to be real, and in turn, persuaded herself to believe that her dream self was real. In so doing, however, she still would have to exist. In each case Miraclewoman would be able to say with Descartes: "There is no doubt that I exist."

Descartes continues: "Thus, after everything has been most carefully weighed, it must finally be established that this pronouncement 'I am, I exist' is necessarily true every time I utter or conceive it in my mind" (18). As he more famously puts it in his 1637 *Discourse on Method*: "I think, therefore I am" (18). Nearly as famous is his Latin: "Cogito, ergo sum." If she spoke Latin, Miraclewoman could say the same. For Descartes in particular, this is a metaphysical discovery of the utmost importance.

Playing God

Descartes's argument, called the "Cogito," is first-personal. It doesn't prove that other people or the world exists. If it works, the Cogito proves only that "I" exist—whether I am Miraclewoman, Descartes, or someone else— leaving other arguments to prove the rest. The Cogito doesn't even prove that I'm not being controlled by an evil genius. The argument presupposes that, for all I know, I might be. If I am being deceived, then I exist. If I am not being deceived, then what I take reality to be matches reality itself, so I exist then also. Since those are apparently the only two possibilities, I exist.

But Descartes doesn't stop there. He wants to justify our belief in reality overall. All those metaphysical claims that we normally take to be true—not just that I exist, but that other people and the world around me do too—are his target of support. That's why, having established the Cogito, Descartes next tries to show that what I take reality to be matches reality itself. He does so by attempting to remove the worry about the evil genius. Once that worry is out of the way, we can be assured that we're getting reality right. Descartes tries to get it out of the way by proving in the Third Meditation that someone else exists—namely, God.

For this, Descartes turns not to a thought experiment but instead to a logical argument. Superhero stories—even Alan Moore's—typically avoid arguments for or against, or any discussions generally of, God's existence. As comic book scholar Tom Morris notes:

> We don't see Superman sitting in church or Bruce Wayne poring over a Bat-Bible for inspiration and guidance. The Fantastic Four don't have prayer times together to discern the direction their work should take. [. . .] There is very little mention in any mainstream comics of a Creator. (45)

And yet, as we saw in the previous chapter, a wide range of comics do include gods and Godlike beings. As we see here, some of these beings even play a role similar to the one that God and the evil genius play for Descartes.

During his 1977–78 run of *The Avengers,* Jim Shooter plotted the character Starhawk, a member of the Guardians of the Galaxy traveling from the future to 1978 in pursuit of the cyborg criminal Korvac. Unknown to Starhawk, Korvac downloaded infinite knowledge from an alien supercomputer and evolved into a god: "As a new-made god, his position was unique. As long as he concealed his presence from other near omnipotent beings, he would be free to make subtle alterations in the fabric of reality, eventually taking control..." (#175: 17). Korvac is free to act as a god—a benevolent one according to himself, a malicious one according to others—as long as he isn't caught by other godlike (or Godlike) beings. When Starhawk tracks Korvac to a seemingly banal suburban house, the new god—now calling himself "Michael"—makes his first alteration:

> Of all the great powers in existence, you alone are aware of me! I cannot allow your knowledge to spread! [...] You must be obliterated. Thus I must convert your ethereal spirit form into basic substance—substance which can be rent—shredded by talons of naked energy! [...] Now in order to insure my secrecy—I shall restore the one I have destroyed! [...] You live again, remade, molecule by molecule... exactly as you were—but henceforth, you will not remember this incident, nor the fact of my existence... and never again shall your senses perceive me! Go now—aid your friends in their petty "mission" in this era—reassure them that it is imperative! (#168: 16, 29, 30)

The altered Starhawk reappears seconds later: "Nearly a mile above the upper east side, in midst of a graceful loop, Starhawk pauses—suddenly noticing his location, but unable to recall flying hither. It seems to him that he was troubled a few seconds ago—and yet, now he feels a comfortable sense of purpose" (30). When returning to the Avengers and asked if has found out anything, Starhawk answers: "Only... that we must proceed with our mission! It is imperative!" (31). As Descartes wondered about himself, Starhawk is the victim of Michael's evil-Godlike deception. (Worse, the remade Starhawk's words may also lack meaning—which we discuss in chapter 7.)

Shooter's cocreators, penciler George Pérez and inker Pablo Marcos, suggest these skeptical worries visually by continuing to render Starhawk in the

same style after Michael destroys him, literalizing Michael's claim to restore
Starhawk "exactly as you were." Were the restored Starhawk instead rendered
with some stylistic variation, the division between reality and false perception would also be visually represented. The absence of variation suggests the
impossibility of detecting the manipulation of a deceiving god.

Seven issues later, Iron Man requests Starhawk's help in finding Michael:
"Unless your cosmic insight can help—the universe may crumble before our
very eyes" (#175: 1). Starhawk reluctantly agrees: "I still believe the true enemy
is Korvac—but I will try" (2). But he soon reports, "I'm sorry, Iron Man, but
I found...nothing!"

> IRON MAN: Wha—? But these others with lesser psychic abilities at
> least came up with bits and pieces! How could you possibly not—
> STARHAWK: I merely reveal what I sense...(14)

Despite Starhawk's failure to help them, the Avengers do eventually locate
Michael's house, but their combined "psychic and cybernetic probes" find
"no danger!" in his reality-shrouding appearance (26). Starhawk, however, ex-
poses Michael's identity through his inability to perceive him at all: "Enough!
I don't know what your game is, but no one makes a fool of Starhawk! For
minutes you've been talking, probing, pretending to receive responses! But
from whom? There's nobody there!" (27). So Starhawk accidentally proves
the presence of Michael by sensing his absence, and we might read this as a
thought experiment about the power of divine expectations. All the same,
all that trouble could have been avoided had "other near omnipotent beings"
detected Michael themselves. They wouldn't have let Michael's power go un-
checked. That's why Michael concealed his presence from them.

To show that I am not myself being deceived by an evil genius—and, like
Shooter's Michael, Descartes's evil genius has been equated with a deceiving
god—Descartes needs to disqualify the possibility of a Godlike Michael deceiving me. He does so by using logical argumentation to try to prove that
such a being could not exist if an actually all-powerful being—that is, God—
existed. Descartes's argument in the Third Meditation for God's existence is
both more complicated and more contentious than the Cogito. Having established that "I" exist, he notes that I also have the idea of a perfect being in my
mind. Whether or not such a being actually exists, I have the idea of it as all
knowing, all powerful, and all loving. Where did this idea could come from?

To answer that question, Descartes appeals to a metaphysical distinction between formal and objective reality.

Though the distinction is technical, the idea behind it isn't. Formal reality is the reality of an original. A *tree* is formally real. Objective reality is the reality of an object derived from the original. A *picture* of a tree is objectively real. According to Descartes, ideas are like pictures. They come from originals. Descartes adds that an object can't have more objective reality than its original has formal reality. A picture of a tree can't be more real *as* a picture of a tree than a tree is real *as* a tree. If the picture is of a fake tree, then it isn't a real picture of a tree. The realness of the object can't exceed the realness of the original.

Descartes next considers what the original of the idea of a perfect being could be. It couldn't be himself, since Descartes isn't perfect. His formal reality is less than the idea's objective reality. It couldn't be his religious teachers or priests, for the same reason. Because the idea of a perfect being is perfectly objectively real, it can come only from some original that's perfectly formally real. But the only perfectly formally real being is a perfect being—namely, God. So God must exist. That's the only place where his idea of God could have come from.

Whether or not we agree with them, logical arguments for God's existence are central in the history of metaphysics. While religion counsels faith, people with religion who are philosophers seek proof. Even philosophers who are not religious study these arguments, because they reveal people's assumptions about reality. Believing that he's proved that God exists, Descartes himself concludes that I (who, as per the Cogito, exist) am not being systematically deceived by an evil genius. Given that God is all knowing, God would know whether I'm being deceived. Given that God is all powerful, God would be able to prevent me from being deceived. Given that God is all loving, God would in fact prevent me from being deceived. God would not allow there to be an evil genius at all.

Unlike Descartes, Starhawk apparently does not exist in a universe with an all-knowing, all-powerful, and all-loving God because his evil genius, Michael, does deceive him. Though Michael's existence isn't threatened, his ability to deceive, and hence to act like Descartes's evil genius, is. "Michael knew" that he would be free to enact his schemes, "as long as he concealed his presence from other near omnipotent beings" (#175: 17). That included "the most important entity to be observed! The celestial vastness of—Eternity himself! Eternity! He who is the universe personified . . . within whom all the stuff of this reality exists" (#173: 13). Michael adds, "He's so confident, so serene in his omnipotence! He would pay little attention to a mote such as I, even had I not shielded myself from his sight!" (13). Still, Michael was able to shield himself from Eternity's intervention. Had Eternity been truly all knowing like God, then Eternity would have detected him.

Indeed, had Starhawk not accidentally revealed Michael's presence by its absence, then Shooter's deceiving god would have continued to deceive his victim. The deception stops not because of Eternity's intervention but because of Michael's miscalculation about Starhawk. Eternity himself fails to fulfill the role of Descartes's God. Many people think that Descartes's proof for God's existence itself fails too. Neither Descartes nor Starhawk, then, can trust that reality is what he thinks it is. The skeptical worry about reality returns.

Paying Attention

Why do many people think that Descartes's argument fails? In part it's because the argument appears circular. Frans Burman, interviewing Descartes in 1648, explains: "It seems there is a circle. For in the Third Meditation the author uses axioms to prove the existence of God, even though he is not yet certain of not being deceived about these" (Cottingham 5–6). Burman is worried about Descartes's metaphysical claims about formal and objective reality. How does Descartes know that an object can't have more objective reality than its original has formal reality? This worry is especially pressing, since, on the assumption that an evil genius is possible, Descartes must allow that the evil genius could have made him think that. For all he knows, thinking it could be part of the evil genius's deceptive plot—as Michael makes Starhawk think that he must continue to pursue the now-nonexistent Korvac. That's why Burman maintains that Descartes is using axioms—especially those about formal and objective reality—to prove the existence of God, even though he's not yet certain of not being deceived about those axioms.

Burman is taken to have identified what's now called the "Cartesian Circle." Descartes tried to break the circle in his reply to Burman:

> [The author of Meditations] does use such axioms in the proof, but he
> knows that he is not deceived with regard to them, since he is actually

paying attention to them. And for as long as he does pay attention to them, he is certain that he is not being deceived, and he is compelled to give his assent to them. (Cottingham 6)

So according to Descartes, he's safe in believing what he does about formal and objective reality because he's actively paying attention to what he believes.

Philosophers are even less enthusiastic about Descartes's reply than about the argument itself. If "actually paying attention" to something is sufficient to remove the skeptical worry, then why did Descartes worry in the First Meditation about being deceived at all? Why did Descartes try to prove in the Second Meditation that I exist and in the Third Meditation that God exists? By his own reasoning to Burman, couldn't Descartes have simply paid better attention? Descartes had responses to these questions too. The important point here is how Descartes tried to break the circle. He argued that actually paying attention to something lets us know that it's true.

Like Burman, writer-artist John Byrne presents a challenge to Descartes by depicting a story arc concerning the mutant superhero Wanda Maximoff. Unlike Burman's question, though, we can read Byrne's addition itself as a thought experiment. Beginning in 1985, in the limited series *The Vision and the Scarlet Witch*, Steve Englehart scripted Wanda's pregnancy. After Dr. Strange confirms that Wanda is "going to be a mother!," her husband, the Vision, asks: "It was the magick, wasn't it? The force that got away from the witches of New Salem, that you funneled through yourself?" (#4: unpaginated). Wanda responds: "I think so! As it was happening, I made—a little wish! And felt that it would work!" Though Wanda "used magick to make it happen," Dr. Strange assures her that "magick's nothing but directed energy—and you directed it! I'm a better magician than a physician these days, and I'm not worried. The baby will be fine, believe me!"

In the twelfth and concluding issue, Wanda gives birth to twins. During his 1989 run of *Avengers West Coast*, however, John Byrne reveals through Wanda's mentor Agatha Harkness:

Wanda longed all her life for the kind of normal existence forever denied her by her mutant powers. She so greatly desired a family—in her mind the perfect symbol of a peaceful, happy life—that she suffered what in a human woman would have been a hysterical or imaginary pregnancy. In such cases there is usually no child to be born ... but Wanda's power to change probabilities created Thomas and William. (#51: 29)

As a result, when Wanda is "not thinking about them . . . they disappear!" (#51: 6). Like Pérez and Marcos rendering Starhawk, Byrne pencils and Mike Machlan inks the twins in the same style as other characters and objects around them, visually establishing that false insertions are indistinguishable from reality. Though Harkness acknowledges that there "are many kinds of reality," the twins are only "manifestations of Wanda's will. One small step beyond illusion," so the "children are not real" (#51: 15).

Descartes believed that, as long as he thinks about his axiom about formal and objective reality, he can trust it enough to use in his argument for God's existence. Similarly, as long as Wanda thinks about Thomas and William, they exist too. Descartes's appealing to a premise in an argument, while Wanda features in a thought experiment in which believing that something is so makes it so. But Descartes faces another problem. If thinking about something is needed to trust it, then Descartes can't trust any axiom or claim he *isn't* thinking about. Like Wanda and her twins, the trustworthiness of everything that Descartes believes ceases to exist if he breaks his concentration. Because she's not a skeptic, Wanda needs to concentrate only on her children. Unlike Descartes, she's not trying to prove that reality as a whole is real.

Descartes isn't deterred. He believes that he can think about the Cogito and proof for God's existence and that that's enough to prove his reality is real. When Burman wrote: "But our mind can think of only one thing at a time, whereas the proof in question is a fairly long one involving several axioms," Descartes replied:

> It is just not true that the mind can think of only one thing at a time. It is true that it cannot think of a large number of things at the same time, but it can still think of more than one thing. For example, I am now aware and have the thought that I am talking and that I am eating; and both these thoughts occur at the same time. (Cottingham 6)

Descartes can maintain that thinking of the Cogito and argument for God's existence together can assure him that the world exists. Likewise, Wanda needs to think of her two children for them to exist. Like Burman, however, Byrne suggests that Wanda too is unable to keep her concentration focused. When she is unconscious or battling supervillains with the other Avengers, her twins literally vanish. That's because, as Roy and Dann Thomas later script, Wanda "had been living a lie" (#61: 26). Even in thought experiments, lies don't pay.

Unless Descartes's attention stays fixed, then he can't himself—though for logical reasons—know whether he's been living a lie too.

Dreaming Again

Byrne's story concludes with another variation on Descartes's evil genius, leading to a fourth and final related thought experiment. Harkness reveals to Wanda that her children were parts of the shattered "essence" of the demon Mephisto after he had been destroyed by the child of Sue and Reed Richards, the Godlike Franklin Richards: "Since her power cannot create true life, she reached out unconsciously to snare anything which would function as souls for the newborns" (#52: 19, 29). When Mephisto "reabsorbed the portions of his essence which had become" her twins, Harkness defeats him again: "Knowing them to be still bound by the spell Wanda used to create them, I was able to erase them from her memory. The resultant shock to Mephisto's system was enough to disperse him again" (29). Since, "when she returns to consciousness, her first thought is almost sure to be of her children . . . ," Harkness exchanges her unreal children for new, unreal memories: "To spare her that pain, I have closed that corner of her mind for all time. The little creatures she created are gone, restored to their original state. For Wanda . . . it will be as if they never were" (30).

Unlike Gargunza's, Michael's, or Mephisto's, Harkness's intentions are benevolent. Franklin Richards is similarly benevolent, but his powers affect an entire universe of characters in Marvel's *Heroes Reborn* series. For the single 1996 issue *Onslaught: Marvel Universe*, writers Scott Lobdell and Mark Waid depicted the deaths of over a dozen of Marvel's most popular heroes. When the supervillain Onslaught achieves "his final form" of "pure psionic energy," he declares: "Onslaught is no longer a physical creature who can be bludgeoned into submission! I am thought itself! I am perception! Perception is reality—and reality rejects you!" (unpaginated). To defeat him, the Fantastic Four and the Avengers sacrifice themselves by absorbing his energy, ending in an explosion "loud enough to swallow the world."

Yet readers saw Franklin's parents again the following month in *Fantastic Four* vol. 2 #1 (November 1996), one of the four titles that Marvel outsourced to its former employees Jim Lee and Rob Liefeld before declaring bankruptcy that December. Jim Lee and cowriter Brandon Choi's script restores the characters in a new, contemporary origin story that replaces their previous history. Echoes of the past, however, remain. Prior to his transformation into the Thing, Ben Grimm narrates the opening sequence:

> The dream's always the same. It begins with a perfect launch. But this time it takes a fantastic twist. Suzie and Johnny? What're they doing here? It's too dangerous. [. . .] That's when the warning indications start lighting up like a Christmas tree! Radiation's flooding into the main compartment. [. . .] My friends! My ship! They're all dying—when there's suddenly—a phone call for me? (Unpaginated)

Ben wakes in his cockpit to discover:

> No. Not a phone. It's the intercom.
> "You can get up now, Major Grimm. We've completed the simulation."
> "Huh?! Oh. Right! I told you that I could do this with my eyes closed."

Ben is dreaming a memory of his past existence. Instead of a World War II veteran, in his new existence he is a major who flew "combat sorties" before being "wounded during the Gulf War." Before the end of the issue, his dream repeats: "Except this time—it's not—a dream!" He and his teammates are bombarded by radiation and transformed into the Fantastic Four.

The four *Heroes Reborn* series ran for thirteen issues each, then Marvel returned the characters to their main continuity in the 1997 miniseries *Heroes Reborn: The Return.* Each of the four issues begins with Julio Soto's summary of writer Peter David's story:

> All those who had jumped into Onslaught seemingly perished as the rest of the world watched! But all was not as it seemed. In fact the Heroes were anything but dead, as they were actually whisked away to another universe!
>
> It was young Franklin Richards, son of Reed and Sue Richards of the FF, who was unwittingly responsible for the disappearance of the Heroes. Franklin's amazing powers were obviously even more far-reaching than anyone had imagined, as he was unintentionally able to create a pocket universe in which the Heroes now exist. [. . .]
>
> For the last year, immediately following the defeat of Onslaught, the Heroes have been leading new lives which were, to the best of their knowledge, a continuation of their normal lives. They were not aware of

their previous existence back in the real Marvel Universe. In the pocket universe the Heroes had radically different origins and vaguely resembled their former selves. (Unpaginated)

Apparently, Franklin did hold his family and friends continuously in his thoughts. Franklin's mind was more powerful than even Wanda Maximoff's. While Wanda needed to concentrate on her children for them to exist, whatever Franklin thought exists did exist—at least in a pocket universe. This echoes the work of seventeenth- and eighteenth-century philosopher George Berkeley, who argued that God's thinking about the reality overall is what ensures that it exists when no humans are perceiving it. Indeed, the situation that Franklin finds himself in can be read as a thought experiment that seems to try out Berkeley's rather than Descartes's view. But it does come back to Descartes at the end.

Franklin's reality is really real, because he created it. As a deceiving god, however, he also created false memories that replaced the historically accurate memories of the people he saved. Their new world may be real, but its and their apparent pasts are not. As a result, Sue is plagued by "lousy dreams" and complains, "I'm crying... and I don't know why! I—I think something's happening..." (#1). Similarly, Ben admits after a battle: "I wasn't at the top of my game. I was like ... like somethin' was rattlin' around in my head. Distractin' me." When another Godlike being, the Celestial Ashema, reveals to Franklin what he has done, he enters his own pocket universe and appears to his parents, who have no memory of him. Yet Sue still believes: "He's our son, Reed. I don't know how I know ... but I do" (#2). Reed, wishing to be "reasonable," sends Iron Man to gather samples from the planet's substrata, which reveals that "our world... is less than a year old" (#3, #4). Hawkeye calls the idea "beyond insane," something from "The Twilight Zone," but Reed insists the evidence "verifying the boy's claims" "cannot be ignored" (#4).

Such verifying evidence wouldn't exist, however, if Franklin didn't allow it to exist. Franklin is as powerful as Descartes intended his evil genius to be. Unlike Descartes's evil genius—or Gargunza, Michael, or Mephisto—Franklin intends no malicious deception. He mourned his parents passing without realizing that in so doing he resurrected them in this pocket universe. Regardless, to prevent the Celestials from destroying both universes now, the Heroes must leave the pocket universe and return to their original one.

As a result, Captain America must leave his new female sidekick, Bucky.

Though of different worlds, Bucky and Captain America share a single visual style. Penciler Salvador Larroca and inker Scott Hanna render all characters in a common manner, and their two worlds are visually indistinguishable too—including even Franklin and Ashema, who create and maintain the alternate reality. Partly because the two worlds are nearly identical, Bucky doesn't understand: "Cap, please, why can't I come?!" Peter David explains in captions: "The answers race through his mind: 'Because Sam and I aren't from this world . . . because you're . . . a manifestation of a young boy's imagination, made manifest by an incomprehensible power'" (#4).

Soon the Heroes "remember everything," as Bucky and the other inhabitants of the pocket universe watch:

> As for the girl . . . it is as if a dream were over. There is an appropriateness to that. Indeed, it is believed by some that the world . . . the entire universe . . . merely exists as the dream of a sleeping gnat. That the girl—that everyone and everything—is simply the figment of the imagination of some greater being's dream state. [. . .] Ashema sacrificed her own consciousness, gave it over for the preservation of the other universe, which will exist within her for all time. [. . .] Perhaps the celestials themselves . . . are merely figments of someone or something else's eternal imagination. Indeed . . . in the final analysis . . . perhaps we all are.

We're able to read this closing scene as the conclusion to a thought experiment more skeptical than any that Descartes ever raised. Peter David's worry undermines the Cogito itself. Presumably Bucky could have run the Cogito had she wished. Imagine Bucky thinking, "If Franklin deceives me, then I exist. If Franklin doesn't deceive me, then what I take reality to be matches reality itself, so I exist then also. Since those are the only two possibilities," Descartes would have us believe, "I, Bucky, exist."

We've been agreeing with Descartes that something like these are the only two possibilities. Either I'm being deceived or I'm not. Unfortunately for Descartes, Bucky, and the rest of us, they aren't the only two. There's a third possibility. Franklin is neither deceiving nor not deceiving Bucky, at least how Descartes would have us believe. There simply is no Bucky. There is no one, then, to be deceived or not to be deceived. Franklin merely told himself a story. Bucky is "a manifestation of a young boy's imagination." The Cogito works only on the assumption that deception is possible. In Bucky's case, it's impossible. Franklin is daydreaming it all. Bucky couldn't run the Cogito, because

Bucky doesn't exist. Of course, Franklin could imagine that Bucky ran it. But that would establish merely that Franklin exists, not that Bucky does.

No matter how persuasive we might otherwise find the Cogito, therefore, *Heroes Reborn: The Return* can be read as a thought experiment forcing us to leave open the possibility that, like Bucky, we too are figments of the imagination of some being's dream state. The Cogito works only on the assumption that an evil genius might be deceiving me. A more extreme skeptic, like Peter David, would be skeptical about even that assumption. There might really be no me that can be deceived. Descartes's Cogito is useless against that sort of doubt.

In that respect, Peter David joins Alan Moore, Jim Shooter, and John Byrne as being more skeptical than even Descartes, if we read their comics as thought experiments. While, like Descartes, Moore's Miraclewoman can affirm her individual existence, she can prove nothing about the rest of reality. While Descartes thinks that an all-knowing being can remove the worry of an evil genius, Jim Shooter presents a powerful but not all-knowing being who fails to rescue a victim of malign deception. While Descartes thinks that we can pay sufficient attention to two arguments, John Byrne presents a superhero who can't pay consistent attention to two twins. And, most skeptical of all, while Descartes thinks that I exist—because I either am or am not being deceived—David raises the possibility that, for all anyone knows, I might merely be a figment of someone else's imagination. Reality wouldn't be what it seems to me at all.

FOUR

CLOBBERIN' TIME

S etting aside the previous chapter's skeptical doubts, if the world does exist, what can we say about its most fundamental parts? Of those parts, philosophers have paid particular attention to time. According to Aristotle, while the past and present are fixed, the future remains open. For early Christian theologian and philosopher Augustine, the past and future are just modifications of the present, which is entirely in the mind. Seventeenth- and eighteenth-century philosopher Gottfried Wilhelm Leibniz took time to be nothing other than how objects relate temporally, so that time depends on objects to exist. Leibniz's near contemporary, Isaac Newton, wearing both his scientific and his philosophical caps, argued that time instead has a reality independent of objects. Nineteenth- and twentieth-century philosopher John M. E. McTaggart argued that time isn't real at all.

Though not usually grouped with any of these philosophers, the writers, artists, and editors of Marvel have their own views of time. Reading their superhero comic book stories as various thought experiments illustrates how they explore, investigate, and hypothesize time's realities and properties. This chapter focuses on stories involving Dr. Doom's time machine, the plot device that established the trope of time travel in Marvel continuity. We begin in the early 1960s when Marvel introduced Doom's machine, consider a series of subsequent stories involving the machine, and conclude with the philosophical time-travel challenges facing the rebooted All-New, All-Different Marvel of 2015 and beyond. When Fantastic Four teammate Ben Grimm leaps into battle, he shouts his catchphrase: "It's Clobberin' Time!" When tackling time travel, Marvel shouts the philosophical equivalent.

Eternal Time

What if a brilliant scientist invented a machine that could send people to the past? Stan Lee and Jack Kirby introduced that thought experiment to Marvel in 1962. "I have successfully developed the most incredible invention of the age," declares Dr. Doom in *Fantastic Four #5*, "an actual time travel device!" (*Essential Fantastic Four* 8). Doom holds Sue hostage to force the other members of the Fantastic Four to use his machine: "I want you to go centuries into the past and obtain the legendary treasure of Blackbeard for me!" They obey, and once transported to Blackbeard's time and location (presumably early 1700s, West Indies), the three disguise themselves in period dress, including hat, eyepatch, and fake beard for Ben, the Thing. After he proves himself in battle, the pirates he'd been fighting alongside declare him their captain.

> PIRATES: Hooray for the mighty bearded one! Hooray for Blackbeard!
> JOHNNY: Blackbeard? But they're talking about the Thing?
> REED: Good Lord! I see it now! The Thing is Blackbeard! He came
> back to the past to find . . . himself! (16)
> BEN: I'm the guy who started the legend of Blackbeard! The kids will
> read about me in school some day! (17)

What should we make, philosophically, of this?

There are two broad views of the nature of time, both established well before Marvel published Lee and Kirby's story. The first is presentism. Only the present exists. While the past *did* exist, and the future *will* exist, neither exists *now*. Traveling to the past or future doesn't involve going to a ready-made spot. There is no spot—at least not until the time traveler gets there, effectively making that spot her present. Many philosophers think this has implications for the mutability of events in time, and we agree. If neither the past nor the future itself exists, then facts about the past and the future don't exist either. They too would be susceptible to the time traveler's arrival. Presentism therefore may be understood as permitting past and future facts to be changed. Since neither those times nor facts are ready-made, the time traveler can affect them when (as moments of her present time) they come into being.

Presentism isn't the view that Lee and Kirby present in their Fantastic Four thought experiment. Instead they presuppose the second broad philosophical view: eternalism. All moments in time exist, past and future as much as present. For the eternalist, the past, present, and future don't have distinct natures.

They're all metaphysically on par—simply earlier than, simultaneously with, or later than the speaker's own (arbitrary) time. Different points in time are like different points in space. We can travel to Amsterdam if we're currently in New York, because Amsterdam exists in space as much as New York does. Likewise, we can travel to the eighteenth century if we're currently in the twenty-first, because the eighteenth exists in time as much as the twenty-first does. Traveling to the past or future does involve going to a ready-made spot—a spot that exists regardless of who goes there. For the eternalist, all spots are eternally real.

Presentism may be understood as permitting past and future time to be changed when the time traveler travels there, effectively making that time her present. By contrast, philosopher David Lewis in his 1976 "The Paradoxes of Time Travel" relies on eternalism to conclude that past, present, and future are fixed. Because all times already exist, so do all facts about those times. None can be changed. Kirby and Lee agree. In Ben's present of 1962, Blackbeard's is already set. It's *always* (that is, "eternally") already set, just as much as Ben's history is. Ben *always* is Blackbeard. He *always* travels from his day to Blackbeard's heyday. Ben no more becomes Blackbeard at the moment he travels from 1962 to the 1700s than Amsterdam becomes Amsterdam at the moment a New Yorker sets foot there. Had Ben not traveled back in time, then no Blackbeard legend would have existed. But since Ben does (eternally) travel back in time, the Blackbeard legend does (eternally) exist.

According to Lee and Kirby, Blackbeard isn't the English pirate Edward Teach but the time-traveling Ben Grimm. The eternally fixed nature of the past, however, also applies to historical events outside Marvel invention. When in *Marvel Team-Up* writer Bill Mantlo has Spider-Man use Doom's time machine travels to 1692, Spider-Man defeats the supervillain Dark Rider but fails to save the lives of the Salem citizens accused of witchcraft. A caption explains that "Salem hung its witches . . . on August 19, 1692" (#44: 31). Spider-Man consoles himself afterward: "There wasn't anything you could've done to keep those people from being hanged—history's written them off long ago!" (#45: 1). That's because history's already "written." Spider-Man eternally goes back to 1692, eternally defeats the Dark Rider, and eternally fails to save the witches.

Lewis's "The Paradoxes of Time Travel" was published the same month as Mantlo's Spider-Man's adventure (and two months before Roy Thomas scripted the Fantastic Four's travel to 1942), eliminating the possibility of influence in either direction. A year after creating the Blackbeard adventure, and also independent of Lewis, Lee and Kirby depicted the Fantastic Four using Doom's device to travel to ancient Egypt, where they encounter a time traveler from their future. The pharaoh Rama-Tut (later renamed "Kang the Conqueror" and "Immortus") secretly originates from the year "3000 . . . one thousand years further in the future than your own century!" (#19: 10). The Fantastic Four unknowingly inspired him: "It was while watching ancient films, presented by our historical society, that I learned of the Fantastic Four! How I envied your dramatic careers!" (10). As a result, Rama-Tut constructed a time machine inside a Sphinx, established his headquarters in ancient Egypt, and become "a time looter" (10).

So far none of these events speaks for or against presentism or eternalism. In time-travel stories, people move between points on a timeline whether or not those points are always there. For eternalism, they are *always* there. For presentism, they *come to be* there when the time traveler arrives. What happens next, however, indicates that Lee and Kirby are again siding with eternalism. Once defeated, Rama-Tut escapes, leaving behind his empty Sphinx, which will "mystify mankind for centuries to come! And, when I leave, the memory of my reign shall fade into oblivion . . . as though I had never existed!" (20). His prophecy fulfills the observation Reed makes earlier at the Museum of Natural History *before* the adventure: "There are a few years of ancient Egyptian history completely unaccounted for by historians, as though those years just didn't exist!" (4). So Rama-Tut always is inspired in 3000 by the Fantastic Four in the 1960s to travel to ancient Egypt. The Fantastic Four always defeat Rama-Tut, and Rama-Tut's empty Sphinx always mystifies humanity for centuries to come. There do remain those "few years" of history unaccounted for—the ones where all the time traveling occurs—but they would be the years where all the time traveling always occurs.

Kirby's depiction of Dr. Doom's time-travel device further suggests an eternalist metaphysics. Though initially in *Fantastic Four* #5 the time travelers appear to fade as they stand atop Doom's platform and then vanish in a burst (9), Kirby next draws the platform descending around them incrementally so that their feet and legs remain in the past while their heads and torsos appear in the present (19). Kirby repeats the effect in #19, placing the characters simultaneously in ancient Egypt and 1963 (22). The shared panels merge two time periods spatially, requiring both moments to exist as the Fantastic Four occupy each. Through both their words and images, all these stories can be understood as thought experiments designed to get their readers to think through the consequences of eternalism.

Changing Times

But what if time isn't eternal? What if time travelers could alter their own pasts? We understand Marvel elsewhere as presenting thought experiments that get readers to think through the consequences of presentism instead. In 1968, six years after Lee and Kirby introduced Doom's device, writer Roy Thomas sent the Avengers to Doom's castle to use his machine again. The characters travel to World War II to learn whether Captain America's former sidekick, Bucky, died in a plane explosion, as Captain America has believed: "How can I be sure? I saw only a single, searing blast! If I survived it . . . couldn't he have too?" (*Avengers* #56: 5).

Thomas might seem to be, like Lee and Kirby, working with eternalism. Captain America insists that "we're only here to observe!" because "I know we can't change fate" (8). All points in time and facts about them are set. That artist John Buscema initially draws the Avengers as ghostly figures, invisible and intangible to the characters in the past, visually reinforces an eternalist interpretation. But then Captain America says something that suggests that Thomas regards the philosophy of time behind Doom's device as presentist. Why can the Avengers not change fate? Captain America continues: ". . . it'd be dangerous to try" (12). The prohibition against changing the past isn't metaphysical—it's not because the nature of time is eternal—but prudential. Doing so might lead to bad results.

The Avengers do witness Bucky leaping atop the booby-trapped plane just before it explodes: "It had to end this way . . . there was no other way! We couldn't be allowed to affect history . . . to play the role of gods!" (18). But those exclamations have prudential rather than metaphysical force. It isn't that the Avengers *couldn't* play the role of gods, but that they couldn't *be allowed* to play it. That would be unwise. Admittedly, the characters do more than observe. Though they don't save Bucky from the Nazi supervillain Baron Zemo's bomb, their intervention does delay Zemo from launching the plane with the unconscious Bucky and Captain America strapped to it. That gives the time-traveling Captain time to free his past self and sidekick. Those two in turn pursue the launching plane, resulting in Bucky's death as predicted.

On closer inspection, however, the Avengers don't actually change a thing.

Like the Fantastic Four, they travel to a previous point in their own timeline. Yet Marvel continuity seems committed to the Fantastic Four *always* traveling to that point. They *always* are part of the past and as a result don't change it. Though the Avengers apparently *believe* that their timeline is mutable and thus express a presentist view, their intervention *is* ultimately the same as the Fantastic Four's. It causes the past events to occur just as Captain America remembers them, since he was unconscious when his future self freed him and thus has no memory of his own intervention. The Avengers' being in the past is integral to the way that the past always plays out. Contrary to appearances, Thomas—like Lee and Kirby, and later Mantlo—gets his readers to think about eternalism when exploring Doom's time machine as a plot device.

Artist John Buscema's rendering of Dr. Doom's time machine, however, does challenge Kirby's eternalist depiction. After the Wasp presses the control switch and the other Avengers "are instantaneously hurled long, silent years away . . . !" (6), Buscema draws an ambiguous space where the characters' color-drained bodies tumble through swirls and circles before reappearing in the next panel. The Avengers never occupy the two time periods simultaneously. Instead they transition through a middle panel that's an aspect of neither. For the duration of that middle passage, neither 1968 nor 1942 exists. That might support a presentist view of time where a time traveler's presence alone determines the reality of any moment.

The characters themselves also think in presentist terms, since during their adventures they assume that they can change the past, whether or not they actually can. This conflicting attitude expands in Marvel's 1970s stories. In the 1974 *Two-in-One* #4–5, Steve Gerber employed Doom's device to send the Thing and Captain America to the future to meet the Guardians of the Galaxy. Mantlo next used the device for Spider-Man in his 1976 *Team-Up* #41–46, which, as already discussed, supports eternalism. Yet when Gerber reintroduced the Guardians of the Galaxy in *The Defenders* the following year, he depicted a competing philosophy according to which time isn't eternal. Shortly after the future events depicted in the 1974 issues, Major Vance Astro, "1,000-year-old survivor of our own century," travels with his fellow Guardians of the Galaxy, "freedom-fighters from the alien-occupied Earth of 3015 A.D.," to the twentieth century to recover "historical records" that will aid their fight against the alien invaders (*Defenders* #26, *Giant-Size Defenders* #5 in *Essential Defenders*, unpaginated). Gerber scripted Major Astro's "history lesson" of the future, one that brings Astro's preadolescent past self to tears,

From *Avengers* #56.

asking whether "all that stuff . . . it could happen here, too—couldn't it?" The Major consoles him: "It could, Vance . . . Yes, but it doesn't have to. It's difficult to explain . . . but no world's future is predestined. Only the past is absolute." Dr. Strange concurs that the Major's story is "just one possible destiny," "paradoxical though it may seem."

Though flashbacks are typically rendered in differentiated panel shapes, artist Sal Buscema (brother of artist John Buscema) draws the panels of Major

Astro's narration in the same straight-edged and sharp-cornered frames as the present actions that precede and follow them. Kirby, by contrast, drew Rama-Tut's narration of his past experiences of the year 3000 in scallop-edged panels. Differentiated panel frames suggest that the past events depicted inside them are different from the present events depicted inside standard frames. Retold past events have already occurred and so are immutable, while present events are unfolding for the first time. This is true for Rama-Tut even though his past events actually occur in the distant future. Major Astro's memories of the future, however, are framed no differently from any event unfolding in the present. Visually the past and the present are represented as identical.

Gerber and Buscema get us to imagine a different philosophy of time. The Major's explanation, which Dr. Strange agrees with, voices a hybrid view. While presentism maintains that only the present exists, and eternalism maintains that all times exist, the growing-block view maintains that both the past and the present exist while the future does not. Time is like a growing block. Once its pieces are in place, they're immovable. But the block does grow as new time comes into being. The growing-block view might have been Aristotle's understanding of time, when he argued in his *On Interpretation* that it was neither true nor false that there will be a sea battle tomorrow. "Paradoxical though it may seem," Dr. Strange presumably thinks the same regarding whether there will be an alien invasion in his future. Because the future remains open, the facts aren't yet in. They're partly the young Vance's to write. Not wanting Vance's actions to be influenced by what from his perspective is one merely possible future, Dr. Strange erases his memory: "The boy will remember nothing of what you told him. My spell saw to that." Vance will then be unencumbered when, thirteen years later, he rockets into space on "a thousand-year journey to the stars" to create his own destiny.

Marvel's mid-1970s writers, however, don't consistently portray time as a growing block. Sometimes their philosophy of time appears presentist. While Dr. Strange's actions show that only the future doesn't exist, so only its facts are up for grabs, the same might be true of that past also. Though Mantlo's 1976 Spider-Man believes that "history's written" (*Marvel Team-Up* #45: 1), according to a *Fantastic Four* story scripted by Thomas the same year, what has happened in the past can be *re*-written. After a cylinder of the supermetal vibranium is accidentally transported by Doom's machine to 1942 Germany, Reed explains: "Time is a delicate quantity, Johnny—and one we know little about as yet. Who knows what disturbances might be caused in the relative time-stream" (Thomas, Buscema, and Grainger, *Fantastic Four Annual* #11: 8). The arrival of Nazi soldiers from 1946 London reveals that the displaced vibranium could "re-write history, so that the Axis won the war" (11).

For an eternalist, neither past, present, nor future can be rewritten, since the distinction among those time periods is metaphysically moot. All times equally exist, all facts about them equally set. By allowing past and future to be altered—and presumably by allowing those in the present to be masters of their own fate—Thomas appears to have abandoned both the original eternalist position and the growing-block view to embrace presentism outright. His readers are invited to sort the elements of that thought experiment out.

Branching Time

While Marvel creators begin by endorsing eternalism, their views wobble among eternalism, presentism, and the growing block. But what if time travel isn't what it appears to be? Thomas's 1976 time-travel story may not reflect any of these philosophies of time. When Doom's machine shows German buzz-bombs "making a direct hit on London" in 1942, Ben and Reed debate the implications:

> BEN: We all know the buzz-bombs didn't start hittin' England till June of '44—and the V-2 rockets even later!
> REED: That's what happened in our memory, Ben . . . But there may be other time-continuums of which we've previously known nothing—continuums in which Nazi scientists somehow licked the problem of long-range missiles at a far-earlier date! Such a thing might have changed the course of the war in one continuum . . . (16–17)

Instead of rewriting the past, the Fantastic Four of Roy Thomas's 1976 story travel to an alternate 1942, where they team up with Captain America, Sub-Mariner, and the other members of the Invaders to defeat Baron Zemo, who had acquired the vibranium to make rockets. Afterward, Ben wonders, "How come Subby an' the rest don't remember us from '42 when we met a few years back?" (46).

> REED: You forget, Ben—this was a different time continuum—one which came into existence because of that vibranium sample which got sent back into time. (46)

Here Thomas is embracing a branching theory of time. When the vibranium went back in time, it created an offshoot, or branch, of the original timeline (or continuum). That branch isn't the Fantastic Four's home timeline, which we might now understand as simply another branch.

So, besides traveling in time, we now seem to have traveling to different time branches. Thomas's script involves *three*. There's the *first* branch, the Fantastic Four's home, which they remember. There's the *second* branch, which came into existence when the vibranium was sent back in time, resulting in Germany winning World War II. But there's also now apparently a *third* branch, which comes into existence when the Fantastic Four go back in time and defeat Baron Zemo, preventing the German victory. The Fantastic Four appear to believe that events in all of the branches are changeable, as when Reed says that the vibranium "changed the course of the war in one continuum . . . and might eventually affect all of them!" and Ben responds: "If we don't change what's happened back on this other time-path . . . it's just possible that the America we come back to ain't gonna be celebratin' any bicentennial!" (17). But according to the story's internal logic, if the time-traveling vibranium caused time to branch, then the time-traveling Fantastic Four would have done so too. They can't change events in the second branch because their attempt to enter that branch instead creates the third branch. And contrary to their expressed fears, events in one branch are never shown to affect other branches and logically should not.

Separate branches do, however, increase complexity. When the Fantastic Four defeat Baron Zemo by traveling back in time, they don't defeat *their* Zemo but that branch's Zemo, causing that branch's Germany to lose the war just as Germany loses the war in the Fantastic Four's timeline. But if the restored events then continue to unfold the same, that branch must eventually have its own Doom device and its own sample of vibranium that will be accidentally transported back to 1942—causing the creation of a *fourth* branch, in which Germany wins the war. That branch will then be observed by the Fantastic Four of the third branch, who will attempt to travel to the new 1942—causing the creation of a *fifth* branch, in which the Fantastic Four of the third branch defeat that Zemo and cause that Germany to lose the war. But when the fifth branch also eventually produces its own Doom device, vibranium sample, and Fantastic Four, a *sixth* and *seventh* branch will follow— with the process cycling endlessly. When Ben says: "Boy, this is real confusin'!"

he's right. There's an infinity of universes where the Allies/Fantastic Four win *and* an infinity where Nazis/Zemo do. The score would then be tied: infinity–infinity.

These calculations don't factor in Ben's next adventure in *Marvel Two-in-One* #19–20 (1976). There Roy Thomas appeals to Doom's device again, allowing Ben to retrieve the other half of the missing vibranium to prevent a *different* Germany victory, triggering *more* branching. Worse, while the 1976 Fantastic Four and the 1942 Invaders are battling Baron Zemo in 1942, Captain America knocks a vat of Adhesive X onto Zemo, permanently affixing Zemo's mask to his face—fulfilling an event retroactively established in *Avengers* #6 (July 1964). Had the Fantastic Four of 1976 not traveled to 1942, then Captain America wouldn't have faced Zemo at that moment and his mask wouldn't have been affixed. And had the vibranium not been transported to 1942 first, then the Fantastic Four wouldn't have traveled there at all. How, then, was Zemo's mask affixed in the Fantastic Four's own branch where no vibranium from 1976 ever appeared in 1942? Alternatively, vibranium from another branch did appear in what we previously identified as the *first* branch—meaning the endless cycling not only didn't originate from that branch after all, but, more confoundingly, didn't originate from anywhere. It's an infinite branching time loop paradox.

As we said in our introduction, one difference between the thought experiments employed by academic philosophers and those that we're reading into superhero comics is that the first set tends to change only certain details and are more careful in holding other ones constant. Marvel, on the other hand, changes so many details that their writers apparently don't notice the proliferation of branches. To avoid complexities such as these, David Lewis rejects the idea of branching time altogether. Echoing Ben's confusion, Lewis would in this case observe that we don't want to know what happens to some other Germany, let alone some *other* other Germany ad infinitum.

The branching theory of time is a view about the *shape* of time. While nonbranching time treats time as linear, branching time treats it as having tributaries—where branches can themselves have branches. Branching time isn't a view about the *reality* of time or its parts. It's not a view about whether past, present, or future exists. Marvel writers can embrace a branching theory of time and presentism, eternalism, or growing-block simultaneously. It might be that the only existing time for the Fantastic Four is their present (even

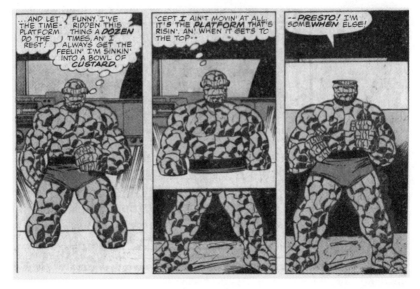

From *Two-in-One* #50.

when that present from our perspective would be the past), branching or otherwise. Or it might be that all times—and now we have to specify *in their branch*—(eternally) exist for them, but that time travel causes a new branch to shoot out from their own. So-called time travel is actually branch creation.

In 1979 writer-artist John Byrne clarified the reality of time as it relates to Doom's device by depicting Ben's attempt to travel to his own past to try to cure himself from being the Thing. Reed explains that "this latest formula of mine would have cured you as you were years ago," but not now because "your basic appearance has been constantly changing" and "your body is becoming 'comfortable' as the Thing" (Byrne, Sinnott, and Mouly, *Marvel Two-in-One* #50: 2). Ben decides: "If this woulda worked on me in the past, I'll give it to me in the past! Courtesy of Doc Doom's time machine" (3). After setting "the dial for a couple of months after our joyride in Reed's rocket" that exposed him to cosmic rays and turned him into the Thing, Ben succeeds in giving his former self the formula (3). But when he returns to his present he is "still the Thing!" (31). Reed explains: "Your past is immutable, Ben. You are what you are! Any change you make in the past results in another reality—a new one caused by your presence" (31).

For Byrne, time does branch, though the events in each branch are immutable. Ben thinks he is changing *the* past, but he's merely in a *different* past. Unlike Thomas's Reed, who expressed presentist fears about the pasts of multiple branches changing, Byrne's Reed is confident about the eternal past. Byrne also echoes Kirby's rendering of the time travel by drawing Dr. Doom's platform rising up Ben's body so that his feet and legs appear in 1961 while his head and torso are still transitioning from 1979. The two time periods once again appear in a single panel (3). Byrne makes clear narratively and visually that, unlike Thomas's Fantastic Four's time-travel adventure to World War II, his story combines a branching theory of time with either eternalism or the growing-block view. There is more than one timeline, and either all points in time (according to eternalism) or only past and present ones (according to the growing-block view) are real and fixed.

For Marvel to depict a thought experiment in which the philosophy of time was fully eternalist, the future would also need to be fixed. Byrne says nothing about the future, but later writers do, showing that the future is itself changeable. Captain America prevents what Gerber's Astro termed "the Bionic Wars of the 1990's," which produced the supersoldier Deathlok, who traveled to Marvel's central time branch via Doom's device in *Two-in-One* #26 in 1977 and was then reprised by writer J. M. DeMatteis for *Captain America* in 1983.

CAPTAIN AMERICA: This future of yours . . . from what he told me, it's a living hell! How did it happen? How did it happen in so short a time? [. . .]
DEATHLOK: Mister, every blasted super hero on Earth—up and vanished back in '83. It was all downhill from there! (DeMatteis, Zeck, and Beatty, #287: 18)

When Captain America prevents all of his fellow heroes from vanishing as they did in Deathlok's timeline, Captain America's and Deathlok's times diverge, so that Deathlok's world is not the future of Captain America's world. Deathlok still exists, just in a different branch of time. Had Captain America not acted, however, his timeline would have unfolded as Deathlok predicted. Captain America could influence his future only because that future didn't yet exist. DeMatteis combines branching time with a growing-block view. The past and present are eternal but the future is open. And there can be more than one branch of each.

Creating Time

What if time travel creates parallel worlds? That's the nature of the thought experiments we've just now been considering: branches *come into* existence when time travelers create new offshoots of already existing branches. Reflecting this central philosophy, in 1977 Marvel premiered its series *What If?*, using the alien character of the all-knowing Watcher to narrate realities that come into existence at points of divergence independent of Doom's device. As scripted by Roy Thomas, the Watcher explains that any moment can produce a range of divergences:

> Consider if you will, a speeding car—a hapless pedestrian frozen in surprise—and a startled on-looker. The instantaneous decision made by the on-looker, made virtually without conscious thought, will affect not only his life, but those of others. He might, for instance, stand helplessly, fearfully by, to see the man struck by the careening vehicle. Or, his adrenalin pumping, he might leap to the rescue—only to see both of them struck and maimed, and perhaps killed. Or, leaping one split second sooner, he might carry both of them to safety—saving the driver from consequences of his own carelessness. Nor are these more than three paths out of countless millions upon millions. (Thomas, Craig, and Marcos 13)

The Watcher's street-crossing example is a variation on a thought experiment proposed by nineteenth-century philosopher William James. Discussing his "choice of which way to walk home after the lecture," James writes:

> Imagine that I first walk through Divinity Avenue, and then imagine that the powers governing the universe annihilate ten minutes of time with all that it contained, and set me back at the door of this hall just as I was before the choice was made. Imagine then that, everything else being the same, I now make a different choice and traverse Oxford Street. You, as passive spectators, look on and see the two alternate universes—one of them with me walking through Divinity Avenue in it, the other with the same me walking through Oxford Street. (18)

It's no coincidence that James's thought experiment, which is similar to our analysis of branching time, speaks of "alternate universes." A branch is like a universe unto itself. Branching time brings with it both space and objects.

Yet James's thought experiment can be understood in two different ways. The first is that James's choice *creates* the branch. It causes the branch to be, which matches the branching theory of time that Marvel writers at this point invite us to imagine. The Fantastic Four create a new branch when they battle Zemo, just as Captain America creates one when he prevents superheroes from vanishing as they do in Deathlok's branch. The second way to understand James's thought experiment is that his choice *finds* the branch. The branch already exists. Instead of being created, it's discovered. James happens upon it. That doesn't match Marvel's mid-1970s branching theory of time at all.

So there turns out to be *three* relevant notions of Doom-related time. First, there's the reality of time: Are past, present, or future real? Next, there's the shape of time: Is it linear or branching? And now, finally, there's the reality of the branches: Do people living in one branch cause another branch to come to be, or do all branches always exist?

We can think of the third notion, concerning the reality of the branches, as the question of presentism, the growing-block view, or eternalism applied not to points on the timeline but to time branches or lines themselves. Does only the present branch exist, and when people from that branch move to another, does that new branch come into existence? If the new branch comes into existence but the previous branch ceases to exist, then this is like presentism for branches. Only the branch that we are now in exists. That appears to be Reed's original assumption about the branch where Germany wins World War II: it vanishes once the Fantastic Four remove the vibranium. However, this presentist view doesn't match the pattern for other branches, which do continue to exist—notably Deathlok's branch, which continues to exist after Captain America prevents its events from occurring in his own branch. If the new branch comes into existence and the previous branch continues to exist, then this is like either a growing-block view or eternalism for branches. It's like a growing-block view if only branches that we are or were on exist. It's like eternalism if all branches exist, independent of whether we are, were, or will be on them.

As we see next, Marvel's decided view is that all branches—all universes—exist. The thought experiment that we're invited to entertain is that the reality of time branches is eternalist. Branches aren't created when characters move between them. They're found.

Finding Time

What if time travel is really universe travel? Marvel writers established the existence of preexisting alternate universes as early as 1968. In *Fantastic Four* #118 (January 1972), Ben travels to a world where Reed was mutated into the Thing instead—an event that occurred prior to and thus was unrelated to Ben's arrival. Writer Roy Thomas returned Ben there in 1975, using not Doom's device but the superpowered dog Lockjaw: "Now pay attention, pooch! I got ya here because ya can travel through dimensions an' all that crud" (*Fantastic Four* #160: 15). Instead of time traveling, Ben understood himself as dimension traveling.

Though Reed's 1979 explanation that Ben created a new universe by attempting to cure his past self contradicts branch eternalism, John Byrne later reinterprets time in light of this eternalism. When Byrne revisited his 1979 Thing story in 1983, Reed reconsiders his earlier conclusions: "I think my original assessment may have been erroneous. I now believe that you did not create that reality" (*Marvel Two-in-One* #100: 3). That reality, or time branch or alternate universe, is always there. Reed deduces this by studying the recorded footage and sees a copy of what should be the *New York Daily Bugle* but is instead the *New Amsterdam Daily Bugle*. He concludes: "The basic data would seem to support that this was an already existing alternate universe" (4). Where eternalism likens different points in time to different points in space, Byrne's revised philosophy allows Ben to travel to New Amsterdam from New York because New Amsterdam exists in space as much as New York does. It just exists in space on a different time branch—thus in a different universe. The thought experiment's been reimagined.

The same revised insight could be applied to other previous adventures. Instead of traveling to their own World War II past or to a parallel World War II past created by time-traveling vibranium, the Fantastic Four instead traveled to an alternate universe that existed prior to their or the vibranium's appearance there. Neither event produced any branching. So is this kind of travel to alternate universes that resemble our universe's past the same as traveling in time? Byrne gets at that point through Ben: "Are you sayin' our time machine ain't a time machine at all?" (4).

> REED: . . . it would appear that any attempt to travel back into one's own past activates some kind of temporal safety-valve. Thus, the traveler is actually shunted sideways, into a universe almost identical to his own. (4)

Though the dialog may look simple, the thought experiment that we're invited to entertain expresses a philosophy of time that is not.

On the question of the reality of time, Reed might be a growing-block theorist or eternalist. The growing-block theory maintains that only past and present exist and are immutable. Eternalism maintains that past, present, and future all exist and are immutable. Or Reed might instead be a presentist, believing that only the present exists—and is what we make it to be. If Reed is a presentist, then his discussion of the "temporal safety-valve" makes a prudential rather than a metaphysical point. As Captain America says that traveling to the past must be limited to observation, because changing fate is "dangerous," Reed would mean that Doom's machine prevents time travel to the past for our own protection.

On the question of the shape of time, Reed is affirming a branching view. Time has different tributaries. Since each is accompanied by space and objects, they may be thought of as alternate universes. Byrne has rejected Stan Lee and Jack Kirby's view that time is linear.

Finally, on the question of the reality of the branches, Reed's earlier discussion makes clear that branches are there to be found. So Reed is either an eternalist or a growing-block theorist about branches. Using Doom's machine to travel to the past must cause the machine to shunt the traveler sideways into an already-existing universe, one "almost identical to his own" (4).

If Byrne's storyline generally revises Marvel continuity, the ramifications are significant. If all previous time travelers are actually dimension travelers, there's a sense in which Spider-Man could have saved the accused Salem witches and the Avengers could have saved Bucky—but only the accused witches and Bucky of different dimensions, not those of the travelers' own immutable pasts. Ben would have created the Blackbeard legend in a different universe as well. That might even suggest that the Blackbeard legend of his own universe could be based on a different Thing visiting from a different universe. Similarly, the time-looting Rama-Tut would have traveled from a different universe after being inspired by the historical films of a different Fantastic Four, meeting our Fantastic Four in the past of yet another different universe.

Characters now also appear to return to dimensions they previously visited without causing new offshoots. In *Marvel Two-in-One* #100 (June 1983), Byrne has Ben use Doom's device to return to the universe that he believed he had created by curing his past self. When he originally traveled there, he set the dial to a few months before his transformation—so, about 1961. Since it was 1979 in his own universe, Ben thought he was traveling backward in time. Instead he moved laterally to a universe with a present of 1961. When he returns, several years have passed there, further establishing the permanence of that other dimension. Ron Wilson's visual reiteration of Kirby's and Byrne's eternalist time platform rising up Ben's body merges the two alternate worlds in a single panel—not because the two moments exist eternally in the same timeline but because they exist eternally in two different worlds, each with its own eternal or growing-block time.

While this makes sense of the philosophy behind Doom's time machine, there's something strange in describing Doom's device as time-related. Universe travel doesn't seem like time travel at all. Do Byrne and those who adopt his view believe in time travel at all? Even Byrne's Ben ponders: "'Course if Reed's right about this doo-hickey not bein' a time machine, that kinda raises a whole lot more questions than it answers . . . I wonder if we've ever really travelled in time? Heck, maybe I never became Blackbeard, or fought in World War II, or . . . Boy, this is real confusin'!" (6).

Reading this as a thought experiment, it's pretty easy to sympathize with Ben. Not only hasn't Marvel's metaphysics of time always been consistent, but—and this is Ben's deeper point—no one is really talking about time travel. Ben never goes into his own past. He goes to an alternate universe that resembles it. Admittedly, universe travel vs. time travel might seem like a distinction without a difference. Ben's past, some other past—they're close enough. Ben recognizes the people in the alternate universe, and his readers do the same. Both allow for the same adventures. So, as far as the narrative goes, they seem the same. But Ben doesn't travel to another universe's past either, since his point of arrival is its present. He moves from the present of his world to the present of another world. In other words, though his destination appears to be the past relative to his own timeline, it is the present relative to the destination itself.

Double Time

It's unclear whether other writers adopted Byrne's understanding of time travel—or "time travel," since it doesn't really involve traveling in time. When in 1981 David Michelinie depicts Doom's time device, referred to now as his "time cube," his narrator and characters refer ambiguously to "the past" (*Iron Man* #149). While the time platform still rises and lowers around its travelers, artist John Romita Jr. also draws Doom and Iron Man tumbling through a surreal space reminiscent of Buscema's rendering in *Avengers* #56, only in addition to orbs and spirals it now includes demons and fanged bubbles. The omniscient narrator declares: "Time is not a glamorous dimension. It is a thick, sticky world peopled by possibilities, by maybes, by could-have-beens. It is an angry, uncertain place" (*Iron Man* #150: 1). This could align with either the branching theory of reality, with travelers facing the uncertainties of infinite alternate universes (created *or* found), or presentism, with the same universe's past and future in constant flux.

So when, in their 1981 joint adventure, Doom and Iron Man traveled to ancient Camelot, it's impossible to tell whether this is the Camelot of a parallel universe or their own timeline. In 1989, Michelinie sends them to Camelot again, but now of 2093. Because the reincarnated King Arthur recalls their past encounter, this presumably involves the same timeline as the one in which their earlier adventure takes place—unless this is a parallel Arthur unknowingly recalling a Doom and Iron Man of a parallel universe, as branching theory would suggest.

Michelinie's adventure seems to reject eternalism. While Iron Man battles his apparent descendant, Doom faces his apparent future cyborg self.

> 1989 DOOM: How can this be? That we could both exist in the same place at the same time?
>
> 2093 DOOM: Scientific theory is just that. Theory. Obviously whoever devised this one has never traveled through time. (*Iron Man* #150, 40)

When Doom kills his future self, an outcome that his future self anticipates because "I did the same a century ago," Doom rejects eternalism: "The future is fluid. It can be changed. And by all the power in my soul, I swear I'll not become—that" (43). That presupposes either presentism or the growing-block view of time, which suggests that there is only one timeline involved. But is Doom's vow or understanding of time accurate? Merlin, duplicating Doctor Strange's earlier intervention with Major Astro's younger self, erases Doom's and Iron Man's memories before returning them to 1989. So the reality and shape of time, as well as the reality of any branches, remain unclear.

Likewise, after Doom is presumed dead in 1997, writer John Francis Moore sends X-Force to Doom's castle to destroy the time device. Because of the explosion, they and the entire castle are "hit by waves of temporal energy" and "hurled back in time" to 1941. But because the castle already exists then, X-Force and the 1997 castle "do not exist in temporal synchronicity with this era," so they're "like a ghost image of the future superimposed on the past" (*X-Force* #64). Since synchronicity requires that two things be aligned, temporal synchronicity suggests two stable time periods. Moreover, when X-Force's Dimitri attempts to prevent his grandfather's death by the group of Nazis he is working with, he gets caught in a paradox:

> SIRYN: Seems to me they didn't succeed, or we'd not be talkin' t'ye now.
>
> DIMITRI: I don't believe in predestination. If we can travel in time, then history can be changed. The only question is will it be changed by us or the Germans?
>
> SIRYN: Maybe the Germans' attempt on the Baron's life didn't succeed because we were here to intervene. (Unpaginated)

This appears to be the case, because X-Force does save him before returning to their own time. Though Dimitri's view is presentist—we can change the past because its facts and existence are not set—Siryn's observation suggests that there wasn't really any change at all. Maybe Dimitri always prevented the Germans' attempt on the Baron's life. That presupposes either eternalism or, because only the reality of the past is in question, the growing-block view. There's similar vagueness about the shape of time and the reality of its branches, if any. Did Dimitri save his grandfather of his own timeline or one of another timeline? If he saved his grandfather of another timeline, did that timeline—with his grandfather—come into existence at the moment of their arrival, or did it always exist? The episode gives little basis for judgment, though past episodes have primed us for figuring out the consequences of whichever thought experiment we read this as.

Later stories offer little more clarity. In 2008, writer Brian Michael Bendis depicts Doom traveling repeatedly to ancient Camelot to continue his alliance and affair with Morgan Le Fay, whom he first encountered in the 1981 *Iron Man* #150.

> LE FAYE: When next we meet . . . I want you to bring me something. From the future time. [. . .]
>
> DOOM: If I brought you something you could keep . . . its very existence could cause a chain reaction in the timestream. By no fault of your

own it could disrupt the natural order of things as they are now and
how they are meant to be.

LE FAYE: But you coming back in time to be with me does not?

DOOM: We're alone. It's contained.

LE FAYE: So it's okay when it suits your purpose. [. . .]

DOOM: I could reappear yesterday and turn this conversation another
way. (*Mighty Avengers* #9)

Because Doom maintains that the past is mutable, their dialog implies presentism. It also suggests that Doom has used his device to travel to her time period on multiple occasions—unless, as Reed Richards understood in *Two-in-One* #50, the device actually created a new universe with each use. Alternatively, according to Reed Richards in *Two-in-One* #100, Doom may have traveled to a preexisting universe instead, and as with Ben Grimm's two visits to the universe in which he cured another Ben Grimm of being the Thing, he has returned to this preexisting universe and so to the same Morgan Le Fay each time.

Regardless, Doom appears to believe that he is traveling within his own timeline, which he can alter. Iron Man later expresses the same belief when he, Doom, and Sentry are transported to New York of only a few years earlier:

You know anything you do in this time period will severely damage the
space-time continuum. [. . .] So let's not do or say anything to anyone
that could alter the course of human history. [. . .] We have to get out of
here before we're discovered . . . or before we accidentally do any damage
or interact with anything or anybody that could "butterfly effect" what
happens to the future as we know it. (*Mighty Avengers* #10)

If the timeline may be altered—and in fact is altered, even if largely unnoticed—then the reality of time is presentist. Though it's less clear whether or not time branches, Iron Man's speaking of "*the* course of human history" and "*the* future as we know it" suggests that there is only one timeline. His worry seems to be not that the future will branch but that the future will change.

Yet until 2015 Marvel continuity included a vast branching multiverse of parallel universes. Marvel.wikia.com lists over 1,400, with number designations peaking with Earth-931113. Though numbering was instituted in the 1980s, prior universes were retroactively designated. The world in which the

Thing cured a younger version of himself—introduced in 1979 and revisited in 1983—is Earth-7940. Lee and Kirby's original future world—the 3000 A.D. birthplace of Rama-Tut—became Earth-6311. So collectively Marvel employs two philosophies, running two distinct thought experiments, simultaneously. Characters could travel within their own timeline and also to alternative universes. Genuine time travel occurs only given the first. The stories of Michelinie, Moore, and Bendis depict time travel within characters' own malleable timeline, returning to a kind of presentism that Thomas introduced in 1968. Other stories depict alternate universes, though not necessarily ones branching from points of divergence as Thomas introduced in his 1970s stories. When Byrne revised Doom's time-traveling device into an alternate universe-traveling device, he ended Thomas's branching reality. Because the device no longer created branches but instead traveled to preexisting worlds, points of divergence no longer mattered. Alternate universes were not created but existed independently, whether encountered by outside travelers or not. The *Ultimate* universe of Earth-1610, which was introduced by Bendis in 2000 and expanded to four series, was never a branch of Marvel's primary universe, Earth-616, as depicted in 1961.

All-New All-Different Time

So what kinds of thought experiments about time does Dr. Doom's time machine illustrate? While Lee and Kirby and later Mantlo seem to be eternalists who think that time does not branch, Thomas introduces presentism in 1968, but actually maintains eternalism until adopting the growing-block view with Gerber and later DeMatteis. Thomas also introduces branching time, which Byrne of 1981 combines with either the growing-block theory or eternalism. While Thomas believes that time branches at points of divergence, including those points created by time travelers, Byrne of 1983 believes that all branches exist eternally. Finally, Michelinie, Moore, and Bendis reject both branching time and eternalism in favor of a multiverse of presentism.

Taken collectively, Marvel poses a question unasked by traditional philosophers: What if time does not have a single metaphysical nature? Dr. Doom's device seems to have (at least) five modes. It sends travelers sometimes to preexisting parallel universes, sometimes to new parallel universes triggered into existence by the attempt to travel within a previously existing timeline, sometimes to the previously nonexistent future of their own timeline, sometimes to the eternally existing past or future of their timeline, and sometimes to the past or present of their presentist or growing-block (and so ever-changing) timeline. Perhaps Doom's device accesses different metaphysical modes randomly or even intentionally. Regardless of the mechanism, they all follow from Marvel's decades of thought experiments.

Because analyzing all of Marvel's time-travel stories is a book-length project, we've limited our focus to the philosophy behind Doom's device. We do, though, make one exception—and that's to consider Marvel's (recent) present. For the 2015 miniseries *Secret Wars*, Marvel destroyed its multiverse of alternate universes and with it all its time branches. Even Earth-1610, its multiseries *Ultimate* universe, and Earth-616, its original continuity introduced in 1961 with *Fantastic Four* #1 (or arguably Timely's *Marvel Comics* #1 in 1939), were erased and replaced by a new, merged universe. (We discuss this and other multiverses in chapter 5.) Rather than starting completely over, however, Marvel's 2015 continuity combined elements of Earth-1610 and Earth-616. Given the complexities and ambiguities in the nature of time in its half century of previous stories, Marvel writers could take years and even decades of new storytelling to establish how exactly time now works. But how time *should* work is a philosophical question that we can use their thought experiments to ask ourselves.

Whether or not their stories involve Doom's device, Marvel writers might reject branching time and revert to taking time's shape to be linear, especially since eliminating a confusing multiverse was one of Marvel's motives for the rebooted, single-universe continuity. Marvel writers might also revisit its view of time's reality: eternalist, growing-block, or presentist. Like the original 1960s Marvel, All-New, All-Different Marvel writers could again opt for eternalism and make all points in time exist and all facts about time set—so that neither past, present, nor future can be changed. Because nothing about any time could be changed, most of Marvel's former time-travel stories could be repeated as long as Marvel continuity maintained eternalism. Ben might still go into the past and find himself, but only if Ben always goes into the past and finds himself. This allows Ben to travel to Blackbeard's time to discover that he *is* Blackbeard, but not to the past of his own memory if his own memory doesn't already include an interaction with his future self trying to administer a Thing-curing formula.

Yet eternalism isn't how the Marvel universe unfolded after Stan Lee and Jack Kirby's initial stories, and there are two reasons it shouldn't be the reality of time that Marvel writers adopt moving forward. First, a universe where everything a time traveler does is already fixed isn't particularly interesting. Second, eternalism presents barriers to new writers who would have to conform to all events established by their predecessors.

Should Marvel writers adopt the growing-block view instead? As a hybrid of eternalism and presentism, this theory inherits problems from each of these others. Spider-Man's, the Avengers', and the Fantastic Four's time-travel adventures would remain futile, because not only can they never change the past, but also their attempts to do so *are* the past. Besides being uninteresting, this too presents barriers to writers.

Admittedly, for the growing-block theorist, unlike for the eternalist, time travelers can change the future. But *changing* the future isn't where the narrative action is. The future is unknown to us, so writers need not change it to explore new and interesting ideas. They can simply describe how they think the future will turn out. That's why so many time-travel stories involve the past and time travelers changing it—or being warned against doing so. The growing-block view also complicates stories about time travelers from the future, like Rama-Tut, Major Vance Astro, and Deathlok. According to the growing-block view, because there *is* no future—only the past and present are real—future travelers don't exist until "the future" *becomes* "the present." Rama-Tut can't travel from the year 3000 until 3000 is the present. Given the growing-block view, however, neither the present nor the past can be changed. But that means that Rama-Tut can't change 3000 or the 1960s, since they're the present time when he's there. On the growing-block view, time traveling from the future, because it would have to be present to travel from there, would ultimately be as uninteresting and creatively inhibiting as time traveling to the past. The same would hold for traveling to the future.

Maybe Marvel writers should adopt presentism. Presentism, though, faces an arguably bigger problem: it's vulnerable to paradoxes. Nothing would seem to prevent Ben from setting the dial of Dr. Doom's machine a couple of months before his transformation and stopping himself from ever becoming the Thing. But if he had done that, then Ben from the present would never have used Doom's machine. And this would mean that he would never have prevented himself from becoming the Thing in the first place. So Ben would seem to become the Thing if he doesn't, and not to become the Thing if he does. Philosophers love contemplating paradoxes. That's why so many of their thought experiments involve them. But they also usually advise us to avoid them.

No matter how time should work, All-New, All-Different Marvel has already made suggestive moves. Four titles—*The Ultimates*, *All-New X-Men*, *Old Loki*, and *Age of Ultron*—contain stories where characters appear to travel within a single timeline. So Marvel writers seem to have decided against branching time. Because the shape of time is linear, questions about the reality of time branches are moot. All that remains is whether time is presentist, growing-block, or eternalist.

To determine this, consider a summary that Al Ewing scripts for Ultimates team member Blue Marvel:

> We have people living together—long-term—with their own past selves. We have visitors from this future regularly attempting to alter their past. We have historical figures exploring our time and taking knowledge back with them. Occasionally, present-day people become historical figures. Even after the so-called "Age of Ultron" incident—when time nearly shattered under this strain—we continue to abuse it. It can't go on. Of course much of this can be laid at the feet of Victor Von Doom—his quasi-mystical "Doomlock" being what allows these travelers to cross their own timelines. (Qtd. in Johnston)

The Doomlock was introduced by Peter David in *X-Factor* #46 (September 2009), but Ewing employs it in the All-New, All-Different universe to explain Marvel's latest philosophy of time. What philosophy is that?

Marvel has a long history of eternalism, which can explain how the X-Men can live together with their past selves. Since there are no time branches, Ben now must have traveled to his own past to become Blackbeard, though eternalism can handle that too. But why don't the X-Men recall traveling to their own future? Though their past selves are adventuring with their current selves in the present, their current selves don't remember having done so in the past. Will Dr. Strange have to erase the younger X-Men's memories as he did young Vance's before they return to the past? Or are past and future unwritten? If so, then Marvel creators are now presentists. If only the future's open, then they're now growing-block theorists. With so much room for exploration, only time will tell how Marvel will continue clobberin' the philosophy of time.

PART III

MEANING

FIVE

REFERENTIAL RETCONS
VS. DESCRIPTIVIST REBOOTS

As we observed in the previous chapter, when Marvel decided in 1979 that Dr. Doom's so-called time travel device didn't time travel but instead leapt through universes, the revision altered a two-decade-old story. When Marvel decided in 2015 that their entire multiverse was replaced by a new continuity, the revision altered a half century of stories. For the characters inside all of those stories, their world, the metaphysics of their reality, changed. In our world of creators and readers, something changed too: how we understand those stories, including the meanings of their words and pictures. By exploring how stories mean what they mean, this chapter introduces readers to another branch of philosophy: the philosophy of language.

Superhero comics provide a distinct thought-experimental laboratory for the philosophy of language, and especially for philosophical views on the meanings of proper names. Unlike isolated novels or movies, superhero comics develop their stories issue by issue and thus are parts of series. Of course, comics writers didn't invent serial fiction. Detective readers started following Sherlock Holmes's adventures in 1887, and Charles Dickens's 1836 *Pickwick Papers*, originally a proto–comic book of captioned illustrations, popularized by publishing chapters of longer works in monthly installments. Today many movies and television shows too, not to mention book series, are serialized. But few genres demonstrate seriality so fully as superhero comics do—plots developing over decades, new characters interacting with old, forgotten villains resurfacing, and favorite heroes continually redeveloped.

As with any form of serial fiction, new issues of superhero comics build on older ones. Often their additions are linear, with new installments simply adding to existing plots. Such linear developments continue established characters and storylines without changing anything. But what if a new installment instead alters a previous installment by forcing the reader to reinterpret events already described? Or, more radically, what if the new installment overwrites older events entirely? This way of developing serial stories is nonlinear. The installments are revisionary: rather than simply adding to existing plots, the writers have to make changes to, or even nullify, the story as previously told.

Revisionary installments can also make words change meanings. We indirectly introduced the philosophy of language in chapter 2 with Twin Earth, Putnam's thought experiment about the use of "water," and Moral Twin Earth, Terence Horgan and Mark Timmons's thought experiment about the use of "good." In that case, we borrowed their thought experiments to understand the metaethical foundations of the superhero universe. In this chapter, we delve deeper by focusing on two schools within the philosophy of language, referentialism and descriptivism, to understand nonlinear revision in superhero comics in terms of the proper names of characters in them.

Retcons vs. Reboots

As a first pass, nonlinear story developments seem to come in two varieties: (a) retcons, which reveal the past in new ways, sometimes by filling in details, other times by correcting them; and (b) reboots, which replace the past with new information altogether.

Marvel's Thor illustrates the first. In *Journey into Mystery* #83 (August 1962), Stan Lee and Jack Kirby introduce a man named "Donald Blake," a mortal who happens upon a stick that transforms itself into a magical hammer and Blake into someone with the power of Thor. Though Blake is called "Thor" when transformed, he remains mentally himself, with all of his memories unchanged. When not battling monsters and supervillains, Blake retains his mortal physique too.

But what if Blake were actually Thor all along?

In *Mighty Thor* #159 (December 1968), Lee and Kirby reveal Blake to be the actual Thor, the Norse god and son of Odin—who temporarily made Thor mortal and altered his memory (not unlike the evil geniuses of chapter 3). Though Lee and Kirby don't change any of the surface details from Thor's first episode—a person who calls himself "Donald Blake" still discovers a magic stick and gains the powers of a god—they do correct those details by creating a larger context. Now we understand the earlier story as being not about a mortal but about a god who didn't know that he was a god. It turns out that our first impression of Blake—a mortal who gains godly powers—was wrong. No such being ever existed. Blake always was Thor, because the original story is now retroactively continuous with the new one: Marvel retconned Blake the mortal out of existence. And that sense of continuity is accentuated by Kirby's art. Though his manner of representing Blake and Thor evolves in the six years between the series' introduction and retcon, the series' overall style remains consistent, suggesting story unity despite the reinterpretation of its central character.

Mighty Thor #159 amounts to a thought experiment exploring the properties of retcons. As the story illustrates, retcons are nonlinear developments because, by revealing new information, they require reinterpreting facts established earlier. "Retcon" is an abbreviation of "retroactive continuity." At the moment of retconning, the details in the continuum are all past. Rather than restarting the story, retconning reinterprets old details to be part of the same continuum as the new details, standing in retroactive continuity with them. Filling in details counts as retconning if the details reveal the past in new ways. While all retconned reinterpretations of old stories reveal new information, only revelations that imply a change in authorial intent are retcons. Writers seem originally to have had one thing in mind, only later to have come up with something else that contradicts the old plan. In non-retconned revelations, intent doesn't change. Writers seem instead always to have had the new information in mind, holding back merely for dramatic effect. Think of the dramatic plot twist that often comes at the end of a crime novel. Non-retconned revelations are most common in single works by single authors like novels and plays. Retcons, on the other hand, are most common in multiauthored serial works like comics, often as the result of new authors assuming control of ongoing characters.

New authors may also reboot stories, the second variety of nonlinear development of a serial story. In DC's *All Star Comics* #8 (December 1941) and *Sensation Comics* #1 (January 1942), William Moulton Marston and Harry G. Peter introduce a woman named "Diana," an Amazon native of Paradise Island and daughter of Queen Hippolyte, who rescues Steve Trevor, a young American navy captain fighting in World War II, and returns with him to the United States, where she begins to battle evil as the costumed Wonder Woman.

But what if these events instead occurred forty years later?

In *Wonder Woman* #1–3 (1987), George Pérez and Greg Potter restart the story. Though this Diana is again the Amazon daughter of Hippolyte from Paradise Island, and again rescues Steve Trevor and returns him to the United States, where she will battle as Wonder Woman, this Trevor isn't a young captain but an older colonel. It's also now not World War II but the 1980s. There's no retroactive continuity, only allusions to the previous story. The story itself restarts, the second Diana replacing the first. So DC rebooted Diana. In this case the sense of discontinuity is accentuated by Peter's and Pérez's contrasting art. Both draw a character whose appearance identifies her as Wonder Woman, but the authors' style and the details they render differ greatly, suggesting story disunity despite major similarities between the two Wonder Women.

Wonder Woman #1–3 amounts to a thought experiment exploring the properties of reboots. Reboots are nonlinear developments because, nullifying the contents of a story, they require restarting the story. "Reboot" was taken from computer jargon for turning a computer off and on, closing all programs in the process. In serial fiction, rebooting occurs when an author effectively turns a story "off" then turns it back "on," starting the story over. While the new story alludes to certain elements from the previous one, that previous story is nullified. Though a rebooted story is untethered from anything that comes before, it alludes to and repeats elements of the pre-rebooted story. It wouldn't exist without it. Yet from the perspective of the new, rebooted story, the slate is wiped clean, so the allusion exists only in the reader's mind. No allusion in a reboot can have meaning to a character within the new story because the object or character that the allusion refers to doesn't exist there. Like retcons, reboots are most common in multiauthored serial works, often as the result of new authors refashioning old characters for new audiences.

Though both are nonlinear revisions, retcons and reboots differ significantly. Installments of a retcon share a single continuity and thus are units within the same larger story. Installments of a reboot are units in a continuity separate from a previous continuity—even if much of their content is identical. A reboot disavows the earlier storyline in its entirety, but a retcon disavows only an earlier interpretation of a story element within the same continuity.

A retcon establishes that previously canonically portrayed events didn't occur only by introducing new facts that so deeply reinterpret previously portrayed facts as to show them to have never been true. A reboot, by creating a new continuity, is composed entirely of new facts, even when those facts repeat old ones.

A reboot usually introduces many unique story facts, but what if one introduces hardly any at all? When Marvel launched *Fantastic Four: Season One* as the first of eleven origin story "updates" in 2011, it publicized the series as a "refresh" not a "reboot" of Lee and Kirby's original work. The series moved the 1961 events to the 1980s, nullifying the Cold War space race as the motivating context for the Fantastic Four's rushed and nearly fatal rocket launch, while retaining many other narrative details from the original. Such a "refresh," however, is no different from a reboot. Any nullification of a past story element constitutes a reboot, regardless of what it is called.

We've already discussed several examples of retcons. In chapter 3 we explained that in 1985 Steve Englehart scripted Wanda Maximoff's twins to be her actual children, while four years later John Byrne retconned the revelatory fact of their being only illusions. More boldly, Alan Moore revealed in 1982 that all of the Marvelman adventures scripted by Mick Anglo in the 1950s and early 1960s were just dreams produced by Dr. Gargunza's somatic inducers. Likewise, we described in chapter 4 how John Byrne also retconned a philosophy of branching universes into the entire Marvel multiverse, revealing that previously scripted time travel didn't create new worlds but was actually universe travel between preexisting worlds. We discuss another bold Moore retcon in the next chapter.

Except for philosophers Andrew McGonigal and Ben Caplan, who touch on retconning—though sometimes confusing it with rebooting—philosophers haven't said anything else about retconning or rebooting. That's strange, because the differences between them also appear at the deepest philosophical level of language, at the nature of words and their meaning. Do the names "Donald Blake" and "Diana Prince" mean what they do because each refers directly to a specific individual, or because each is instead associated with descriptions of that individual? This is the kind of question that philosophers of language ask, and the answer divides such philosophers into two camps: referentialists and descriptivists. Regardless, thought experiments about retcons and reboots can serve to test out referentialism and descriptivism as views of proper names. To see this, we'll consider some of the history of retconning and rebooting in superhero comics before turning to the philosophy of language directly.

A Brief History of Superhero Histories

The first known comic book retcon appeared in *Action Comics* #13 (June 1939), when Jerry Siegel and Joe Shuster introduced Superman's first supervillain, the Ultra-Humanite. After thwarting a gang of racketeers, Superman follows the gang leader to a remote cabin, where a man in a wheelchair awaits (*Superman Chronicles* 1:185, 187).

> ULTRA-HUMANITE: We meet at last, eh? It was inevitable that we should clash!
>
> SUPERMAN: Who are you?
>
> ULTRA-HUMANITE: The head of a vast ring of evil enterprises—men like Reynolds are but my henchmen. You have interfered frequently with my plans, and it is time for you to be removed. (1:190)

Superman interfered with a range of illegal enterprises during his first year—senator-bribing munitions dealers, corrupt bankers, phony stocks swindlers—all of which Ultra reveals were secretly under his control. When in *Action Comics* #2 (July 1938) Superman forces a bribing lobbyist to confess, "Who is behind you in corrupting Senator Barrows?" a reader understands his answer, munitions magnate Emil Norvell, to be correct. The reader's impression is confirmed when the plot concludes after Norvell promises Superman to stop manufacturing weapons (1:19, 29). After Ultra's revelation, however, Norvell—like Reynolds—is now just one in a series of minor henchmen. The change is retroactive, so we understand that Novell was always just a henchman and that the impression that he was the gang's leader was false—a fact we accept even if we also believe that Siegel did not originally intend it.

The first known comic book reboot occurred in *Showcase* #4 (October 1956), when DC reintroduced the Flash. Gardner Fox and Harry Lampert had introduced a character of the same name in *Flash Comics* #1 (January 1940), which ran until 1949. The character also appeared as a member of the Justice Society in *All Star Comics* until 1951. The first Flash possessed superspeed, his secret identity was Jay Garrick, and he wore a yellow thunderbolt on his chest. Robert Kanigher and Carmine Infantino created the second Flash, who, besides having the same superhero name, possessed the same super-powers and roughly the same chest symbol. The new character, however, wore an otherwise different costume, and his alter ego, Barry Allen, acquired su-perspeed through an origin story different from Jay Garrick's. Allen is a police scientist struck by lightning and doused in chemicals. Jay is a college football player who accidentally knocks over a beaker while monitoring his professor's laboratory experiment and inhales the fumes.

Showcase #4 also reveals that the Jay Garrick Flash is a comic book char-acter in Barry Allen's world—which is a retcon, since it reinterprets rather than nullifies those original stories. The second Flash also led to the most influential retcon in comics. For *The Flash* #123 (September 1961), the first Flash writer (Fox) and second Flash artist (Infantino) explained why the two versions of the same superhero exist within the history of DC. Though the second Flash was created as an independent character, effectively overwrit-ing the first, "Flash of Two Worlds" established the old Flash in the second Flash's continuity, now named "Earth-1." All issues of DC published in the late 1930s through the early 1950s were retconned into DC's current continu-ity but assigned to an alternate universe called "Earth-2." After the Earth-1 Flash traveled to Earth-2, more travel followed. Because Earth-1 no longer re-placed Earth-2 but existed simultaneously with it, Earth-1 versions of Earth-2 characters were no longer reboots but new characters in the same larger story. The new Flash existed on Earth-1 and the old Flash on Earth-2. (These are the same Earth-1 and -2 that the Crime Syndicate and Justice League fought on, as discussed in chapter 2.)

Though it had not yet been named, retconning became a central norm of superhero comics. Umberto Eco described it when reviewing *Action Comics* in 1961:

> The stories develop in a kind of oneiric climate—of which the reader is not aware at all—where what has happened before and what has hap-pened after appear extremely hazy. The narrator picks up the strand of the event again and again, as if he had forgotten to say something and wanted to add details to what had already been said. (17)

This has continued to be a standard technique of comic book storytelling. Bill Finger and Bob Kane established Batman's origin story in *Detective Comics* #33 (November 1939)—itself a retcon that provides an explanation for Bat-man's unmotivated first six episodes. Bruce Wayne's parents were murdered by a mugger, so he vowed to avenge them by warring on criminals. Elements of Batman's origin story have been retconned numerous times since, notably by Frank Miller through flashbacks in *The Dark Knight Returns* (1986) and with David Mazzucchelli in *Batman: Year One* (1987). In both, Miller extends the Finger-Kane origin sequence by inserting a range of additional details. The four-issue *Year One* takes place between the final four panels, filling in the gaps of the gutters. The approach is formally limitless, since new writers can continue to fill in other gaps, including gaps within *Year One*, in principle allowing never-ending insertions in Eco's dreamlike climate.

Eco's review of Superman included *Action Comics* #252 (May 1959), where Otto Binder and Al Plastino introduced Supergirl, who then continued as a regular feature in the series. Eco recounts:

> At a certain point, Supergirl appears on the scene. She is Superman's cousin and she, too, escaped from the destruction of Krypton. All of the events concerning Superman are retold in one way or another to account for the presence of this new character (who has hitherto not been mentioned, because, it is explained, she has lived in disguise in a girls' school, awaiting puberty, at which time she could come out into the world; the narrator goes back in time to tell in how many and in which cases she, of whom nothing was said, participated during those many adventures where we saw Superman alone involved). (17)

Supergirl's first appearance, in "The Supergirl of Krypton," also retcons an entire city of Kryptonian survivors who study Superman from their mobile city before it too is destroyed. Though the term was not yet coined, Eco offers an early definition of retcons: "stories that concern events already told but in which 'something was left out'" (18).

The phrase "retroactive continuity" traces to biblical scholarship. In 1968, coincidentally the year that Lee and Kirby retconned the son of Odin's identity, theologian Wolfhart Pannenberg published *Jesus—God and Man*, which examines Jesus Christ's initially mortal identity. E. Frank Tupper in his 1973 study of Pannenberg summarizes the issue: "Did Jesus become the Son of God at some point in his history, or conversely, was he the Son of God from the beginning?" (169). From the perspective of Jesus's family and other Gospels characters, Jesus was understood to be a fellow mortal and then later revealed to be divine. Pannenberg asserts that his divinity as Christ "comes into force retroactively from the perspective of the [Easter] event" (qtd. in Tupper 170).

Tupper clarifies that though "a continuity of the pre-Easter Jesus with the exalted Lord is perceived," the resurrection's "retroactive power" establishes his divinity (169, 170).

Pannenberg also argues that the New Testament essentially retcons Jesus—now Christ—into the God of Israel. Jews describe the God of Israel in the Tanakh. Christians, however, who from Pannenberg's perspective retcon Jesus into that God, retcon the Tanakh into, and then rename it, the Old Testament. That makes the New Testament a continuation, chronicling Jesus's life and reactions to it. Pannenberg explains the retconning process: "The Old Testament idea of God became something preliminary" because "in the view of Jesus everything previously thought about God appeared in a new light" (qtd. in Tupper 168). Christians didn't reboot the pre-Easter Jesus but instead retconned Christ into Jesus's seemingly mortal history. They likewise didn't reboot the God of the Tanakh, but instead retconned the New Testament understanding of God into the Tanakh, making the Tanakh the Old Testament in the postresurrection continuity.

Though Tupper coins the term "retroactive continuity," he attributes the concept to Pannenberg. In his 1970 *Basic Question of Theology*, Pannenberg describes "the backward-reaching incorporation of the contingently new into what has been" as "the primary connection of history" (qtd. in Tupper 99–100). Tupper concludes: "Pannenberg's conception of retroactive continuity ultimately means that history flows fundamentally from the future into the past, that the future is not basically a product of the past" (100). From a Christian perspective, the New Testament retcons the Tanakh into the Old Testament. However, from a Jewish perspective, the New Testament reboots the story of God's involvement in human affairs—a reboot they reject. From a Jewish perspective, not only is there no New Testament, but there is also no Old Testament. The Tanakh remains the Tanakh. By contrast, when Kanigher and Infantino rebooted the Flash, they meant the reboot to be true, and Fox and Lampert's initial story nullified. From a Jewish perspective, when Christianity reboots the story of God's involvement in human affairs, the reboot is false. In comic book reboots, there might be people who prefer the original version to the reboot. In the Judeo-Christian case, there certainly are.

According to the *Oxford English Dictionary*, "reboot" dates to the early 1970s in computer programming, before expanding to more general uses by the late 1980s. The *Oxford English Dictionary* identifies the first appearance of "retcon" in the letter column of DC's *All-Star Squadron* #18 (February

1983), where Roy Thomas credits a fan for the term: "We like to think that an enthusiastic *All-Star* booster at one of Adam Malin's Creation Conventions in San Diego came up with the best name for it, a few months back: 'Retroactive Continuity.' Has kind of a ring, don't you think?" The truncated form appeared on a comic book discussion board six years later in a comment about another DC series, *Legion of Super-Heroes*, which underwent multiple revisions following *Crisis on Infinite Earths*: "Wow! Talk about a retcon by another name! . . . The Time Trapper never existed! Does this mean that Triplicate Girl is still Duo Damsel?"

Thomas's pre-*Crisis* series *All-Star Squadron* was set on Earth-2 during World War II and inserted new Justice Society adventures into DC's post-1956 continuity. The series, despite providing the first known use of the word "retcon," also combines rebooting. Thomas took characters from the narrative continuity of the defunct Quality Comics—which had gone out of business in 1956 and its properties sold to DC—and placed them into the Justice Society as long-standing though never previously mentioned members, making them all retcons. But Thomas also nullified the characters' former Quality Comics history of stories and replaced them with different histories, also making them all reboots.

Superhero Names and Retconning

The history of retconning and rebooting is complicated partly because it's intertwined. Regardless, the two cases we opened with—Donald Blake as Thor and Diana Prince as Wonder Woman—are relatively clear. With some philosophical work, it should also be relatively clear that each story requires a different understanding of how language functions. Though there are many different categories of words, the two major schools of thought, referentialism and descriptivism, focus on proper names.

What if a name refers to an individual directly?

Referentialists understand a proper name as a rigid designator. A rigid designator is a word whose meaning is the object which it refers directly to, in every world where the object exists. If "Jerry Siegel" is a rigid designator, then its meaning is Jerry Siegel, the object—here, the person—that exists in this world and any other possible one. On this view, the actual world is a possible world just as Earth, Moral Twin Earth, and Bizarro World from chapter 2 are all Earths, and all the possible Earths involved in time travel from chapter

4 are also. In fact, they're *all* possible worlds. A possible world that's not the actual world would be one where, for example, Siegel is correctly described as "co-creator of Wonder Woman rather than Superman," "native of Columbus rather than Cleveland," and "son of Romanian rather than Russian Jewish immigrants." But if "Jerry Siegel" is a rigid designator, then changing how he's described doesn't change who the name refers to or what the name means. "Jerry Siegel" refers to and means the same person, regardless of career, place of birth, and family background.

But what if a name instead refers to an individual through descriptions?

In contrast to referentialists, descriptivists understand a proper name as a nonrigid designator: a word whose meaning is not what it refers to but the descriptions associated with it instead. If "Jerry Siegel" is a nonrigid designator, then its meaning includes "cocreator of Superman," "native of Cleveland," and "son of Russian Jewish immigrants." If those descriptions differed, then "Jerry Siegel" would refer to and mean someone different from whom it actually does. If it's a rigid designator, then Jerry Siegel doesn't have to have cocreated Superman, because there's a possible Jerry Siegel who didn't. If it's a nonrigid designator, then there's only one Jerry Siegel, the actual one, who did cocreate Superman. Had the person whom we're now calling "Jerry Siegel" not cocreated Superman, then he wouldn't be Jerry Siegel—just someone else a lot like him.

Philosophers of language have nuanced views about how proper names function in fiction as opposed to fact. They argue that there are differences between the use of, say, "Jerry Siegel" in a history book and "Donald Blake" or "Diana Prince" in a comic. Those differences don't matter here, since referentialism and descriptivism can each be applied to factual and fictional proper names. Philosophers of language also tend to endorse referentialism or descriptivism but not both. They think that a proper name's meaning either is the thing it names or the descriptions associated with the name. But retcons and reboots challenge that. Taken as a series of thought experiments, the history of superhero history overturns both camps. That's because retconning presupposes referentialism about proper names, while rebooting presupposes descriptivism. Each kind of narrative revision presupposes a different philosophical account. The meaning of a proper name depends on how it functions narratively. If we read reboots and retcons as thought experiments involving descriptivism and referentialism, respectively, then we see that we need both of these philosophies of language.

Look again at our introductory case of retconning, noting the wide range of exact descriptions associated with Blake and Thor. Thor's premiere issue begins by introducing "a frail figure," "Dr. Don Blake, an American vacationing in Europe" (*Marvel Firsts: The 1960s* 115). Soon Blake is chased by alien invaders and, helpless after losing his cane, hides inside a cave. There he discovers a "gnarled wooden stick" (118). Angry at being trapped, Blake strikes the stick against a rock, causing the stick to become a hammer and Blake to become immensely strong. Blake declares: "I can feel my body bursting with power—such as I've never known" (119). The inscription on the hammer reads: "Whosoever holds this hammer, if he be worthy, shall possess the power of . . . Thor" (119). Blake wonders: "The God of Thunder! What do I remember of him from my school days?" (121). Because Blake's transformation doesn't give him Thor's memories, he must rely on his own memory of mythology that he read as a child to learn his new abilities. Blake understands himself to be a mortal who can at will take on the appearance and physical prowess of Thor. This understanding remains when in subsequent adventures he travels to Asgard, where he is treated as though he were the actual god Thor. When in the form of Thor, Blake, like the other Asgardians, even speaks faux-archaic English. But, according to the 1962 origin story, Blake merely adopts Thor's persona from time to time.

Six years later, however, Blake wonders: "My life as Thor began a few short years ago—when I found that enchanted hammer! But Thor has lived for ages!! So who was Thor before I found the mystic mallet?? . . . and, who was Dr. Blake??" (reprinted unpaginated in the 1976 *Thor* #254). Blake again transforms into Thor and travels to Asgard, where he is as usual welcomed as the Norse god. He continues to muse: "But if it be home to Thor . . . what of the mortal Donald Blake? Why was it him who didst find the hammer? And . . . what of me? Where then was Thor . . . upon that fateful day??" Odin responds by lifting "the veil which clouds thy memory . . . that thou may see the past!!" Blake now recalls that he had always been Thor but, having angered his father, was stripped of memory and power and sent to Earth as Donald Blake:

> It all comes back to me now! My first memories that day I found myself upon the campus . . . of the State College of Medicine! I introduced myself . . . as Donald Blake! The name sounded so right . . . so proper . . . I was strangely unaware that I had never known of it before!

Odin explains Blake's discovery of the magic cane:

Yet ever were thou son of Odin . . . though thou knew it not! 'Twas I who placed thy hammer in an earthly cave . . . so thou wouldst one day find it! And find it though didst . . . when thy lesson had been learned!

What does this mean philosophically? In 1962 "Blake" is associated with the following descriptions: "a naturally frail figure," "an American vacationing in Europe," "gaining the power of Thor by coincidentally happening upon a gnarled wooden stick with powers," and "learning about Thor in his school days in America." In 1968 "Blake" is associated with these descriptions instead: "a naturally strong figure," "an Asgardian exiled on Earth," "regaining his power as Thor by rediscovering his hammer disguised as a gnarled wooden stick," and "not learning about Thor in his school days in America but actually being Thor in his youth on Asgard."

Each later description contradicts an earlier one. But Blake in 1968 is the *same* Blake as in 1962. We are provided a retroactively continuous explanation. Odin deceived Thor, and us, into associating one set of descriptions with "Blake" and its variants when the other set actually applied. That set of descriptions replaces the first, we figure out, because the first resulted from Odin's deception. The story's been retconned and requires referentialism to make sense of it.

Referentialism was articulated by Saul Kripke in his 1970 *Naming and Necessity*, and in his 1973 *Reference and Existence* Kripke applied referentialism to fiction. Anticipated by John Stuart Mill's 1843 *A System of Logic*, Kripke's view was roughly contemporaneous with Hilary Putnam's 1973 "Meaning and Reference," which voiced similar themes. Referentialism treats proper names as rigid designators, directly referring to the same objects in every possible world (factual or fictional) where the objects exist. The meaning of proper names is the objects which they refer to. Descriptions that happen to be associated with those names are not part of their meaning. Though they may help us learn more about the referent, those descriptions aren't definitive of the referent and so can be altered while the referent remains fixed. According to referentialism, the meaning of a proper name is independent of what we believe it to be—and thus also the descriptions we associate with it.

This applies to "Blake" both before and after the 1968 retconning. The meaning of "Blake" is the object Blake, no matter what a reader knows or doesn't know about him. When the first 1962 set of descriptions associated with the name is revealed to be wrong, "Blake" still refers to Blake—the same fictional individual. According to the internal logic of Odin's plans, a reader gets the descriptions wrong, even though she gets the person whose adventures she follows right. The second set of descriptions isn't necessarily right either. A future story might rework the 1968 one—revealing that Odin lied or left out some other significant fact that reinterprets the story further. But as long as any future story establishes retroactive continuity, it would still concern Blake. The name does the essential work. Since descriptions change, without the name we wouldn't be talking about the same person.

Read as a thought experiment, Kirby and Lee's use of "Blake" poses a major problem for descriptivists. Descriptivism was articulated by Bertrand Russell's 1905 "On Denoting" and 1919 "Descriptions." Russell's view was anticipated by Gottlob Frege's 1892 "On Sense and Reference." Descriptivism treats proper names as nonrigid designators, which don't refer to the same object in different possible worlds (factual or fictional). Because "Blake" is associated with different descriptions in different stories, "Blake" wouldn't refer to the same person in different stories. Descriptivism treats proper names as non-rigid *because* it maintains that the meaning of proper names is the descriptions associated with them. The Blake discussed in 1962 wouldn't be the same Blake discussed in 1968. While referentialism allows descriptions to help us learn more about the referent, descriptivism identifies the name's meaning with those descriptions themselves. So the meaning of a proper name would depend on what we believe it to be—and therefore its associated descriptions.

This time "Blake" in 1962 would mean an American vacationing in Europe but in 1968 an Asgardian exiled on Earth. Further, referentialism is a direct-reference theory of proper names. Names refer without the mediation of their associated descriptions. Descriptivism, meanwhile, is an indirect-reference theory. Descriptions mediate between names and referents. Because the meaning of "Blake" in 1962 includes the description "an American vacationing in Europe," according to descriptivism, that description directly refers to Blake in 1962. The name itself refers indirectly. Yet, given the retconning, Blake *wasn't* an American vacationing in Europe. The description is wrong. The description doesn't refer to Blake in 1962, even though Blake in 1962 is meant to be retroactively continuous with Blake in 1968. Worse, because after the retconning no one matches the descriptions associated in 1962 with "Blake," a proponent of descriptivism has to conclude that Blake didn't exist in 1962. However, Blake in 1962 and Blake in 1968 were meant to be the same person.

So descriptivism violates the logic of retconning altogether. According to the retconned stories, we're to incorporate what we learn about the 1968 Blake into our understanding of the 1962 Blake. "Blake" rigidly designates, and so continuously names, the same person. Only the descriptions associated with the name change. But then those descriptions can't determine the meaning or referent of the name. Retconning therefore requires referentialism rather than descriptivism as a theory of proper names, as the comic book thought experiment shows.

Superhero Names and Rebooting

Now reconsider our initial rebooting case, with special attention to the descriptions attributed to the central character's name. The 1941 Diana and the rebooted 1987 Diana share a wide range of characteristics, including similar abilities, commitments, and costumes. In addition, though, there's a wide range of differences establishing each as distinct.

After the 1941 Diana transports Captain Steve Trevor to the United States in her invisible jet and delivers him to a hospital, she communicates in English as she did on Paradise Island, expresses her love for Trevor, and assumes a secret identity by trading places with a nurse. Because the nurse needs money for a plane ticket to join her fiancé in South America, Diana asks: "If I gave you money would you sell me your credentials?"

> NURSE: You—you mean you want to take my place here at the hospital?
> DIANA: Look—by taking your place I can see the man I love and you can marry the man you love! No harm done, for I'm a trained nurse, too—just a little money and a substitution— (Marston and Peter 15)

The nurse, who without glasses looks "a lot like" Diana, is also coincidentally named "Diana."

The second Diana shares none of these characteristics. As she carries Colonel Steve Trevor in her arms, the god Hermes magically transports them to the United States. There she speaks only Themyscirian, the language of the Amazons. When she tries to communicate with an American woman, the woman exclaims: "What the—? She's speaking some sort of gibberish—mixed with ancient Greek—!" (Pérez, Wein, and Patterson, *Wonder Woman* #3: 6). Fortunately, the woman is a language professor, and soon "her new student consumes her first lessons—absorbing in mere minutes the rudiments of" English (19). After secretly leaving Trevor in the hospital, Diana expresses no romantic feelings for him and makes no attempt to see him again. She doesn't pay off any similar-looking nurse who's also named "Diana," either.

The first "Diana" is associated with the following descriptions: "flying an invisible jet," "always communicated in English," "disguised in the secret identity of a nurse who wears glasses," and "in love with Steve Trevor." The second "Diana" is associated with these descriptions instead: "not flying an invisible jet," "only now learning English," "having no disguise or secret identity," and "having no feelings of love for Steve Trevor."

Again, each later description contradicts an earlier one. Yet here DC intends the later Diana to *replace* the earlier one. When DC changes the descriptions associated with "Diana," it changes the 1941 Diana for the 1987 one. The earlier version has been rendered null and void, the narrative slate wiped clean. The story begins again from year one. Though the later iteration alludes to elements of the earlier one, the characters are unaware because the story's been rebooted.

Descriptivism rather than referentialism explains how this is possible. Because "Diana" is not a rigid designator, it refers to noncontinuous, and therefore distinct, people in the 1941 and 1987 stories. Those distinct people are referred to directly not by "Diana" but by the different descriptions that Marston and Peter, and Potter and Pérez, associate with "Diana." In fact, the latter two writers' changing the descriptions associated with "Diana" *constitutes* the reboot. Their describing the 1941 Diana and 1987 Diana differently is definitive of their leaving the old story behind and starting the new one. And the descriptions do the essential work. Without them, we wouldn't be talking about different Dianas at all.

Descriptivism also explains why Potter and Pérez, and their readers, have no interest in the previous story. The 1941 "Diana" is associated with the description "flying an invisible jet," while the 1987 "Diana" is associated with the description "not flying an invisible jet." Because after the reboot the 1941 descriptions don't apply to anyone—the story has been rebooted so that the second Diana doesn't fly an invisible jet, and no one else in the second story does so either—that and other descriptions associated with the 1941 "Diana" refer to nothing within the new story world. Since, according to descriptivism, proper names refer to objects only indirectly via their descriptions, after the reboot the 1941 "Diana" doesn't refer to anything, which is the point of the reboot.

To the 1987 characters, the 1941 Diana never existed. Nor do DC's writers or fans consider those early adventures part of the same continuity. In the new narrative they never occurred. DC rebooted them out of existence. Rebooting therefore requires descriptivism rather than referentialism as a theory of proper names, as this particular comic book thought experiment shows.

Multiverses

So if you want to understand the difference between referentialism and descriptivism, superhero comics provide thought experiments for each in terms of retcons and reboots, respectively. No one else has connected retconning and rebooting with referentialism and descriptivism either. But we can't conclude just yet. Remember that retcons and reboots are nonlinear developments in serial stories. Linear developments occur when stories simply unfold, with new adventures added to old, where it's not necessary to reinterpret or nullify what came before.

But what if retcons, reboots, and linear developments can exist, or appear to exist, all together?

At least three combinations are possible, so we have three types of story developments vying for a single term: "multiverse." (a) What initially were reboots are retconned into the story world of another story. (b) Apparent reboots are not actually reboots but, instead, linear development where the history of the story world is mostly forgotten but not categorically nullified. And (c) multiple reboots exist independently. Cases (a) and (b) have been called "multiverses," but we extend the term to cover all three cases — (a), (b), and (c).

Regarding (a), recall what happened with the Flash. Initially Jay Garrick was the lone Flash in his story world. When his series and other series which he appeared in were canceled, his serial installments ceased, as did his character. When a new Flash series began in 1956, Barry Allen was the lone Flash in his newly created story world. The new Flash was therefore a reboot. But beginning in 1961, all issues of DC stories published in the late 1930s through the early 1950s were retconned into DC's then-current continuity but narratively relegated to Earth-2. Jay Garrick's Flash was retconned back into existence. Does that mean the new Flash changed status too, or did Barry Allen remain a reboot of Jay Garrick — even though both characters now existed in the same story world?

The complications continue, as the first "multiverse" case, (a), morphed into the second, (b). The Flashes' two-world system expanded as writers invented additional alternate Earths. At the same time, DC acquired the story worlds of other superhero publishers, retconning everything into the increasingly immense DC multiverse. After a quarter century of retconning, however, the result had grown so complex that DC reimagined all of its stories. The 1985–86 limited series *Crisis on Infinite Earths* erased the multiverse of alternate Earths and introduced New Earth—a restart of the DC continuity using a combination of previous Earths.

This sounds like a reboot, only at a larger scale. Yet, because *Crisis* provided an internal explanation for the destruction of the old worlds, from the characters' point of view these worlds were actually being destroyed. New Earth was formed as a result of the same process, so while it replaced Earth-1, Earth-2, and all of the other alternate Earths, it didn't nullify their history. New Earth was not a reboot—and it wasn't a retcon either. *Crisis* didn't nullify previous events, and it didn't reinterpret them in light of new ones. It was simply a new installment building on older installment, therefore a linear development.

Writer Marv Wolfman explains in the post-*Crisis* 1986 two-part comic book *History of the DC Universe*:

> What began as a single universe grew to become a multiverse in danger of annihilation at the hands of demonic forces. Heroes from many universes banded together and destroyed the evil at the dawn of time, and because of them, the single universe was born anew.

Though in "that rebirth, the histories of planets were changed," those changes continued to exist in the narrator's history of the history and thus also in the larger story known to the reader. Wolfman's narrator insists: "No one is permitted to know of the multiverse that had been," except of course for the narration and a reader of the chronicle that details where the histories of the pre- and post-*Crisis* worlds differ.

Despite this prohibition, however, the wizard Shazam also recalls the past. After Shazam transforms Billy Batson into Captain Marvel, Roy and Dann Thomas script Billy's reaction: "You talk like you've done this boy-into-man bit before." Shazam: "I have! Once, there was a whole family of beings such as you—once—but no! That never happened! That is, it did—but now it did not. I must push such memories forever from my mind—for that way lies madness!" (*Shazam: The New Beginning* #1: 19). If Shazam didn't recall the altered past, then from the perspective of Billy and its other characters the new series might be a reboot. But George Pérez and Greg Potter's *Wonder*

Woman #1 (February 1987), like the majority of DC's post-*Crisis* series, makes no reference to the earlier history, so if read in isolation, it may be considered a reboot. Yet, if read as part of the entire DC continuity, the second *Wonder Woman* continues the same story world—though no one in the story world knows that. Read within their companywide contexts, all of the apparently rebooted 1986 and 2011 series are continuations of preexisting stories. They also aren't retcons because no retroactive content has been revealed. From Shazam's semi-all-knowing perspective, and the reader's fully all-knowing one, the "New Beginning" is simply the next installment of an ongoing linear progression. The same is true of the DC's 2011 post-*Flashpoint* continuity, its 2015 post-*Convergence* continuity, and Marvel's 2015 post–*Secret Wars* All-New, All-Different continuity. They're all linear developments where the history of the story world is mostly forgotten but not categorically nullified. That's the second type of "multiverse."

The third type, (c), is more common in serial films. Unlike their comic book counterparts, superhero franchises tend to avoid internal explanation. Christopher Nolan's 2005 *Batman Begins* reboots Tim Burton's 1989 *Batman*, and Zack Snyder's 2013 *Man of Steel* reboots Richard Donner's 1978 *Superman*. Snyder's 2016 *Batman v. Superman* then reboots Nolan's entire Batman trilogy. Looking further back, the 1989 *Batman* rebooted the 1966 *Batman*, which rebooted the 1949 *Batman and Robin* film serial, and the 1978 *Superman* rebooted the 1951 *Superman and the Mole Men*, which rebooted the 1948 *Superman* film serial. Each later film replaces without internally referencing the earlier film, and the earlier film never narratively triggers the later. All of the character incarnations are narratively independent. They're reboots. For audiences, they exist simultaneously and in a complexly interwoven allusive relationship. Multiple, independent reboots occur in comics too. DC's post-*Crisis* imprint *Elseworlds* presents a range of Batman reboots—a Victorian Batman, a pirate Batman, a Cromwell Batman—but each exists in narrative isolation. The series taken as a whole presents a serialized multiverse.

Though associated primarily with comics and films, (c) appears in other narrative forms too. *Hamlet* provides a prominent example. The play first appeared in print in 1603 in a quarto edition designated "Q1." A second, much longer version, designated "Q2," appeared the following year. Q2 reboots Q1, replacing multiple passages with new passages that nullify the originals. Hamlet's most famous soliloquy begins "To be, or not to be—ay, there's the point" in Q1, but "To be, or not to be, that is the question" in Q2 (92). The folio version, designated "F," appeared in 1623, rebooting Q2 by subtracting 230 lines and adding 90 new ones. Since the nineteenth century, most performances of the play have used scripts that insert the 230 lines into F, creating a fourth, conflated text. Each *Hamlet* exists in narrative isolation from the others, but together constitute a *Hamlet* multiverse with no single, definitive variant.

Playwright Jemma Levy combines the variants in her 2015 play *Believe None of Us* by placing the *Hamlets* of Q1, Q2, and F in conversation with each other and thus positioning their three continuities in a single, shared story world. This makes it a "multiverse" of the third kind. Book editions that include Q1, Q2, and F are multiverses of this kind as well, because the narratively independent texts are explicitly in parallel. Ursula Le Guin first coined the similar term "multiplied realism" for her short story "Half Past Four" in 1996 because her eight-part story featured the same four characters rebooted into eight scenarios, another example of the same phenomenon.

Superhero Names and Multiversing

Retcons require referentialism, and reboots require descriptivism. Read as thought experiments, what theory or theories of proper names do multiverses require?

Consider multiverse (a), a reboot retconned into the story world of another story.

The 1956 Flash rebooted the 1940 Flash, and then the 1940 Flash was retconned into the larger, 1956 story world, by situating one on Earth-1 and the other on Earth-2. Because from the 1956 Flash's *rebooted* perspective we have to distinguish him from the nullified 1940 Flash, descriptivism is the right view of proper names. The 1940 "Flash" means its descriptions: "Jay Garrick," "college football player," and so on. The 1956 "Flash" means "Barry Allen," "police scientist," and so on. The change in descriptions constitutes the reboot.

But from the 1940 Flash's *retconned* perspective, referentialism is operative. We learned things about the two Flashes, each of whom now exists, that we didn't know before. Jay Garrick and Barry Allen were always different versions of the Flash, existing on different worlds—just as Donald Blake always was Thor (though existing on the same world). In each case, the name is the bearer of meaning, not its descriptions, which is especially apparent since their descriptions were initially wrong. The only philosophical difference is that "Donald Blake," because it names one person (who always was Thor), is one name. "Flash," because it names two people (who always were two), is two.

"Flash" as used on Earth-1 and "Flash" as used on Earth-2 are homonyms, just as two "Jerry"s as used on Earth-0, *our* world, would be. They sound the same but mean different things—now because they refer to different objects. Retconning revealed new things about *each* Flash, including, even, that they're different.

Consider multiverse (b), a linear restart of a story world where the history of the story world is mostly forgotten but not categorically nullified.

There's no retconning or rebooting, just linear development. Without the explanatory events of *Crisis on Infinite Earths*, the 1987 Wonder Woman is part of a reboot. In that larger context, she is part of a linear installment of an ongoing story—even though she's unaware of it. We already know that from the *rebooted* perspective the meaning of each "Diana" is its descriptions. From the *linear development* perspective, the meaning of "Diana" is Diana, the referent of the name. That's because the descriptions associated with the name were wrong, but the name still managed to refer, as with the "Flash" example. Further, also as with "Flash," we have to specify *which* "Diana" (and Diana) we're talking about. The linear development made clear that there are two, when based on the descriptions initially associated with each, we'd previously thought that there was one.

Finally, what about multiverse (c), independent reboots, including Nolan's, Burton's, and Snyder's versions of Batman?

As viewers watch each movie individually and learn more things about each version of Batman, descriptivism is presumably the operative philosophy of language. As with the two Dianas, these three Batmen are distinguishable via their descriptions. In each case "Batman" means those descriptions. The different uses of "Batman" are themselves homonyms. We have Burton's "Batman," Nolan's "Batman," and Snyder's "Batman."

Regardless of whether superhero comics are involved in (simple) retcons or reboots, or multiverses, we've been understanding each as amounting to a thought experiment in the philosophy of language. And that's led us to a conclusion that should be interesting to academic philosophers too. Because all these forms of revision exist, both referentialism and descriptivism are here to stay. Though philosophers don't need to read comic books to reach this conclusion, reading them as thought experiments about referentialism and description in particular reveals that each theory of proper names is required for any complete philosophy of language.

SIX

MINDING THE SWAMP

The previous chapter analyzed the meaning of superhero names according to the rebooted, retconned, or multiversed story worlds they appear in. This is the meaning the names have to a reader. But what do those or any other words mean to the characters themselves? Do those characters even have minds in which their words mean anything? More importantly, what makes our own words meaningful in our thoughts? In this chapter we treat the character type of swamp creatures and their subgenre of horror and superhero comics as a series of thought experiments answering those questions.

Because they concern meaning, the questions that we're asking fall under the philosophy of language. Because they also concern thought, they overlap with the closely related philosophy of mind. One of the most famous philosophers of language, who himself dabbled in this philosophical overlap, was twentieth- and twenty-first-century philosopher Donald Davidson. Davidson explored interconnections among language, thought, and reality more deeply and systematically than perhaps any other analytic philosopher. Because Davidson introduced two different thought experiments—one involving a swamp creature, the other not—bringing his academic thought experiments to bear on these comic book ones illuminates both.

There's another reason to appeal to Davidson in the context of comic book swamp creatures. Tracing back in the non–comic book literature to Theodore Sturgeon's 1940 short story "It," the swamp creature subgenre culminates in Alan Moore's *Saga of the Swamp Thing*, a comic book series that ran from

1984 to 1987. In 1986, the third year of its run, Davidson delivered "Knowing One's Own Mind" as the Presidential Address for the Sixtieth Annual Pacific Division Meeting of the American Philosophical Association. Davidson there introduced his own swamp creature:

> Let me tell my own science fiction story—if that is what it is. [. . .] Suppose lightning strikes a dead tree in a swamp; I am standing nearby. My body is reduced to its elements, while entirely by coincidence (and out of different molecules) the tree is turned into my physical replica. My replica, The Swampman, moves exactly as I did; according to its nature it departs the swamp, encounters and seems to recognize my friends, and appears to return their greetings in English. It moves into my house and seems to write articles on radical interpretation. No one can tell the difference. ("Knowing One's Own Mind" 18–19)

Did Davidson come up with The Swampman while reading Moore? Davidson gave his address on March 28, 1986, and it was published in the *Proceedings and Addresses of the American Philosophical Association* in 1987—five months before DC released the first compilation of *Saga of the Swamp Thing* issues #21 (February 1984) to #27 (August 1984). If Davidson knew Moore's work before writing "Knowing One's Own Mind," then he had to have read *Swamp Thing* in its original format.

We can't know whether Davidson read Moore's comics, but we do know that Moore read philosophy. Though Moore is not an academic philosopher, the *Guardian*'s Stuart Kelly writes, "One underestimates Moore at one's peril: yes, he may have written *Swamp Thing*, but he did so while reading continental philosophy." But continental philosophy differs from analytic philosophy and thus from Davidson's work—which Moore likely did not read.

So while there's no evidence that either Moore or Davidson read each other, Moore's series appears to be philosophically influenced, and Davidson's thought experiment appears to be pop-culturally influenced. The name of Davidson's creature echoes the names of many superheroes—Batman, Spider-Man, Superman, and so on—and the capitalization, "The Swampman," gestures to earlier pulp heroes like The Shadow and The Spider. Davidson also apparently borrows from a comic book subgenre whose general criteria, write Jon B. Cooke and George Khoury, includes "reanimated corpses taking the physical characteristics of swampland. In other words, creatures of once living and breathing flesh, but through whatever horrid process, they are transformed from man into monsters, now composed of mud, debris, and muck 'n' mire" (10).

Further, similarities between Davidson's and Moore's two creations extend beyond the genre-specific surface details and into philosophical depths. The Swampman and its mind-revealing relationship to Davidson's thought-experimental version of his deceased self also resembles Moore's retcon of the original Swamp Thing character created by Len Wein and Bernie Wrightson in 1971 and slightly revised by them in 1972. After placing Davidson's Swampman historically in the subgenre of swamp creatures, we describe the philosophical end that motivated Davidson to propose his thought experiment. We then turn to Davidson's *other* thought experiment, which he mentions when introducing The Swampman: radical interpretation. By comparing Davidson's Swampman and radical-interpretation thought experiments with comic book stories about other swamp creatures, we reveal a tension in Davidson's description of Swampman that other swamp creatures don't face. As a result, we conclude that the comic book stories are better grounded philosophically than what emerges as Davidson's overall view.

Swamp Creatures

In 2014, *Comic Book Creator* published *Swampmen*, an issue devoted entirely to the swamp creature character type. The editors' timeline includes over fifty swamp creature incarnations, beginning with Sturgeon's "It," first published in the August 1940 issue of the pulp magazine *Unknown*. Marvel adapted the story for *Supernatural Thrillers* #1 (December 1972), and Sturgeon was invited to the 1975 San Diego Comic Convention, where Ray Bradbury presented him with a Golden Ink Pot, the convention's highest award. "I learned for the very first time," Sturgeon later wrote, "that my story 'It' is seminal; that it is the great granddaddy of *The Swamp Thing, The Hulk, The Man Thing*, and I don't know how many celebrated graphics" (384).

As a subgenre, swamp creatures are not typically superheroic. They're monsters designed to be overcome by heroes. But when the character type entered comics from horror fiction, it did so in a superhero context, producing a hybrid: a do-gooding monster. Some comic book swamp creatures are heroically ambiguous—the Heap and Man-Thing may be too mindless to have any mission, let alone a prosocial one. And Alec Holland, the man transformed into the 1972 Swamp Thing, wants to cure himself and return to his old form, so he's not entirely selfless either. But the serial form endlessly postpones his goal, focusing him instead on episodic, do-gooding adventures where he uses his monstrous abilities to help others, as other superheroes would.

By contrast, Davidson's Swampman, because it doesn't have special powers or a special moral mission, is no more superheroic than Davidson, whom it replicates. Superheroism is not how the swamp creature subgenre began either. Sturgeon's short story depicts "the mold with a mind," a creature that "grew and moved about without living" and that resembles "an irregular mud doll" because a man "had died and sank into the forest floor where the hot molds builded around its skeleton and emerged—a monster" (306, 303, 324, 327). Sturgeon says no more about the creature's fantastical creation, and though human bones "had given it the form of man," those remains aren't the "part of [it] which thinks," therefore it "will stop being" when the molds are washed free of the skeleton (303, 327).

Though the origin point for swamp creatures, It only partly meets Cooke and Khoury's first generic criterion, "reanimated corpse" (10). To that extent, It resembles Joseph Payne Brennan's 1958 Slime, "a blob of liquescent ooze" that "had evolved out of the muck and slime of the primitive sea floor" before a volcanic wave "deposited it in the midst of a deep brackish swamp area" (34, 4–5). Brennan explains the "living slime" as an "experiment of nature," but the creature is "as alien to ordinary life as the weird denizens of some wild planet in a distant galaxy" (4, 5). Brennan's story inspired the 1958 film *The Blob*, part of a horror and science fiction subgenre distinct from swamp creatures, but Slime also contrasts with It through the unambiguous absence of the "reanimated corpse" trope. Both Sturgeon's and Brennan's creatures are driven by singular desires. It has "a thirst for knowledge" (306), Slime an "insatiable hunger" for prey (4). In each case, these desires are unrelated to memories, identities, or consciousnesses of any human remains contained or consumed.

This contrasts comic book incarnations of the character type, which typically (though not always) imply continuity between the creature and the deceased human being. When Harry Stein and Mort Leav introduced the Heap in Hillman Periodicals' *Air Fighters Comics* #3 (December 1942), a World War I German pilot crashes in the lonely swamp. His body is thrown clear of the plane and lies silently in the slime. It merges with the other dreary vegetation. But Baron Emmelmann's will to live has been a powerful force. And brings an unearthly transformation that has drawn its oxygen food from the vegetation. A fantastic heap that is neither animal nor man. (Thomas, *The Heap* 19)

Besides the pilot's "will to live," uncredited writers later offered two other fantastical explanations for the creature's existence: a zoologist's "serum" that reanimates the Heap in his fourth episode and the supernatural intervention of the goddess Ceres retconned into the Heap's origin in the seventeenth episode (54, 171). Though the Heap isn't explicitly Emmelmann, the creature likes the sound of German and is drawn to a model plane similar to the plane flown by the pilot, suggesting that some portion of Emmelmann lives on through its memories and inclinations (24, 65).

The Heap appeared four times from 1942 to 1946 and then, beginning in the October 1947 issue of the retitled *Airboy Comics*, was a regular feature until 1953. When Roy Thomas—a former childhood fan of the Heap—reprised the character type in *The Incredible Hulk* #121 (November 1969) and #129 (July 1970), he added radioactive waste to a Florida swamp that transforms the corpse of an escaping convict into the Glob. Skywald's *Psycho* #2 (March 1971) features an updated version of the Heap, because, as Thomas explains in a 2008 interview, he suggested to Skywald cofounder Sol Brodsky that Skywald revive the character (25). Skywald could then benefit commercially from Marvel, which was creating the Man-Thing, a new Heap-like character that would premiere in *Savage Tales* #1 (May 1971). Stan Lee initiated the name and project in keeping with his pattern of recycling Golden Age character types, and Thomas developed the character with scripter Gerry Conway and artist Gray Morrow, who pays visual homage to the Heap by reproducing its vine-like nose.

Similar to the Heap, Man-Thing is a human transformed by an untested supersoldier injection that merges his body with the swamp that he drives into while escaping criminals:

Once you were a <u>man</u>! But now—even that memory fades to join the others which once gave you <u>sanity</u>—Now, you do not even try to scream your frustration . . . Now, as you <u>struggle</u> for breath and life, the last of your humanity leaves you—and you <u>become</u>, truly, the— ... Man-Thing! (Thomas 31)

When Man-Thing loses its last human memory, it ceases to be human and thus becomes a new entity.

Len Wein and artist Neal Adams created a second Man-Thing episode, but Marvel canceled *Savage Tales* after its first issue. Wein also worked at DC where he created Swamp Thing with artist Bernie Wrightson for an eight-page story in *House of Secrets* #92 (June–July 1971). The Wein-Adams Man-Thing appeared in Marvel's *Astonishing Tales* #12 (June 1972), shortly before Wein and Wrightson revised their *House of Secrets* Swamp Thing for DC's *Swamp Thing* #1 (October–November 1972).

Both versions of Wein's Swamp Thing feature a human being who, after transformed by an explosion and the combined effects of a "bio-restorative formula" and "swamp ooze," retains his memories and consciousness (Wein and Wrightson 22, 32). Swamp Thing narrates as he tries to communicate with his former lover: "I stretch out my arm to her—to calm her—to comfort her—I open my mouth to tell how much I care—but what once had been my vocal cords have been silent too long—I cannot make a sound" (14). Swamp Thing is a man monstrously disfigured, so even though it's the longest-running and most commercially successful swamp creature, it doesn't meet the Cooke-Khoury "reanimated corpse" subgenre criterion either—arguably a result of the character's simultaneous presence in the superhero genre.

This early 1970s surge in swamp creatures is likely the result of multiple influences, including the rise of the ecological movement. Activist John McConnell proposed the first Earth Day celebration during a national UNESCO conference in October 1969, while Roy Thomas's first Glob issue of *The Incredible Hulk* was on newsstands, and in the Winter 1968 issue of the *International Journal of Parapsychology* Cleve Backster even argued for the extrasensory perception of plants. The subgenre's comic book popularity also coincides with the 1971 change in the Comics Code Authority guide-lines: "Vampires, ghouls and werewolves shall be permitted to be used when handled in the classic tradition such as Frankenstein, Dracula, and other high calibre literary works written by Edgar Allan Poe, Saki, Conan Doyle and other respected authors whose works are read in schools around the world" (Comic Code Revision of 1971). Though the word "horror" still could not ap-pear on a cover, the horror work of Theodore Sturgeon entered comics for the first time since the Code had been established in 1954.

Len Wein and Gerry Conway, Man-Thing's first scripter, shared an apartment, widening the range of possible cross influence. Because production periods for any single comic average four months, with sometimes radical variations from creator to creator, it is impossible to determine order of composition of any comics published within several months of one another. Skywald's new Heap is cover dated (March 1971) two months before Man-Thing (May 1971) and three months before the first Swamp Thing (June–July 1971), yet Thomas recalls urging Brodsky to create the character as a way to enter a popular trend. Wein conceived Swamp Thing in December 1970, but, he confessed, "Why I decided to make the protagonist some sort of swamp monster [. . .] I can no longer recall. [. . .] Coincidentally, Joe [Orlando]," then-editor of *The House of Mystery* and *The House of Secrets* at DC, "had been thinking of doing a story along the lines of Theodore Sturgeon's classic fantasy tale 'It' [. . .] a story I had actually never read" (Wein and Wrightson 4). Wein insisted that his 1972 Swamp Thing was also coincidental to his earlier scripting of Man-Thing.

Though expansively influenced, the swamp creature subgenre was relatively short-lived. *Man-Thing* ran until 1975 and was revived from 1979 to 1981. *Swamp Thing* was canceled in 1976 and revived as *Saga of the Swamp Thing* in 1982 to capitalize on the Wes Craven film adaptation of the same year. Though the film proved commercially unsuccessful, the comic book continued. Now an editor at DC, Len Wein contracted Alan Moore to replace writer Martin Pasko with issue #20 (January 1984).

Moore began by retconning a new interpretation of the title character, "making it that he was never human" (interview by Cooke and Khoury 134). Where Kirby and Lee's 1968 retcon of Thor revealed that Donald Blake had *always* been Thor but that he just hadn't realized it, Moore's retcon reveals that Swamp Thing had *never* been Alec Holland but that he just hadn't realized it. The character of a scientist assigned to study Swamp Thing's apparent corpse tells the origin to his employer:

> The combined effects of the blast and the reflex muscles in his legs propel him through the door and into the swamp. But Alec Holland is already dead. His body goes into the swamp along with the formula that it is saturated with. And, once there, it decomposes. A patch of swampland like that would be teeming with microorganisms. It wouldn't take long, General. But what about the plants in the swamp? The plants that have been altered by the bio-restorative formula? The plants whose hungry

root systems are busily ingesting the mortal remains of Alec Holland? Those plants eat him. They eat him as if he were a planarian worm, or a cannibal wise man, or a genius on rye! They eat him and they become infected with a powerful consciousness that does not realize it is no longer alive! Imagine that cloudy, confused intelligence, possibly with only the vaguest notion of self, trying to make sense of its new environment, gradually shaping the plant cells that it now inhabits into a shape that it's more comfortable with. It remembers having bones, so it builds itself a skeleton of wood. It remembers having muscle and constructs muscles from supple plant fiber. It remembers having lungs, and a heart, and a brain. And it does its best to duplicate them. You see, we were wrong, General! We thought that the Swamp Thing was Alec Holland, somehow transformed into a plant. It wasn't. It was a plant that thought it was Alec Holland! A plant that was trying its level best to be Alec Holland. (#21: 11–12)

Moore collaborated with artists Stephen Bissette and John Totleben, who joined the series on #16. As a result, the retconned Swamp Thing revealed in #21 maintains roughly the same visual style as the Swamp Thing of the previous six issues—much as Kirby's retconned 1968 Donald Blake continues the visual style of the 1962 Blake. And as discussed in chapter 5 in the context of Thor, this visual continuity corresponds well with Swamp Thing's newly revised but retroactively continuous origin.

Other elements of Moore's retcon, however, are more ambiguous. If the plants are "infected" by a "conscience," is that consciousness the defining element of the new creature's identity? If the environment is "new" to the "intelligence," then the intelligence isn't an aspect of that environment—though might the intelligence also be new since any environment is new to a newborn? And when "it" "remembers," is "it" the altered plants or the preexisting intelligence or consciousness that does so?

Ultimately, though, both in the text and in an interview, Moore states that his Swamp Thing isn't a former human being transformed. Swamp Thing is and always was a new entity. Therefore, Moore too breaks the comic book swamp creature tradition of altered humans seen in the Heap, Man-Thing, and Wein's Swamp Thing. Because Alec Holland's corpse was destroyed as it was digested by plants, there's not even a scaffolding of human bones inside the body of the 1984 Swamp Thing.

Admittedly, this new entity happens to possess a previous entity's memories and urges, retroactively the same Swamp Thing who reached out its hand to comfort the woman Alec Holland had loved and thus whom Swamp Thing experienced as continuing to love. According to Moore, however, Swamp Thing was mistaken. The creature wasn't Alec Holland, so it couldn't have *continued* to love the woman. Just before introducing his own swamp creature thought experiment, Davidson asks "whether we can [. . .] think we have a belief we do not have" (18), and Moore seems to answer: yes we can. Though Swamp Thing once thought it had Alec Holland's beliefs, when it learns the nature of its origin, it abandons those beliefs as not really its own. As a result, it no longer thinks it loves Holland's girlfriend. In fact, the creature thinks it had never loved her. Davidson worries that we can be wrong about the content of our beliefs, and Moore provides a thought experiment illustrating that worry.

The Swampman

Davidson's Swampman shares several defining features with Moore's Swamp Thing. Swampman's own genesis occurs with Davidson's "body [being] reduced to its elements" when lightning strikes a dead tree beside him. None of Davidson's elements transfers to Swampman, who is composed "of different molecules." Swampman isn't Davidson but the dead tree transformed. Like Moore's Swamp Thing, Davidson's Swampman is a new entity.

But unlike Moore's and all other prior swamp creatures, Swampman is so convincing a replica that Davidson's friends mistake it for him. Swampman even appears to mistake *itself* for Davidson, carrying on Davidson's life just as Moore's Swamp Thing wished to carry on Alec Holland's. Swampman seems "to recognize [Davidson's] friends, and appears to return their greetings in English. It moves into [his] house and seems to write articles on radical interpretation. No one can tell the difference. But," and it's now necessary to conclude the description of Davidson's thought experiment, "there *is* a difference." Davidson explains:

> My replica can't recognize my friends; it can't *re*cognize anything, since it never cognized anything in the first place. It can't know my friends' names (though of course it seems to); it can't remember my house. It can't mean what I do by the word "house," for example, since the sound "house" Swampman makes was not learned in a context that would give

it the right meaning—or any meaning at all. Indeed, I don't see how my replica can be said to mean anything by the sounds it makes, nor to have any thoughts. (19)

Davidson would, had he not been destroyed according to the thought experiment, recognize his friends, know their names, and mean things by his sounds. But Swampman wouldn't. That's because—Davidson deduces—Swampman has no history of interactions with Davidson's friends or anyone else. Swampman has never met them, has never learned their names, and even if the creature utters their names or any other words, Swampman doesn't know what the sounds it produces mean. Swampman is, to borrow an image from seventeenth-century philosopher John Locke, a blank slate.

Davidson relies on his thought experiment to conclude something about the nature of thought and meaning generally. Merely acting *like* someone with a history of interactions with the world isn't enough to think or meaningfully speak anything. And this is so even though Swampman's brain is configured identically to Davidson's and therefore would apparently encode the same "stuff." That stuff, however, doesn't have any historical connection with the world, so it is just stuff. Because Swampman's origin was "entirely coincidental," the mental content of its brain states, like the mental content of Moore's Swamp Thing's brain states, doesn't count as actual memories. Having never learned anything, Swampman has nothing to *re*member. Were we in Swampman's spot, neither would any of us.

In fact, we wouldn't possess any language or thought at all. As Davidson explains, "All thought and language must have a foundation in [. . .] direct historical connections" (29). Davidson and Swampman are "two people [. . .] in physically identical states," yet Swampman's physical states have no history prior to its fantastical creation (18). While Swampman and Davidson might make the same sounds, only Davidson can mean anything by them. Davidson acquired those sounds by learning English, which is why his sounds count as words. Since thought is something like internalized speech, the content of Davidson's brain states count as thoughts, while the content of Swampman's don't. Swampman neither means nor thinks anything. Eventually Swampman's sounds might become meaningful and its brain states might become thoughtful, assuming it creates its own history of worldly interactions. But initially Swampman has no history. Though visually indistinguishable from Davidson, Swampman is historically a newborn babe. When it comes to meaning, or semantics, Swampman is a blank slate. While Moore's Swamp Thing initially mistakes itself for Alec Holland only later to realize that it isn't Alec Holland, Swampman never mistakes itself for Donald Davidson. It only *appears* to do so. If Davidson is right, Swampman thinks no thoughts. It can't *think* it's Davidson because it can't think at all.

Minding the Swamp

Questioning whether external sounds count as language and internal sounds as thought—questioning whether each has semantic content—ultimately questions what it means to have a mind. That's where the philosophies of language and mind overlap. According to Davidson, Swampman doesn't have a mind, and if Davidson's reasoning is applied to Moore's revision of Swamp Thing, then his Swamp Thing doesn't have a mind either.

What if we analyzed the other comic book swamp creatures as thought experiments along the lines of Davidson's?

Though Moore's Swamp Thing, because it's a new entity, has no history of worldly interactions, Wein's 1972 Swamp Thing does. Wein's Swamp Thing retains the memories and consciousness and even some of the same body of its former human self. Though this Swamp Thing looks different from the man who transformed into it, the creature shares a history with that man. Its altered body is composed of some of the same molecules. This fits with Davidson's requirements for Swampman to have memories, as well as to mean or think things generally. Wein's Swamp Thing can be said to have learned what his sounds mean before he transformed. By Davidson's lights, therefore, this Swamp Thing thinks and means things: "All thought and language must have a foundation in [. . .] direct historical connections" (29), and the 1972 Swamp Thing's thoughts and language have that.

Indeed, by Davidson's reasoning, Wein's Swamp Thing thinks and means things for the same reason that Swampman and Moore's Swamp Thing do not. Meaning and thinking require having a history of worldly interactions. Wein's Swamp Thing has such a history, while Davidson's Swampman and Moore's Swamp Thing don't. Though the genesis of Moore's Swamp Thing is somehow triggered by Alec Holland's body, the stuff of Alec Holland's memories and consciousness are somehow configured into a new plant body—one, like Swampman, composed of "different molecules." Moore's Swamp Thing doesn't share a physical history with Alec Holland. So even though Moore's

Swamp Thing might think (or act as if it thinks) that its memories are Alec Holland's, they aren't. Moore's Swamp Thing would be as clean a slate as Davidson's Swampman.

If we apply the importance of history to other swamp creatures, we see that the Heap also means and thinks things—or does so to the degree that it inherits Emmelmann's body and so his history of worldly interactions. When the creature hears a German character speaking, the "words strike a familiar chord in the Heap's consciousness" (Thomas, *The Heap* 23). When the creature witnesses the death of Emmelmann's presumed widow, the captions ask: "Can the creature who once was a man still know grief? Who can guess what passes through the Heap's mind as he holds the lifeless form of the woman who once was his wife?" (51). The Heap answers both questions by taking revenge on the Japanese soldiers who killed her. While the Heap doesn't speak and its thoughts are not represented in thought balloons or captioned first-person narration, its other behavior, according to Davidson, would have meaning.

Though Gerry Conway scripts Man-Thing's thoughts in second- rather than first-person narration, a mental muteness further suggested by Gray Morrow's drawing its face without a mouth, Man-Thing too has the potential to mean and think things. Its body inherits the supersoldier inventor's history of worldly interactions. Man-Thing *recognizes* the woman who betrayed him: "And again, memory stirs. This one. This one is special. This one has caused you the deepest pain . . ." (Thomas, Conway, and Morrow 39). When Man-Thing's "memory fades," its capacity for thought also fades because it's losing its history of language learning (31). The remnants of its human brain are still composed of their previous molecules, but those molecules dwindle or take on new history to the degree that their, and so Man-Thing's, history of worldly interactions is severed, reducing Man-Thing to a semantic blank slate. When the creature loses track of its history, it loses its mind.

Sturgeon's It is more ambiguous. This mostly new creature inherits only its human predecessor's skeleton. Since bones don't have a capacity for language acquisition, It should itself be a semantic blank slate. Sturgeon does represent the creature as a curiosity-driven newborn, describing the creature's explorations as the first events in its history. The creature also doesn't recall memories of its past human self or understand the language of the humans it encounters. Yet It does appear to have thought. Though Sturgeon represents those thoughts in the third person, even this indirect form of internalized speech should be impossible in Davidson's view. Perhaps the inclusion of a human skeleton with a history of worldly interactions contributes to the creature's semantic existence. The "mold with a mind" apparently needs the bones to arrange itself in a shape that enables thought. When the mold is stripped from the bones, It dies. This original swamp creature can't exist, semantically or otherwise, without its human skeleton.

Interpreting the Swamp

According to Davidson, history and meaning go hand in hand. Bracketing It because of its ambiguity, if the significance that Davidson's Swampman thought experiment places on history is correct, then the Heap, Man-Thing (until it loses its memories), and Wein's Swamp Thing are all thinking creatures. They all share a history of worldly interactions with a human who engaged in those interactions directly. On the other hand, Man-Thing (after it loses its memories), Moore's Swamp Thing, and Davidson's Swampman are not thinking creatures. They are historically new entities and thus are semantically blank slates.

Yet regardless of Davidson's view about the importance of history, Moore's Swamp Thing certainly seems to mean and think things. Swamp Thing acts as if it does, and everyone around the creature responds to it in kind. Moore doesn't represent Swamp Thing as one of philosopher Robert Kirk's zombies, behaviorally indistinguishable from humans but lacking consciousness. Rather, he depicts Swamp Thing in such a way that readers take Swamp Thing's internal sounds as thought.

While Davidson's analysis applied to Moore's Swamp Thing is counterintuitive, the same analysis is counterintuitive even when applied to Davidson's own Swampman. Readers don't take Swampman's sounds, internal or external, as thought or language, but that may be partly because Davidson the philosopher tells them not to do so. Those who encounter Swampman in Davidson's tale, however—the people in his thought experiment—do take Swampman to be a creature that means and thinks things. The creature doesn't behave as a newborn, semantic or otherwise. Swampman "moves exactly" like Davidson and "seems to recognize" Davidson's friends, "appears to return their greetings," and even "seems to write articles." Moore's narrator considers Swamp Thing's actions in similar terms: "That's what a rational man would do. And a walking pile of mold and lichen and clotted weeds that thinks it's a rational man? I guess it would do pretty much the same thing" (Moore, Bissette, and

Totleben 17). Yet, according to Davidson, Swamp Thing isn't thinking, only behaving as if it is. But if such replicas duplicate human behavior so perfectly, is there really a difference between merely *acting as if* one means and thinks things and *actually doing so*? Could Swampman and Moore's Swamp Thing be semantic swamp creatures too, like the Heap and Man-Thing—even though they are composed of entirely new molecules with no history of worldly inter-actions? In other words, does Davidson's thought experiment succeed?

Philosophers are divided on the issue. Those who think that it fails may be more sympathetic to the lessons that Davidson drew from an earlier thought experiment that inadvertently challenges the semantic status of Swampman years before introducing it. Davidson even alludes to this other thought exper-iment in his description of Swampmen. In his 1973 "Radical Interpretation," Davidson introduces a thought experiment in which an interpreter encoun-ters someone who speaks a language completely alien to her. He then asks how the interpreter could interpret the speaker's words. By "interpret," Davidson means figure out what those words mean, and radical interpretation—the process of interpreting a completely alien language—is central to Davidson's philosophy of language. As his description of the thought experiment unfolds (here and in later articles, as Goldberg [*Kantian Conceptual Geography* chap. 4] discusses), Davidson claims that the radical interpreter would eventually identify cases where the speaker says things in response to her immediate en-vironment. Through trial and error, and by determining how smaller units (words) systematically combine into larger ones (sentences), Davidson claims, interpretation would in principle be possible.

Davidson doesn't believe that actual interpreters, who include all of us, are radical interpreters. We don't usually encounter completely alien languages, and even, say, early explorers who encountered previously unknown human cultures still used shortcuts in interpretation. No two human cultures were ever completely different in every way. Regardless, for Davidson, actual inter-preters could engage in radical interpretation, which highlights the minimal evidence required to interpret language. As he explains elsewhere: "The point of the 'epistemic position' of the radical interpreter is not that it exhausts the evidence available to an actual interpreter, but that it arguably provides suf-ficient evidence for interpretation" ("Radical Interpretation" 121).

Radical interpretation is Davidson's second thought experiment—or first thought experiment, chronologically—about how language and meaning work. Because Davidson thinks radical interpreters can determine all the semantic details of a situation, he endorses the importance of interpretability. Meaning requires only interpretability. And ultimately, for Davidson, that's meaning in language or thought. Though we don't interpret thoughts directly, we express our thoughts in words, which interpreters can interpret. So now, according to Davidson the radical-interpretation philosopher, interpretability and meaning go hand in hand.

Davidson then has *two* views of meaning and thinking, one emphasizing the importance of history and the other the importance of interpretability. Davidson uses his Swampman thought experiment to argue that history and meaning go hand in hand. And much of the subgenre of swamp creatures can be read as thought experiments that broadly agree. Swampman neither means nor thinks anything, while the Heap, Man-Thing, and Wein's Swamp Thing do. On the other hand, Davidson uses his radical-interpretation thought experiment to argue that interpretability and meaning go hand in hand, and that's where Davidson's thought experiments get him into trouble. If interpretability is sufficient for meaning and thinking, then Swampman turns out to mean and think things after all. Contrary to what Davidson writes, Swampman *does* "recognize Davidson's friends," "return their greetings in English," and "write articles on radical interpretation," because Swampman is interpretable as such. This time "no one can tell the difference" between Swampman and Davidson himself because there is no difference—at least no semantically relevant one. Swampman and Davidson mean the same things and have the same thoughts, because they're interpretable as such. Davidson's two thought experiments are at odds.

What happens when we apply the lesson from the radical-interpretation thought experiment to Alan Moore's Swamp Thing? Moore himself seems to endorse the importance of interpretability. Since Moore's Swamp Thing makes internal sounds that appear in captions as first-person thoughts and acts based on them, the creature turns out to mean and think things after all. But here too Moore gets in trouble, because if the importance of interpretability is right, then it's not so easy to dismiss Alec Holland's memories as not being Swamp Thing's. At least initially, Swamp Thing acts as if it thinks that it's Alec Holland. It therefore would be interpretable as thinking that, so as per radical interpretation, it *would* think that. Swamp Thing *does* love the woman whom Alec Holland loved. The creature wasn't wrong to experience itself as continuing to love her. Swamp Thing later abandons those beliefs as not really its own. To the extent that Swamp Thing's behavior changes, it would no longer be interpretable as thinking loving thoughts toward the woman whom Alec Holland had loved. Given the importance of interpretability, however, that's because Swamp Thing *changed* its mind, not because it never loved her. The creature loved her and, because Swamp Thing falsely convinced itself that its love was false, the creature fell out of love with her.

Focusing on radical interpretation, and with it the importance of interpretability, also forces reconsideration of other swamp creatures. How interpretable Theodore Sturgeon's It would be is debatable, but to the extent that the creature is, It would mean and think things too. Those meanings and thoughts, however, would likely not be the same as those of the man whose skeleton It formed around. It's and the man's behavior would be interpreted differently. Though the bones remain the same and thus a history of worldly interactions is preserved, interpretability as we're imagining it here trumps that. Stein and Lev's Heap would likewise mean and think things to the extent that the Heap is interpretable. Though Emmelmann and the Heap might or might not be interpretable as the same creature, some of their behavior would be interpretable as manifesting the same memories and inclinations. Thomas, Conway, and Morrow's Man-Thing would mean and think things to the extent that their creature is also interpretable. But unlike the Heap, Man-Thing before it loses its memories means and thinks things according to the importance of history, while after it loses its memories it means and thinks things only to the extent that it's interpretable.

Davidson vs. Davidson

So according to Davidson, two different things make thought and language possible: history and interpretability. And he argues for this by introducing two different thought experiments: The Swampman and radical interpretation. If those experimentations are taken together, then all the swamp creatures would seem to be semantic creatures. Either history or interpretability would be relevant for each. Things are not, however, always as they seem.

Wein's Swamp Thing is apparently a semantic creature because it shares a history with a man who learned what his terms mean. Moore's Swamp Thing is apparently a semantic creature because it's interpretable as such. Moore's Swamp Thing retcons Wein's, so that Wein's is retroactively revealed to have never existed. However, bracketing Moore's retcon, his and Wein's Swamp Thing each might mean and think things for different reasons. Regardless, because Wein's Swamp Thing has a history of worldly interactions, his behavior would reflect those interactions. The same would be true for the Heap and Man-Thing (until it loses its memories). In virtue of that behavior, each would be interpretable as meaning and thinking beings. So any creature that means and thinks things given the importance of history would automatically mean and think things given the importance of interpretability too. That's because history *teaches* interpretable behavior. Davidson himself is interpretable because he learned what his terms mean. The importance of history reinforces the importance of interpretability. Creatures with a history of worldly interactions are necessarily interpretable.

All that's to say that anyone who means things and thinks according to the Swampman thought experiment would turn out to mean and think according to the radical-interpretation one. The opposite, however, is false. While Moore's Swamp Thing turns out to mean and think things too, that's only because its behavior is interpretable. Moore's Swamp Thing, unlike Wein's, is a semantic creature only given the importance of interpretability. But being a creature that's interpretable doesn't require being a creature with a history of worldly interactions. The importance of interpretability doesn't reinforce the importance of history. Interpretable behavior doesn't teach, or in any way confer, a history of worldly interactions. Likewise, post-memory-loss Man-Thing is a semantic creature only through interpretability, since he forgot his history. And while Davidson himself is interpretable because of his history of learning, Swampman is interpretable only because its behavior is indistinguishable from Davidson. According to interpretability, Davidson's and Swampman's thoughts would be as indistinguishable as their bodies.

In short, creatures with a history of worldly interactions are necessarily interpretable, but creatures that are interpretable don't necessarily have such a history. If we accept the lesson of Davidson's Swampman thought experiment, any creature that lacks a history must lack thought and meaning—no matter how meaningfully it appears to act. If, however, we accept the lesson of his radical-interpretation thought experiment, all it takes for a creature's actions to have meaning and for the creature itself to have thoughts is that it's interpretable as such. The importance of interpretation makes sense of the importance of history but not vice versa.

Though not everyone has a history of worldly interactions, all swamp creatures do turn out to be interpretable. This is also good news for the characters in chapter 2's thought experiments. Recall that like The Swampman, which was

Davidson's "physical replica" made "out of different molecules," Starhawk was "obliterated" and then "remade, molecule by molecule . . . exactly" as he was except without the ability to sense his destroyer and re-creator Michael. Because the remade Starhawk is composed of different molecules, he has no history of learning the meaning of the words that he speaks and thinks. If we accept the point of the Swampman thought experiment, then the second Starhawk can't himself mean or think things. Worse, the other inhabitants of Richards's *Heroes Reborn* bubble universe too are all like The Swampman—since all of them came into existence instantaneously. Because their memories are fabricated, they have no history of learning either, so they would be semantic blank slates. And worse still, the rebooted multiverses mentioned in chapter 5, including DC's post-*Crisis* and Marvel's All-New, All-Different companywide reboots, consist entirely of swamp creatures—since *all* of them blinked into existence at the same moment as variant replicas of their previous versions but with false memories of events that had never occurred. When the new Wonder Woman arrives in the United States, she has to learn English before her English words have meanings, but because she has no history of learning her native Amazon language, those words would have no meaning.

Fortunately, Davidson's radical interpreter puts all these worries to rest. All swamp creatures mean and think things, which is good news for many superhero multiverses also. Yet, while this is good news for Davidson's Swampman as a creature, it's not good news for the point of the thought experiment. Davidson introduces The Swampman to illustrate the importance of history, but the importance of interpretability makes Davidson's point moot. Why introduce The Swampman at all?

Davidson might ask the same question of his readers that Moore himself asked of one of his interviewers: "Why shouldn't you have a bit of fun while dealing with the deepest issues of the mind?" (Kelly). In Davidson's case, though, the "bit of fun" is worthwhile only to the extent that it does get at the deepest issues of the mind, and that forces him to decide between his two contradictory thought experiments.

PART IV

MEDIUM

SEVEN

CAPED COMMUNICATORS

The previous three sections have used tools of academic philosophers to analyze the content of superhero comics. This chapter and the next address the comic book medium, setting aside story content and analyzing the philosophical implications of comics as a form. Instead of treating just the stories as thought experiments, we examine larger puzzles presented by comics overall. The medium becomes the thought experiment in which we readers find ourselves, and that's what needs explaining. As a result, we consider more intricate comic book analyses and to some extent more complicated philosophies, and we look at them in greater detail. This chapter will focus on philosopher H. Paul Grice's theory of communication and apply it to the visual communication of superhero comics.

Comics differ from traditional novels, which employ only words, and from forms of visual art that employ only images. In typical comic books and in most if not all superhero ones, words and images occur together, as each communicates story content. These words and images should therefore share certain properties. In previous chapters, we've been taking these properties for granted, discussing artists' visual details in the same ways that we've discussed the words contained in talk bubbles and caption boxes. For example, in chapter 3 we argued that artists communicate whether a character's false perceptions were detectable by using either a consistent or inconsistent style across the two realities. Similarly, in chapter 4 we argued that artists communicate either an eternalist or presentist view of time according to how they draw moments of time travel. But drawings are not words, so how can we argue that these artists are communicating anything? We respond with this real-world thought experiment:

What if comic book artists communicate with images according to the same principles by which speakers communicate with words—and we're the ones they're communicating to?

To explore that "What if?," this chapter applies a philosophical analysis of the meaning of words to the meaning of images. In that sense, we're continuing our examining of the philosophy of language. But we're also respecting the aesthetic norm of naturalism that governs the genre of superhero comics as a form.

Cooperative Principle and Maxims

Recall how in the previous chapter The Swampman and Swamp Thing can be said to speak meaningful words if an interpreter understands their words to be meaningful. But what guides an interpreter's interpretations? Enter Grice. Early in his career, Donald Davidson distanced himself from Grice, but later he embraced the distinction that Grice articulated in his 1975 "Logic and Conversation." According to Grice, speakers and writers implicate (or imply or communicate) the meaning of words in two ways: conventionally when the meaning is communicated by the words themselves, and conversationally when the meaning goes beyond those words by relying on context. Grice calls those implications conventional and conversational "implicatures." Consider this exchange:

> JOE: Do you think that Superman will catch the robbers right away?
> JERRY: No, I don't.

Jerry implicates that he doesn't think that Superman will catch the robbers right away. His words are used conventionally, and their conventional implicature is just what they say. Contrast it with this:

> JOE: Do you think that Superman will catch the robbers right away?
> JERRY: He's fighting Bizarro.

Jerry again implicates that he doesn't think that Superman will catch the robbers right away. Now, however, his words are used conversationally, since this isn't what they literally mean. It's what they mean in the context of the conversation. Jerry's first response is literally answering Joe's question. Even without knowing what it is, we can figure out that Jerry is answering a question negatively. But the meaning of Jerry's second response only makes sense given that previous question. Without it, we would have no way of knowing that Jerry was answering a question at all. While the conventional implicature of "He's fighting Bizarro" just is what it says, the conversational implicature is something like "*I don't think that Superman will catch the robbers right away, because* he's *too busy* fighting Bizarro." How does Joe—and how do the rest of us—figure that out?

Grice observed that communication, whether conventional or conversational, is a cooperative activity. Communicative partners must work together for meaning to be communicated (or implicated). According to Grice, all communication is governed by what he calls the "Cooperative Principle":

> Make your conversational contribution such as is required, at the stage at which it occurs, by the accepted purpose or direction of the talk exchange in which you are engaged. (45)

Grice further specified the Cooperative Principle by identifying four subprinciples or maxims:

> Quantity: Make your contribution as, but only as, informative as required.

If Jerry responds to Joe's question with silence, then he's being uncooperative by offering too little information. If Jerry responds by answering with Superman's full biography, then he's being uncooperative by offering too much.

> Quality: Try to make your contribution true.

Suppose instead that Joe asks Jerry about Superman's secret identity, and Jerry falsely answers that it's Donald Blake rather than Clark Kent. Joe might wonder whether he and Jerry were talking about the same character.

> Relation: Be relevant.

If Joe asks about Superman's planet of origin, and Jerry starts talking about the molecular makeup of water, then he's being uncooperative too, this time because his answer isn't relevant.

> Manner: Be perspicuous by avoiding obscurity and ambiguity and by striving for brevity and order.

While previous maxims concern *what* is said, this last one concerns *how* it's said. There are occasions for more or less concise language, but communication requires that exchanges be clear and on point more often than not. Vagueness, rambling, and murkiness must be the exception. Sure, Jerry could say that Superman's secret identity is the first person to enter the *Daily Planet* building every morning. Though that arguably gives both too much information (Joe wanted only a name) and too little (Joe didn't actually get the name), it may be better to regard it as simply being obscure—it's too obtuse an answer to be of much good.

Look again at Joe and Jerry's first, conventional exchange. Joe asked: "Do you think that Superman will catch the robbers right away?" and Jerry responded: "No, I don't." Jerry's response respects all five maxims, so his meaning is relatively easily communicated. Now look again at their second, conversational exchange. This time Jerry's response, "He's fighting Bizarro," taken conventionally, fails the Cooperative Principle. Joe's question requires a yes or no answer and mentions robbers rather than Bizarro. Jerry's response isn't yes or no and seems to switch subjects entirely. If his words are taken conventionally, then Jerry is violating Grice's Quantity and Relation maxims. Though he's offering more words, understood conventionally those words express less information than required, and what he does offer—understood conventionally—is irrelevant to what's asked. But according to the Cooperative Principle, Joe is to assume that Jerry is *trying* to communicate with him. Joe can therefore work out Jerry's implicature instead not as conventional, but as conversational.

So exchanges that violate the Cooperative Principle if understood conventionally should tip us off to try to understand them conversationally. Of course, not everyone cooperates all the time, and as a result not all exchanges are cooperative. Sometimes communication breaks down. There's no conventional or conversational implicature. Imagine this exchange:

JOE: Do you think that Superman will catch the robbers right away?
JERRY: Lois won a Pulitzer Prize.

The first time Jerry said that, Joe might try understanding him as communicating conversationally. By perhaps appearing again to violate Quality and Relation, Joe might reason, he's letting on conversationally that Lois is good at her job, so Superman should be good at his too. Or, Joe might reason, Jerry's communicating that Superman needs to hurry so that he can attend Lois's award ceremony. Actually, without more context, just what Jerry means isn't clear. But suppose that Joe asks Jerry the question repeatedly and each time

Jerry responds in the same way, or maybe starts uttering gibberish. Eventually Joe would conclude that Jerry was being uncooperative and wasn't communicating anything at all.

Conventional and Conversational Depiction

While Grice used his Cooperative Principle to analyze words, other philosophers have applied the principle to images, arguing that they can communicate cooperatively or uncooperatively also. The same maxims apply too. Though the one-way act of reading a comic may not seem like a conversation, the goals of creators and readers are the same ones identified by Grice for communication generally: "giving and receiving information, influencing and being influenced by others" (49).

If a comics artist wants to communicate a story about Superman to her readers, she would probably not sketch every individual wrinkle in the Superman's costume, but she also would not leave out Superman's head. That would be contributing too much or too little detail. She wouldn't sketch Superman with two heads either. That would be contributing something not true. Her sketch also shouldn't foreground other superheroes and characters that aren't part of Superman's story. That would be contributing something irrelevant. Nor would she sketch the image so lightly that no one can see it. That would be contributing something obscure.

Of course, she might do any of those things to communicate something unconventionally. Maybe all those wrinkles in Superman's costume are meant to communicate his heightened senses, how he can feel each individual wrinkle on his skin. Maybe she draws two heads to communicate his (one) head in motion, or as visual metaphor showing how torn he is between his two identities.

Sometimes it's hard to figure out from an individual image in isolation whether the artist's intent is conventional, conversational, or neither. It can be easier when you're presented with a series of images, like the sequential ones found in comics. The creators of the comic wish to influence and give information to a reader, and a reader wishes to be influenced and receive information back. So comics artists generally draw images that obey the four maxims of the Cooperative Principle.

A comic book artist implicates the meaning of an image conventionally when the meaning is communicated by the strict representational qualities of the image itself. Such qualities approximate what Robert Hopkins calls "pictorial representation" (145–46). When Joe Shuster draws an image of Superman standing atop a skyscraper, we understand that the character of Superman is standing atop a skyscraper at the corresponding moment in the narrative. To take the meaning of an image to be communicated by its strict representational qualities is to take it literally as part of the story world.

A comic book artist implicates the meaning of an image conversationally when the meaning goes beyond the image's own strict representational qualities by relying on context. When Steve Ditko draws squiggly lines emanating from Spider-Man's head, we understand that those lines don't represent literal objects floating around Spider-Man. Instead, they're abstract markers of a psychological experience. His spider senses are "tingling." Similarly, when Carmine Infantino draws long lines behind the Flash skidding to a stop, we understand the character to have been moving at an inhuman speed, even though the image represents a stationary figure. In both cases, each set of lines communicates effectively because the reader has seen such lines used similarly before—in other panels, other issues, or other comics in the superhero genre. From that context, a reader understands that the lines are not literal and thus the implicature isn't conventional. The artists are implicating something conversationally.

To distinguish conventional and conversational implicature when applied to images, let's say that those images are "depicting" something conventionally and conversationally. We can then speak of "conventional" and "conversational depiction." Like implicatures when applied to words, conventional and conversational depictions are governed by the Cooperative Principle. As with words, if one flouts the Cooperative Principle in the conventional depiction case, then a reader should try to work out a conversational depiction instead. That's what happened with Ditko's and Infantino's drawings.

Because we're focused on superhero comics, we need to add something to cover that specific genre. Implicatures communicated in superhero comics also depend on the non-Gricean aesthetic norm of naturalism. Joseph Witek identifies naturalism as "the preferred approach for stories of adventure and domestic romance," which includes superhero comics as its largest subset (28). Naturalism, according to Witek, makes the

> implicit claim that its depicted worlds are like our own, or like our own world would be if specific elements, such as magic or superpowers, were to be added or removed. However cursory the attempts to support its

truth claim might be, that claim supplies the metaphysical structure underlying the visual and narrative strategies of the conventional tradition of comics. (32)

When an image violates naturalism, a reader expects an explanation from within the story world, which the image can't be understood literally without. In those cases, the depiction can't be conventional. A reader may then interpret the naturalistic break as the artist's intentional flouting of one of Grice's maxims to depict something conversationally. If the naturalistic break is too great, however, then nothing is depicted. Confusion rather than communication occurs, just as if Jerry answers each and every one of Joe's questions with "Lois won a Pulitzer Prize."

We can now appreciate how a comic book reader is the subject in a thought experiment about whether depictions are conventional or conversational, or not depictions at all. As she glances at the images, the reader is forced to figure out what they mean. To illustrate, we explore examples of comic book artists flouting each of Grice's four maxims conventionally. Sometimes the artist is understood as depicting an image conversationally. Other times, though, she's understood as not depicting anything.

Quantity

What amount of visual information is the minimum and maximum required for us as readers to understand what's being depicted in a comic book image?

Consider a script written by Neil Gaiman for artist Mark Buckingham for *Miracleman* #17 (June 1990). Gaiman describes a page 1 panel:

> Daylight outside. In the foreground is a small, male figure with his back to us. He's got a backpack, and has put his hands on his hips, and is looking upwards, at the pyramid. The sides of it are black granite, with occasional windows and doors in different architectural styles. It towers above him, vanishes into the clouds, which mask its upper 2/3rds from us. ("Miracle Man #17, Second Story" 3)

Gaiman's description is divisible into three major elements and sixteen supporting details. Buckingham, however, responds by drawing all the major elements but only some of the details (*Miracleman* #17: 1). His panel takes place outside and in daylight as established by the figure's shadow, and the

From *Miracleman* #17.

figure is in the foreground, is small, has its back to us, and is wearing a back-pack. Though ambiguous, the figure may also be male, since its short hair and individuated legs preclude the stereotypical female markers of long hair and leg-obscuring skirt. The figure may have its hands on its hips, though the angle and height of the arms suggest hands in pockets. The angle of the head doesn't indicate that the figure is looking up. Buckingham also doesn't draw an establishing view of the pyramid, which is instead the front of a large build-ing of unknown shape. There are no black granite sides. The obscuring clouds are absent as well, and the building vanishes at the panel edges. It includes windows of different architectural style though no doors, but it does tower above the figure. Of Gaiman's sixteen details, Buckingham eliminates five. He also originates many details not specified in the script, including eight columns, a triangular arch composed of fourteen segments, a stained-glass window with Miracleman's "MM" chest emblem at the center, twelve sur-rounding stained-glass panels composed of numerous abstract shapes, about twenty-five stairs before the entrance, and an open space roughly twice the area of the stairs. Most of the details reflect Gaiman's phrase "IN DIFFERENT ARCHITECTURAL STYLES."

Though Grice's analysis of implicature is applicable to both words and im-ages, the quantity of information that each is expected to convey does differ. As philosopher Robert Hopkins explains:

> It is possible to refer to a particular thing using a word (e.g., the name "Osama Bin Laden") without saying anything about it. Likewise, one can talk about a kind of thing using a phrase (e.g., "a small blackbird") which does not tell us anything else about things of that kind. In con-trast, a picture of Bin Laden, or of a small blackbird, however schematic, must depict much more. It must, for instance, depict a man with certain features, or a small bird of some shape, in some posture. (145)

Gaiman, no matter how detailed his script, can't describe every property of the image to be drawn, so Buckingham must add details to draw anything at all. But does he add the right amount?

While problems with underinformativeness might be obvious, Grice sug-gests that "overinformativeness may be confusing in that it is liable to raise side issues" (46). In comics the side issue is how the image relates to the real-ity meant to be depicted. In *Understanding Comics*, Scott McCloud provides a standard for judging such Quantity norms through his "iconic abstrac-tion." The scale consists of five faces of varying detail, with a "cartoon" face consisting of two dots, a straight line, and an oval at the "iconic" end, and a reproduced photograph at the opposite "realistic" end (46). McCloud identifies only the middle face as the "style of drawing found in many adventure comics," including superhero comics (29). The middle face consists of "outlines and a hint of shading." Neither underinformative nor overinformative, this middle face suggests both the minimum and the maximum amount of visual information expected of a superhero comic book character.

Buckingham's figure, however, doesn't include any hint of shading. It's defined almost entirely by outline, with no distinguishing features within the outline but its backpack and collar. The figure also has no feet. Rather, its legs end in points. If a reader regards the image as a conventional depiction, taking its drawn qualities to be actual qualities of its subject matter, then she would have to conclude that the being walks on legs ending in points. Yet that breaks the naturalistic expectations of the superhero comic book genre. There's too little information depicted, so in Grice's terms the image flouts Quantity conventionally.

But this isn't how a reader likely interprets the image. The conventional violation of Quantity encourages a reader to understand the depiction conversationally. Given the context of a towering building drawn above a contrastingly minuscule figure, as well as other images of characters before and after this panel and issue, a reader may infer that the absent features are obscured by the figure's implied distance. Such depiction, because it relies on the context of the overall image and of a genre governed by naturalism, is conversational. Buckingham's figure compares with Grice's example of conventional violation of Quantity, where the writer of a letter of recommendation states only that a pupil's "command of English is excellent, and his attendance at tutorials has been regular" (52). Because more information is expected, a reader may conclude that the writer is conversationally implicating that the pupil lacks other positive qualities. In Buckingham's image, flouting Quantity conventionally leads the reader to understand that the artist is conversationally depicting distance. The figure is so far away that we can't make out its feet.

Quantity also requires that an artist not give too much information. Gaiman suggests in a subsequent description that Buckingham "USE THE BRITISH MUSEUM FRONTAGE AS YOUR MODEL FOR THE DOORWAY" (3). Instead, Buckingham collages an actual photograph of the British Museum into the panel. Actual photos communicate more detail than drawn images. So this might seem to flout Quantity conventionally. Yet it's unclear whether

it does. Grice himself is uncertain as to whether too much verbal information always flouts the maxim: "It might be said that to be over informative is
not a transgression of the [Cooperative Principle] but merely a waste of time"
(46). In comics too much visual information may not even be a waste of time,
since a reader, not the creators, controls the amount of time spent on content.
Her eyes may pass as quickly over the photo as they would if Buckingham
had instead drawn a simpler frontage. McCloud also notes that "backgrounds
tend to be slightly more realistic," at times even "near-photographic" (42, 44).
Because it follows genre norms, Buckingham's building doesn't conventionally flout Quantity by giving too much information. He's depicting the image
conventionally after all.

Quantity, however, sometimes applies differently to different subject matter in comics. Buckingham's photo collage respects Quantity partly because
the acceptable amount of detail is higher for backgrounds than for characters.
But a photorealistic rendering of the figure approaching the building could
flout Quantity conventionally by giving more information than expected or
required. According to McCloud, most comic book characters are "designed
simply, to assist in reader-identification," so characters "drawn more realisti-
cally" are more objectified, "emphasizing their 'otherness' from the reader"
(44). Other scholars disagree with McCloud's analysis, but to the degree that
it's accurate, it is generally agreed upon that objectifying otherness would be
depicted conversationally by the artist conventionally flouting Quantity with
too much detail.

More generally, a reader appreciates that greater abstraction would place a
character beyond the naturalistic norms of superhero comic book art, while
greater detail would place the character within the non-superhero norms of
photorealism. Eliot Brown produced several conventionally Quantity-flouting
images for his photographic covers for Marvel in the 1980s and early 1990s, including *Amazing Spider-Man* #262 (March 1985). The photograph is meant to
depict Peter Parker. Because photographs are more detailed than drawn comic
book images, the photograph doesn't match the images of Peter Parker within
the pages of #262 and other comics. It is a photograph not of Peter Parker, but
of an actor posed as him. By assuming that Brown is obeying the Cooperative
Principle, however, a reader may still understand the image's implicature as
a Quantity-flouting representation that is conversationally of Peter Parker.

If a photograph of a comic book character flouts Quantity both conventionally and conversationally, however, then a reader might reject the image

as meaningless because it doesn't reflect things as they are in the world of the story. Roy T. Cook concludes similarly that, though a photorealistic image of the Riddler in a Batman comic "suggests a higher level of objectivity, accuracy, or authority" than a drawn image would, it fails to achieve that purpose because an image of the Riddler can't be *more realistic than he is*" ("Drawings of Photographs in Comics" 133). The image "misrepresents his appearance" (134). Cook's claim relies on the assumption that characters "appear, within the fictional world, as they are depicted in typical panels," a view he later contests, concluding instead that "our access to the physical appearance of drawn characters in general is indirect, partial, inferential, and imperfect" ("Judging a Comic Book by Its Cover" 25). But if an image can't be more realistic than its intended subject, then Brown's cover image might fail to depict Peter Parker altogether. If, on the other hand, Cook's second view is correct, then readers ignore overly realistic details as nonliteral and therefore understand the image as communicating conventionally.

Quality

According to Grice's second maxim, a superhero artist should draw what is true. But what is true in the context of a superhero comic? Though the genre is fantastical and therefore violates many truths of our world, it's also limited by the parameters of its own reality, many of which borrow from the parameters of ours. Understood as subjects in a thought experiment, we bring some of our world's parameters with us into the comic book world.

Psychologist James Carney identifies superhero narratives as minimally counterintuitive. This is similar to Witek's norm of naturalism. Though superhero comics feature "supernatural agents," these agents "deviate in one, and usually only one, characteristic trait from intuitive ontological categories." Their way of being is otherwise basically ours. Carney continues: "The figure of the superhero is a stable rendering in the category of 'person,' which is then supplemented with minimally counterintuitive characteristics and abilities" (Carney et al. A202–3). Adhering to minimal counterintuitiveness captures what it is for comic book artists to respect Grice's Quality maxim. This is so even though such overall naturalistic renderings of superheroes do allow specific fantastical elements.

In *Action Comics* #8, Joe Shuster draws a group of juvenile delinquents facing trial. Initially the four are tall, broad-shouldered, and square-jawed,

From *Action Comics* #8.

qualities that conventionally depict adults rather than children (Siegel and Shuster, *Superman Chronicles* 1:99). After eliminating the corrupting influence of an older criminal, Superman attempts to reform the delinquents by bouncing them on power lines to frighten them. They shout for help, but when Superman threatens to do it again, they answer: "You bet!" and "It was fun!" (108). Shuster now draws the delinquents as short, thin-armed, and comparatively round-headed. What meaning is Shuster trying to communicate with the change?

The conventional depiction is that the four somehow become physically younger. Later panels depict the criminals as children because the burly thugs of earlier panels transform within the reality of the story. Yet, while no more or less impossible than a human-looking alien leaping tall buildings, the conventional depiction as to what is being communicated violates Quality. Nowhere within that or other Superman narratives is Superman depicted with the ability to alter characters' ages by bouncing them on power lines. Had *Action Comics* #7 introduced such an age-reducing superpower, then the ability would have been established, and a reader could understand the images of #8 in that context. This isn't the case. An age-transforming ability even threatens to violate Superman as a character type and his naturalistic grounding as a whole, since a superstrong Superman who can also transform adults into children wouldn't be the same minimally counterintuitive character within the same minimally counterintuitive context.

It's difficult to interpret Shuster's depiction conventionally because it appears to flout Quality, so a reader should try to understand it conversationally. Perhaps Shuster wants to communicate that once Superman eliminates the corrupting influence of an older criminal, the juveniles act, or should be regarded, more like children than like adults. While this might suit conversational depiction generally, however, it's problematic for images within a superhero comic. If this is Shuster's attempted implicature, then it fails because he flouts Quality even conversationally by drawing images that depict breaks in naturalism left unexampled by the context of the genre norms. So the counterintuitive elements are too great for the images to be understood as conventional depictions because they can't be taken to be literally true. And they're also too great to be understood as conversational depictions because the context of naturalism constrains nonliteral interpretations. Instead of communicating, Shuster has confused his reader—who likely ignores the images and keeps reading.

Similar Quality concerns arise in depictions of the character Thor. Jack Kirby's 1962 cover and interior art for *Journey into Mystery* #83 introduces the character spinning his hammer in a circle. Other artists—John Byrne, for example, in *The Avengers* #166 fourteen years later—imitate the image, making it so iconic that director Kenneth Branagh re-created it for the 2011 film *Thor*. Because the cyclone-like arm affects other characters, nearly sucking a supervillain into "a hole—a portal leading to . . . another plane of existence!"

From *Journey into Mystery* #83.

(Shooter, Byrne, and Marcos 6), within the story world the spinning hammer has the literal properties of its drawing. So the depiction seems conventional.

But Quality within naturalistic norms challenges an understanding of it as a conventional depiction. While the hammer remains minimally counterintuitive, Thor's shoulder socket doesn't. Humanlike anatomy wouldn't allow a "stable rendering in the category of 'person'" to spin even a magic object in such a way as to produce the circles drawn by Kirby and his imitators. The anatomical impossibility flouts Quality conventionally. If the image is a conventional depiction, then Kirby is guilty of not having tried to make his contribution true in the context of the genre's naturalistic mode. Though Thor isn't human, he is presented as stronger but otherwise no different from humans. He moves his other muscles as humans do, only more powerfully. No explanation is given for how he can move his arm in such a humanly impossible, even superhumanly impossible, way.

Is Kirby engaging in a conversational depiction? In the context of the other frames, perhaps his point is that the perfect circles of Thor's arm should be understood metaphorically. Grice himself includes metaphor as an example of Quality flouting that produces conversational implicature in words (53). When drawn, the simile "his arm spins *like* a cyclone" is indistinguishable from the metaphorical statement "his arm *is* a cyclone." Yet this alleged conversational depiction is itself strained. Thor's arm does create a hole, or portal, leading to another plane of existence. He must therefore (within the bounds of the comic's story) be moving it as fast as he is conventionally depicted as doing. An alleged metaphor that's literally true isn't a metaphor. That suggests that Kirby isn't depicting it conversationally after all. We are to take the image conventionally. But, as we've seen, this too is problematic. Like Shuster, Kirby is confusing his reader. The image of the spinning hammer must be accepted as true, while Thor's shoulder anatomy must be simultaneously ignored as untrue. Ultimately, the image depicts neither conventionally nor conversationally. A reader must choose which elements of the image to ignore and which to accept to maintain the minimally counterintuitive narrative.

There are, though, cases where artists flout Quality conventionally only to depict images conversationally. In *Icon: A Hero's Welcome* (1993), artist M. D. Bright variously renders Icon's cape as roughly his own height, slightly longer than his height, twice his height, and three times his height (Bright, Gustovich, and McDuffie 30, 144, 45, 69). More recent artists' renderings of Ms. Marvel's cape-like sash vary similarly. Though Adrian Alphona prefers conventional depiction where the sash appears to dangle mid-calf and is understood in the story literally to dangle mid-calf, Jacob Wyatt renders it at times as twice or more Ms. Marvel's height, even though the sash is understood to be a stable object (*Ms. Marvel*, 2: unpaginated). Bright and Wyatt may not draw what they think is conventionally true, but their drawings cause no confusion because the context establishes their images as the visual equivalents of hyperbole, a category Grice includes under Quality flouting (53). The cape and sash don't literally change. They're just drawn in an exaggerated fashion. Conversationally, Icon's expansive cape expresses authority and power, while Ms. Marvel's trailing sash functions as motion lines.

Relation

An artist should also draw images that are relevant. What is relevant in a superhero comic? If, as with *Miracleman* #17, a reader may obtain an issue's script, then the drawn images may be compared with the originating instructions. Recall that Buckingham included only Gaiman's three primary elements: outdoor setting, a building, and a small figure. Yet he altered and added details freely, but relevantly, because the details actualized each element. Buckingham, however, didn't improvise new major elements, like a second figure or a second building. Relation requires Buckingham to remain within the script's range of relevancy.

Yet access to scripts is comparatively rare. As a result, a reader generally assumes that all drawn content is relevant. Consider the evolving appearance of the Thing. Jack Kirby's cover for *Fantastic Four* #1 features a bumpy-skinned Thing. The Thing's face on the cover of #7, however, is rocklike. By #20 his cover image is divided into pentagonal and hexagonal segments. And #51 presents the character's canonical appearance now completed with the previously absent eyebrow ridge. Because the images are all identified in the text as the Thing, the varying images seem to flout Relation conventionally. Each image seems conventionally to depict a different character.

Stan Lee's original treatment for *Fantastic Four* #1 describes the character as "grotesque," "shapeless," and physically "ponderous" ("synopsis"). As Hopkins explained, Kirby must depict more than the words describe, giving specific shape to Lee's shapelessness. Of all possible grotesque details, Kirby at first draws the Thing with bumpy skin. Later he apparently draws the Thing's face on the #7 cover with rocky detail—perhaps because the face is large and isolated, inviting greater precision for which rockiness is better suited. On the other hand, Kirby's inker, Dick Ayers, may have been responsible for adding the quality of rockiness over Kirby's ambiguous pencil lines. If so, then that's a stylistic innovation that influenced Kirby's subsequent penciling, so that by #20 the Thing's body appears consistently rocky. Regardless, a reader might ignore and later artists and writers did ignore Kirby's initial rendering as irrelevant. When artists Jim Starlin and Joe Sinnott drew Len Wein's retelling of the Thing's origin in *Marvel Feature* #11 (June 1973), they rendered his skin as rocky rather than bumpy from the first moment of his transformation (*Marvel Firsts: The 1970s* 65).

Assuming that Kirby and his fellow artists are abiding by the Cooperative

Principle, a reader should expect a story-based explanation for changes in the Thing's appearance. Differences in the images would then be relevant, depicting something conversationally. Perhaps, given the context of earlier images, Kirby and Ayers are communicating that the Thing is continuing to mutate—which is what actual readers did assume. Their assumption even influenced later writer-artist John Byrne to retcon that explanation. For *Marvel Two-in-One* #50 (April 1979), Byrne addresses Kirby's variant renderings by incorporating their differences into the narrative. Byrne draws five versions of the Thing's head on a display screen, as Reed Richards explains:

> Remember how, when you first became the Thing, you would sometimes revert to Ben Grimm spontaneously [. . .] that was your body trying to shed the effects of the cosmic rays [. . .] so even your basic appearance has been changing . . . from the something akin to dinosaur hide . . . to its present rock-like state. (Byrne, Sinnott, and Mouly 2)

When the Thing time-travels to 1961 where he encounters his younger self (which we discussed in chapter 2), Byrne and his inker, Joe Sinnott, highlight their differences by depicting both versions of the character together in multiple panels. Colorist F. Mouly further differentiates them by applying a different shade of orange for each. The meaning is clear: the Thing changed appearances over time. Here is a case where imputing a conversational depiction turned out to encourage artists retroactively to regard the depiction conventionally.

A reader, however, does regard many visual inconsistencies as irrelevant when they violate naturalism generally and Relation specifically. For Spider-Man's debut in *Amazing Fantasy* #15 (August 1962), the uncredited colorist filled Steve Ditko's costume design in red and blue. When Marvel moved the character to his own title, the costume is red and blue on the covers of *The Amazing Spider-Man* #1–4, but red and purple inside the same issues. Were the two color designs consistent between each issue's cover and pages, then a reader might interpret the change as a conventional depiction. Spider-Man changed costumes after his first adventure. Yet the contradiction between cover and internal panels prevents this understanding—unless a reader assumes that for a short time Spider-Man maintains two costumes and somehow is drawn wearing the red and blue one only when he's depicted in cover images. But there'd be no narrative reason to assume that. The change in color doesn't suggest any conversational meaning either. The contexts where the changes occur tell the reader absolutely nothing relevant about the color changes. A

From *Marvel Two-in-One* #50.

reader likely disregards them on a naturalistic assumption that objects don't spontaneously change color. The difference between blue and purple, in this specific context, is irrelevant.

The purple shade vanishes entirely with #5. Though conventional depiction is still possible—maybe Spider-Man used two slightly different costumes during his early career but soon settled on one—there's still no reason to believe that. As a result, a reader may continue to dismiss the color variants. Because the changes are more confusing than communicative, they're ignored. Grice describes a similar incident of Relation flouting where a speaker makes a socially impolite statement at a party and a second speaker follows it with an unrelated comment about the weather—implicating that the first "remark should not be discussed" (54). Later Spider-Man writers, by making no references to Spider-Man's color-changing costume, implicate a similar message. In cases like this Relation is flouted both conventionally and conversationally.

Manner

Applied to verbal communication, Grice's final maxim requires speakers to be perspicuous by being brief and orderly and avoiding ambiguity and obscurity. Unlike previous maxims, Manner addresses not what is said but how it's said. With comics, the content of panels is the what and their layout is the how. Just as an artist should depict content in a way that abides by the Cooperative Principle, she should also lay out that content—and so depict its sequence—in a way that abides by the same. Layout should itself be brief, orderly, unambiguous, and unobscure.

How should we understand these principles? Brevity might allude to encapsulation—the division of a narrative into single images—suggesting that a story should be drawn in the minimum number of panels needed. But that directive is already addressed by Quantity. In comics, Manner best describes only layout. So brevity isn't clearly applicable here. Order would concern how to understand panel sequence, including what happens narratively between panels. Ambiguity and obscurity would themselves concern whether that sequence is difficult for readers to follow.

Two elements of layout, reading path and closure, are especially relevant to Manner. Reading path describes how a reader navigates a page of sequential images relative to panel shapes and positioning. Closure describes how a reader processes transitions between images. Both involve whether layout is orderly, unambiguous, and unobscured—or their opposites. Because the norm of naturalism concerns content, it plays no direct role in governing layout.

Early comic book artists sometimes depict panel order conventionally by placing numbers inside panels. George E. Brenner's "Murder by Proxy" episode of the Clock in *Detective Picture Stories* #5 (April 1937) includes numbers in the corners of panels, totaling thirty-one over seven pages (16–22). Joe Shuster follows the same procedure from *Action Comics* #1 through #19, where numbering ceases midstory (Siegel and Shuster, *Superman Chronicles* 2:141). Panel numbering generally ceased by the 1940s, but early artists also conventionally depict order by drawing gutter-bridging arrows between panels. Jack Kirby and Joe Simon's *Blue Bolt* #10 (March 1941) includes three such arrows (177, 178, 180), and though the practice was uncommon by the 1960s, Steve Ditko includes a directional arrow in *Amazing Spider-Man* #23 (April 1965) (16).

Artists more often conventionally depict order by arranging layout according to expected Z-path and N-path reading patterns. Neil Cohn demonstrates that the Z-path (first left to right, then top to bottom) is the default navigation pattern for an English-speaking reader of comics. Such a reader, however, will adopt an N-path (first top to bottom, then left to right) if panel gutters don't align left to right. In either case, layout determines how panels are to be navigated, so the artist conventionally depicts her intended reading path.

Artists may also conventionally depict while challenging but not flouting Manner. Thierry Groensteen terms layouts that avoid regularized panels "neobaroque," lamenting that it "is as if the simple succession of panels was no longer deemed sufficient to ensure the production of meaning." Groensteen attributes the style to "a generation that has turned its back on the ideals of simplicity and transparency that permeated classic Franco-Belgium comics, whose leading practitioners strove about all to tell a story as legibly as possible"

(47). Such neo-baroque works may include "the interpenetration of images," "images that bleed off the edge of the page," "intrusions in the gutter," "multiple insets," "the vertical or horizontal elongation of panels," and the "stacking of very narrow horizontal panels" (47). Such techniques are also common in American superhero comics, though the overall layout style emphasizes legibility—which is to say Manner.

Sometimes, however, a reader must rely on the context of panel images to determine navigation because the artist has flouted Manner conventionally. In such cases an artist depicts panel sequence conversationally. In "The Claw Battles Daredevil" from *Silver Streak Comics* #7 (January 1941), Jack Cole includes no numbers or arrows, and because the second panel begins below the top left panel, a reader may navigate either to the left of the first panel or to the panel beneath the first, resulting in ambiguous sequence and thus confusion (147). Cohn and coresearcher Hannah Campbell investigated a similar layout where 38 percent of readers followed a Z-path to the left, and 61 percent followed an N-path down. The lack of consensus is a result of flouting Manner conversationally. Cole's layout is also sequentially ambiguous, but the context indicates a Z-path and thus resolves the confusion.

Likewise, Jim Steranko opens *Captain America* #111 (March 1969) with a thirteen-panel page that represents scenes from an arcade that defy any set reading pattern. The layout produces a sequence of navigational choices where neither a Z- nor an N-path direction appears correct or even comparatively effective. Whichever navigational choice a reader makes at each transition point, some panels can't be read without breaking the pattern. Steranko therefore conversationally depicts through conventional Manner flouting that a reader may navigate the panels in different orders. This depiction reinforces the image content of the arcade, where characters may also navigate the depicted scene in different orders.

We now turn to the second element of layout under consideration: closure. McCloud defines the Gestalt psychology principle as the "phenomenon of observing the parts but perceiving the whole," though it more specifically indicates a viewer filling in visual gaps between disconnected parts (63). McCloud's notion of closure corresponds to the conversational depiction that occurs between images: "Comics panels fracture both time and space, offering a jagged, staccato rhythm of unconnected moments. But closure allows us to connect these moments and mentally construct a continuous, unified reality" (67). On McCloud's view, closure is so essential to comic book layout that "comics IS closure." Hyperbole notwithstanding, McCloud explains: "Nothing is seen between panels, but experience tells you something must be there!" (67). That experience is gained from context, so it's a form of conversational depiction.

McCloud focuses his analysis on gutters and therefore types of transitions possible between panels. Yet closure can be independent of these, since insets and interpenetrating images too depict conversationally. We identify four types of closure, or conversational depiction, between images:

> Spatial: Subject matter in separate images is conversationally depicted as existing in physical relationship to each other, typically as a result of panel framing. (What McCloud identifies as aspect-to-aspect, subject-to-subject, and some scene-to-scene transitions require spatial closure.)
>
> Temporal: Undrawn events are conversationally depicted to take place outside of events in separate images, typically as a result of panel transitions and so occurring as if in gutters. (What McCloud identifies as moment-to-moment, action-to-action, and some subject-to-subject and scene-to-scene transitions require temporal closure.)
>
> Causal: Action is conversationally depicted to have been caused by an element absent from a current image but present in a preceding image. (None of McCloud's transitions, not even action-to-action, accounts for this type of closure.)
>
> Associative: A metaphorical relationship is conversationally depicted between two images in which one image is understood to represent some idea about the other image. (Though McCloud does not identify this type of closure, Jessica Abel and Matt Madden add "symbolic" [46] to McCloud's list of transition types. Symbolic transitions require associative closure.)

Each type of closure may occur alone or in combination. Consider a three-panel sequence in *Watchmen* #8 (Moore and Gibbons 28). In the first image, Dave Gibbons conventionally depicts the shadow of a statuette cast over the face of a frightened man kneeling on the floor. The second image conventionally depicts the statuette in the fist of an attacker. Taken in context, spatial closure is required to understand conversationally that the two images occur within a few feet of each other, each image drawn from one of the two men's points of view. The second image also requires temporal closure because

From *Watchmen* #8.

the statuette is behind the attacker's head at an angle that wouldn't cast the shadow seen on the victim's face in the first image. Gibbons therefore also conversationally depicts a movement forward in time during which the attacker has cocked his arm back to strike.

The third image conventionally depicts a jack-o-lantern striking the floor with falling books. It also conversationally depicts all four forms of closure together. The pumpkin exists in the same space as the two now undrawn men, an example of spatial closure. The pumpkin is crushed at a moment immediately following the second image, an example of temporal closure. And because it resembles a human head and breaks open at the moment a reader anticipates the statuette striking the man's head, the crushed pumpkin conversationally depicts that the man's head has been similarly damaged, an example of associative closure.

A close reading of the sequence, however, reveals an element of confusion where Gibbons fails to depict images perspicuously. Regarding causal closure, it's unclear how the shelf of falling books was overturned. Was it the victim of panel 1 striking the shelf after he was himself struck? Was it the attacker of panel 2 striking the shelf in the process of striking the victim? Was it another attacker depicted behind the victim in the first panel striking the shelf before the victim was struck? Each possibility requires a different conclusion regarding not only causal closure, but also temporal closure. If the second attacker already struck the shelf, then the pumpkin breaks at the same moment that the victim is struck. If the victim or the attacker with the statuette knocks over the shelf, then the pumpkin breaks after the victim has already been struck. A reader may conjecture that Gibbons was fulfilling a directive in Moore's script, producing this unintended communicative gap in its execution. All the same, the flouting of Manner, in both conventional and conversational cases, results in confusion—which readers likely ignore.

To address panel arrangements that might produce confusion, McCloud includes "non-sequitur" as a type of transition that "offers no logical relationship between panels whatsoever!" (72). A non sequitur produces no closure and thus no depiction of either kind. That could be because the artist's attempt at communication so lacks concision that the transition only confuses, or the artist simply intended to communicate nothing to begin with. Either way, both violate Manner and with it the Cooperative Principle.

Regardless of how we understand individual examples, it's intriguing to consider superhero comics as one big philosophical thought experiment. Their medium presents a scenario to its readers in which meaning is communicated through sequential images—but how? We've argued that Grice's notion of conventional and conversational implicature can be applied to sequential images. An image conventionally depicts when its meaning is communicated by its strict representational qualities. It conversationally depicts when its meaning goes beyond those qualities by relying on context. Like Grice's own notions, conventional and conversational depictions can be demarcated by appealing to the Cooperative Principle and its maxims. Unlike Grice's notions, respecting that principle and its maxims in the context of superhero comics requires respecting naturalism. Regardless, when Quantity, Quality, Relation, or Manner is flouted conventionally, a reader tries to understand the image as depicting conversationally. When the maxims are flouted conversationally too, the image just doesn't communicate.

EIGHT

TRUE BELIEVERS

We've claimed that superhero comics can be understood as treating their readers as subjects in a thought experiment. In the previous chapter, the thought experiment we considered was that their form encourages us to take their words and images as both having meaning. Here, we argue, the form of superhero comics encourages us to treat that meaning as being communicated by a single, individual voice. The premise of this book—that superhero comics can be read as philosophical thought experiments—embeds this second thought experiment especially. From the beginning, we've been reading individual comics as if they were written by individual philosophers. In chapter 1, we examined what makes a superhero good—taking the multiple authors of Superman's first year of comics to be an individual philosopher expressing the ethical view of consequentialism, and the multiple authors of Batman's first year to be an individual philosopher expressing deontology, even though each actual comic explicitly has multiple creators. We've followed through on this in every chapter since. So this "What if?," drawn from the form of superhero comic books, is also one of our book's most fundamental:

What if multiple authors were somehow also an individual author?

Perhaps the most famous academic philosophical thought experiment asks a similar point, though in reverse. In Plato's *Republic*, Socrates and his companions discuss what makes an individual person just. Because the question's so complicated, Socrates proposes answering it by understanding an individual's soul on the model of a city. We should identify where justice is in the city as a whole, only "afterwards look[ing] for it in the individual, observing the ways in which the smaller is similar to the larger" (1008). Instead of examining superheroes, the thought experiment in which we find ourselves examines comic book creators. Are they like cities too? Should we, in flipping Plato's thought experiment around, understand all the citizens of a city—all the writers, artists, and other creators of a single comic—on the model of an individual? Are there ways in which the larger, team of creators, is similar to the smaller, an individual one?

Plato didn't have the last word on how to understand individuals or their souls. About 2,400 years later in his 1995 *Darwin's Dangerous Idea*, philosopher and cognitive scientist Daniel Dennett updates the notion of a mind or soul by focusing on intentionality, the property of beliefs, desires, intentions, and other states with semantic content. In this passage, he explains what it is for an individual human being, or "organism," like each of us, to have intentionality. He even invokes Plato:

> In an organism with genuine intentionality—like yourself—there are, right now, many parts, and some of these parts exhibit a sort of semi-intentionality, or mere *as if* intentionality, or pseudo-intentionality—call it what you like—and your own genuine, fully fledged intentionality is in fact the product (with no further miracle ingredients) of the activities of all the semi-minded and mindless bits that make you up. [. . .] That is what a mind is—not a miracle-machine, but a huge, semi-designed, self-redesigning amalgam of smaller machines, each with its own design history, each playing its own role in the "economy of the soul." (Plato was right, as usual, when he saw a deep analogy between a republic and a person—but of course he had much too simple a vision of what this might mean.) (206)

Plato and Dennett have us understand an individual in terms of a plurality, and we've already said that we're going to flip the order. That's because superhero comics present us with the thought experiment where we're to understand a plurality of creators in terms of an individual one.

How can we understand an author as singular when she is—or they are—really plural? In the previous chapter, we analyzed how artists communicate visually by following the same maxims that apply to writers. Yet every word and graphic mark on a page might result from multiple writers, pencilers, scripters, and inkers. How can we be made to imagine that all these forms of communication combine into a single voice? Likewise, as we saw in the introduction, Scott McCloud maintains that comics are "juxtaposed pictorial and other images in deliberate sequence intended to convey information and/or produce an aesthetic response in the reader" (9). Whether or not we accept his definition, McCloud is right that when they occur in comics images are intended to convey information and/or produce an aesthetic response. They're intended to do this *by* authors. Yet individuals intend things. How can a pluralistic author do so? What is it for a plurality to have intentionality?

These are the sorts of questions this "What if?" thought experiment would have us answer, and doing so engages in the philosophy of mind. While many have written on collaborative authorship and intentionality, we focus on Dennett to solve this thought-experimental puzzle. First, though, we try to identify the author of a comic book by ordinary means, getting into the nitty-gritty of comic book splash pages.

Credited Authors

Ordinarily readers identify the author of a published work by looking at its cover or title page. But before the 1980s, the major publishers of US comics, Marvel and DC, didn't include author names on their covers, and internal credits are complex. The opening page of *Giant-Size Defenders* #3 (January 1975) declares:

> Steve Gerber, Jim Starlin and Len Wein plotted this tale together. Then Jim did the layouts, Steve wrote the script, and Dan Adkins, Don Newton and Jim Mooney finished the art. Charlotte Jetter lettered it, Glynis Wein colored it, Roy Thomas edited it, and aren't these credits ridiculously complicated? (Gerber)

Though the paragraph is unusual, the inclusion of splash-page credits is not. A splash page, Dennis O'Neil explains, is "usually the first page, with one or two images, incorporating title, logo (if any), credits, [and] other such information" (12). A splash page resembles a novel's title page, except that the splash page is also the first page of the story. Further complicating things, credits may appear on splash pages inside drawn boxes, banners, or spaces within images that are part of the story world, with no standard size or shape for letterforms or standard method for their incorporation into surrounding art.

Author roles are equally complex. Consider a year's run of *The Avengers* published by Marvel from November 1977 to November 1978 (which we discussed in chapter 3):

- Issue #165 credits James Shooter as "writer," John Byrne as "penciler," and Pablo Marcos as "inker."
- The contributors remain the same for the next issue, but their categories shift. Besides dropping first names, #166 credits Shooter for "story" and Byrne and Marcos for "art."
- In #167, Shooter (now "Jim") is "writer," but George Pérez is "artist" instead of "penciler," though Pablo Marcos remains "inker." The issue also includes a separate credit for "co-plot."
- In #168, Shooter ("James" again) receives credit for "script," and Pérez reverts to "pencils" and Marcos "inks."
- #169 interrupts the story arc with a stand-alone episode, likely inserted because the intended episode missed production deadlines. Marv Wolfman is "writer," but "layouts" and "finishes" are introduced for Sal Buscema and Dave Hunt, respectively.
- When the story arc continues in #170, Shooter is "writer/colorist," and "George Perez" (no accent mark) shares writing credit as "artist/ co-plotter."
- #171 and #172 feature Shooter as "writer" again, while introducing two new term variations: Sal Buscema's "breakdowns" and Klaus Janson's "finished art."
- #173 divides writing credit, "J. Shooter" for "story" and "D. Michelinie" as "writer," with "S. Buscema" for "layouts" and "D. Hands" as "finisher." But, according to marvel.wikia.com's entry for the issue, seven contributors are missing, because "D. Hands" is short for "Diverse Hands" and includes Pablo Marcos, Win Mortimer, Bob McLeod, Joe Rubinstein, Dan Green, Ricky Bryant, and Klaus Janson.
- Bill Mantlo appears for "story" in #174, with Wenzel's "pencils," Marcos's "inks," and Shooter's "plot."
- Shooter returns in #175 now as "plotter," with Michelinie as

"scripter," while "D. Wenzel" and "P. Marcos" continue for "pencils" and "inker," respectively.

- In #176, Shooter (now "Jim" again) receives "plot" credit, and David Michelinie is "writer," but Dave Wenzel and Pablo Marcos are combined as "artists."
- Finally, for #177, "Shooter" (still "Jim") is again "writer," and Dave Wenzel continues for "pencils," while P. Marcos and newcomer R. Villamonte share "inkers" credit.

Apparently, "ridiculously complicated" is an industry norm. The credits also acknowledge letterers, colorists, and editors, but limiting to writing and black-and-white art, the thirteen issues acknowledge fifteen contributors. Their names also vacillate, especially Shooter's first name, variously "J.," "Jim," and "James." The variations contradict the publishing norm of stable author names. J. K. Rowling is never credited on her novels' titles pages as "Joanna" or "Jo." Less stable author names suggest authorship as a less stable category in comics.

Further, the terms for identifying authorial roles vacillate widely. They include both job titles (artist, finisher, inker, penciler, plotter, scripter, writer) and what those jobs produce (art, breakdowns, finishes, inks, layouts, pencils, plot, script, story). Roles do, however, divide into broad categories: writing and art. When a single author receives writing credit, the categories plot, plotter, story, script, scripter, and writer appear interchangeable and comprise the total writing process. When two authors appear, the terms divide into two categories: (a) plot, plotter, and story; and (b) script, scripter, and writer. The first is the initial stage of composing, conceiving paraphraseable ideas to be executed later; the second indicates the creation of physical script, typically with dialog, narration, and descriptions of panels for a penciler to develop into layouts. So "script," "story," and "writer" may include conceiving ideas and developing them into a script, but "story" may also indicate conception only and "writer" and "scripter" scripting only. "Plot" and "plotter" refer always and only to the conceptual stage.

Shooter is the most consistently credited author, appearing in all but one issue as lone writer or as conceptual writer working with a script writer. As we saw, #169 interrupts the story arc, so it's unsurprising that Shooter would be uninvolved. #167 also credits "Sterno" (whom marvel.wikia.com identifies as editor Roger Stern) for "co-plot," the only example of Shooter sharing conceptual writing with anyone but George Pérez. Stern's name, however, is literally hidden, appearing in a differently colored and angled box that merges with the splash-page artwork, suggesting that his contribution is less than Shooter's, who is credited not as another "co-plotter" but as "writer."

"Writer" itself has an additional meaning that may describe Michelinie's contributions to #175 and #176. Marvel writer and editor Roy Thomas recalls taking the "Marvel Writer's Test," consisting of four pages from *Fantastic Four Annual* #2. Job applicants, including Dennis O'Neil and Gary Friedrich, had to fill in empty caption boxes, talk balloons, and thought balloons with words (Lee and Thomas). To the extent that the test mimics actual work, "writing" includes neither conceptual work nor scripting, but only inserting words into completed artwork—what Stan Lee described as "just putting in the copy after he drew it" (Lee). If Shooter provided only abstract story ideas for #176, Michelinie as "writer" may have produced a script based on them, as he presumably did for #175 as "scripter." On the other hand, Michelinie as "writer" may have only filled in Dave Wenzel's empty talk balloons and caption boxes with words.

Art credits also divide into two stages of production. The first includes penciler, pencils, breakdowns, and layouts; the second, inker, finisher, inks, finishes, and finished art. When the two categories are combined as "art" or "artists," the terms could imply that the jobs of penciling and inking were also combined, but it's more likely that the "art" of #166 was penciled by Byrne and inked by Marcos. In one instance "artist" means penciler when paired with a separate inker. While the year-long run has four pencilers and five inkers, Pablo Marcos "pencils," "co-pencils," or is a "co-artist" on ten of the issues, providing the most visual consistency. Marcos is an "artist" only when his inking is undifferentiated from penciling. Further, while the role of penciler is never divided, inking may be done by multiple artists. When inking is done by more than two artists, they aren't credited individually, since the seven contributors missing from the #173 splash page are collectively credited as "D. Hands."

Penciling may also be a subcategory of "writing," as suggested by George Pérez's "artist/co-plotter" credit in #170, the only instance of *The Avengers* run where an author receives both writing and art credit. Yet it's unclear whether Pérez's penciling is independent of his writing, and whether his coplotting differs from Stern's in #167. Are all pencilers, by virtue of creating breakdowns, "writing"? Most of Stan Lee's credited "writing" involves concepts and words but not scripts, which pencilers bypass by "writing" layouts directly. This so-called Marvel Method was not unique to Marvel, either. Mick Anglo followed the same process when "writing" *Marvelman* comics for London publisher L. Miller and Son in the 1950s: "Mick would instead suggest a basic plot outline to an artist, giving him a specific number of pages to fit the idea into. Once the art was complete, Mick would then write in the actual wording for the letterer" ("Miracleman Alias Marvelman"). Such layout-writing, however, is rarely acknowledged on splash pages. Robert Steibel examined pencil photostats of Jack Kirby's layouts for *Fantastic Four* #61 (April 1967), estimating Kirby's "writing" contribution between 65 and 95 percent and Stan Lee's, who receives sole "writer" credit, between 5 and 35 percent. Lee himself estimates that "90% of the *Tales of Asgard* stories were Jack's plots" (Lee). According to comic book historian Sean Howe, artist Wally Wood left Marvel in 1965 because "drawing an issue before there was a script [. . .] meant that he was plotting the story without being paid or credited" (57).

Though uncredited, one additional artist contributed significantly to all thirteen *Avengers* issues. Starting in the mid-1960s, Marvel used Jack Kirby's work as a house style. "When new artists came to Marvel," writes Howe, "they were handed a stack of Kirby's books or, better yet, a stack of Kirby's rough layouts over which to draw," or Kirby would even "draw basic layouts for the [new artists'] first issue" (84, 50). According to Marvel artist Gil Kane, "Jack's point of view and philosophy of drawing became the governing philosophy of the entire publishing company. [. . .] It was how they taught everyone to reconcile all those opposing attitudes to one single master point of view" (Groth 109). Marcos joined Marvel after Kirby left in 1970, so it's unlikely that he or any of the other 1977–78 *Avengers* artists trained in this specific capacity. But all Marvel pencilers and inker still worked within strict visual norms, what Cohn terms the "Kirbyan" dialect or the "'mainstream' style of American Visual Language" (*The Visual Language of Comics* 139). But are Kirby's influences great enough for him to count as an author?

House style or its management is also contained in the role of editor, adding Archie Goodwin, Marv Wolfman, and Roger Stern to the list of contributors. Editors can contribute during the writing stage as well, implicitly or explicitly shaping content before a penciler begins layouts and again before an inker finalizes them. According to the "undisputed" facts section of the 2011 US District Court ruling on *Marvel v. Kirby*, where Kirby's heirs sued for rights over his cocreated characters, "It was not uncommon for [Stan] Lee to make changes to artwork or script without first consulting the artist or writer" (14). An editor therefore has a level of autonomy traditionally indicative of an author. *The Avengers* splash-page credits don't indicate the degree of Goodwin's, Wolfman's, or Stern's involvement. Is it significant enough for them to count as authors?

Hierarchical Authors

A collaboratively produced comic book title like *The Avengers* therefore has many ambiguously overlapping roles. Such ambiguity also applies beyond the specific title, publishing period, and publisher. It's the industry norm. But not all roles are equal. Does an understanding of comic book authorship require formulating a hierarchy of contributors, only the highest of which count as authors?

The Avengers splash pages imply such a hierarchy, since writing credit precedes artwork except for #174, where Shooter combines "plot/editor-in-chief" in the final position, with editor credit appearing in all cases. In #167 Michelinie's "writer" appears after Shooter's "plot," further suggesting that concept is more important than script. It remains unclear, however, whether Michelinie's contribution is more important than the two artists'. Artwork credits also appears hierarchical, with pencilers always preceding inkers. Is Marcos, despite his inks providing the most visual consistency of the thirteen issues, less of an author than each of the writers and pencilers? Or does the order of splash-page credits only reflect production order: story concept, script, pencils, inks, colors, and letters?

The decade leap to the late 1980s introduces additional complexity to credits. While *The Avengers* includes no author names on covers, the 1987 *Wonder Woman* (which we discussed in chapter 5) reflects the change in industry norms by listing them. Though internal credits still include plotting, scripting, penciling, inking, coloring, lettering, and editing, the covers of #1 and #2 credit only "Potter, Pérez and Patterson," as writer, penciler, and inker, respectively. Because the names are not alphabetized, the order is presumably hierarchal. Though Greg Potter and George Pérez share plotting, Potter's script precedes Pérez's pencils, with Bruce Patterson's inks always third. Letterer, colorist, and editor don't appear, suggesting their contributions are nonauthorial. The #3 cover, however, is ordered differently: "Pérez, Wein, Patterson," as plotter/penciler, scripter, and inker, respectively. Apparently an artist who also plots a story is more important than a writer who only scripts it. Cover credits reduce the number of authorial roles to three and, combined with internal credit order, establish that inkers are secondary to writers and pencilers and that pencilers are secondary to writers.

Contemporary comics suggest a similar hierarchy but with additional inconsistencies. *The Multiversity: Mastermen* #1 (April 2015) (which we discussed in chapter 2) concludes with credits in a banner at the bottom of the final page. "Writer" Grant Morrison and "penciller" Jim Lee are the only ones named in the top line, suggesting that they alone are authors. Their names appear twice the height of the names of those listed in the second line: "inkers," Scott Williams, Sandra Hope, Mark Irwin, and Jonathan Glapion; "colorists," Alex Sinclair and Jeromy Cox; and "letterer," Rob Leigh. That Morrison and Lee are the only or primary authors, however, is undermined by the cover, which lists Morrison, Lee, Williams, and Sinclair by last name and in descending order of apparent role importance: writer, penciler, inker, and (breaking with previous norms) colorist. According to the cover then, only the first of the four inkers and only the first of the two colorists are authors.

Image Comics' *Wayward* (March 2015) further complicates things. Internal credits for the first volume include nine contributors: "story," Jim Zub; "line art," Steve Cummings; "color art," Tamra Bonvillain, Ross A. Campbell, Josh Pérez, John Rauch, and Jim Zub; "color flats," Ludwig Olilmber; and "letters," Marshall Dillon. Cover credits, however, include only five by last names: Zub, Cummings, Rauch, Bonvillain, and Dillon. Though the writer and the photoshop equivalent of penciler appear first, the inclusion and order of Rauch and Bonvillain confuse previous patterns. Both contribute "color art," an ambiguous category likely combining colorist and inker. Names are alphabetized within categories internally but by apparent order of importance on the cover, where Rauch appears before Bonvillain and Campbell, and Pérez (as well as Zub as an artist) are omitted. The inclusion of Dillon on the cover also disrupts the assumption that letterers are not authors.

Despite variations, writer and penciler remain the two primary roles, with penciler subordinate. Yet *Omega: The Unknown* (2008) both supports and disrupts this. The cover of the collected edition credits Jonathan Lethem as sole author: "By the Award-winning author of *Motherless Brooklyn*." Following the norms of book publishing, Farel Dalrymple receives the credit "Illustrated by," dividing art from authorship and placing it before but literally parallel to Paul Hornschemeier's "Colored by." Lethem's name also appears more than twice as large as Dalrymple's and Hornschemeier's. The inclusion of Karl Rusnak, however, confuses norms. His name, smaller than all others, appears directly under Lethem's and is preceded ambiguously by "with." Inside, Lethem and Rusnak receive joint "Words/Story" credit, partly clarifying Rusnak's role, but confusing his authorial significance. Though his name appears smallest on the cover, it's second on the book's spine: Lethem, Rusnak, Dalrymple, Hornschemeier.

While Rusnak's credits suggest that writing, however secondary the writer's contribution, is more significant than art, *Omega: The Unknown* also overturns this conclusion. The original series premiered in March 1976, and according to its splash page the first issue was "Conceived and Written by Steve Gerber and Mary Skrenes," and "Illustrated by Jim Mooney." When the ten issues and two related *The Defenders* issues were collected in *Omega: The Unknown Classic* in 2005, the title page lists seven writers and eight artists. Lethem's 2006 reboot series credits none of them, and because of Marvel's policy not to acknowledge creators, Gerber and Skrenes are mentioned only in the book's promotional material on the front flap. In an included interview Lethem admitted, "I knew I'd have to model my first issue closely on theirs," and added, "I also followed slavishly" a key sequence. Gerber himself condemned the project:

> Writers and artists who claim to respect the work of creators past should demonstrate that respect by leaving the work alone—particularly if the original creator is still alive, still active in the industry, and, as is typically the case in comics, excluded from any financial participation in the use of the work. (Johnston)

Legal and ethical issues aside, Gerber and Skrenes contributed to the rebooted series as writers (seemingly more than the ambiguously credited Rusnak) and therefore are uncredited authors. Their and Mooney's exclusion reveals a further complexity in implied hierarchies.

Since serial comics routinely feature characters and situations by authors not involved in subsequent episodes or series, where would these contributors fall hierarchically? Even when not overtly imitating another artist's house style, artists use other artists' templates to re-create ongoing characters. Bryne's, Buscema's, and Wenzel's individual renderings of Captain America all repeat costume motifs authored by Jack Kirby and Joe Simon in 1940. Dalrymple's style differs more significantly from Mooney's, but Dalrymple's Omega depends on Mooney's original. When an original author is credited— as with Siegel and Shuster in *Multiversity*—it's as creator, not author. Since

The Avengers itself includes a range of preexisting characters from other series created by other authors, the number of uncredited current authors expands exponentially, further undermining any sense of hierarchy.

Implied hierarchies also collapse, since the majority of comics are commissioned works, reducing a primary artist or writer like Jack Kirby to only "an employee for hire" (US District Court 2). According to comic book scholar and lawyer Terry Hart, "Copyright protection initially vests with the author or creator of the work. The exception to this rule is when the work is a 'work made for hire'—in that case, the employer or entity commissioning the work is considered the author under the law" ("Marvel v. Kirby"). In a legal sense then, only Marvel is the author of *The Avengers*. Shooter, Pérez, Marcos, and so on, are not. They merely contributed.

However, even Marvel may not be the author. John G. Cawalti likens an "individual formulaic work" to "a successful production of a familiar play by a gifted cast and a talented director" (10). Extending the analogy, formulaic superhero comics are directed and performed, but not authored, unless the author is the undifferentiated body of earlier authors who shaped the formula. All works of art are influenced by predecessors, but formula writing involves so much influence that the credited author may be less primary than the totality of earlier ones of the genre. Brian Richardson argues similarly:

> The more formulaic a work is, the less of a need to account for an individuated authorial work; that is, no distinctive author is properly implied by such novels. Second rate mysteries, Harlequin romances, and pornography—and for that matter, most Restoration comedies—exhibit no distinctive authorial presence. (121)

When superhero comics are as formulaic as Richardson's examples, they wouldn't have a distinctive authorial presence either. Not only is there no hierarchy of authors, but there might not be any relevant author at all.

Pluralistic Author

Returning to our first example, comic book credits fail to determine how many authors *The Avengers* has and which are primary. Apparently, both answers lie somewhere between well over the dozen credited on its splash pages and, if none are distinctive, zero. Focusing on a single issue doesn't help either, since each individually has a similar range. While anything near the larger end of the range strains our intuitive sense of authorship, the smaller end, zero, breaks it outright. There's no reason to think that the series or any single issue has exactly one author either.

Philosopher Christy Mag Uidhir tries to make sense of comic book authorship and hierarchy through an analysis of "mass-art comics (e.g., 'superhero' comics)." He draws "a principled distinction between collective *production* and collective *authorship*," arguing that the activities of some "significant production roles" are "directed by—or facilitating those activities directed by—the intention of others." Those individuals are therefore not authors. Instead, Mag Uidhir proposes a criterion for "minimal authorship":

> Assume *comic* to be an author-relevant work-description. From this, we get the following:

> > A work *w* is a comic if and only if *w* possesses the features in *C* where *C* is the set of all and only those features essential for being a comic.

> And from this:

> > Someone is the author of *w* as a comic if and only if that someone is directly responsible, at least in part, for *w*'s possession of the features in *C*.

> Further specified by the following:

> > For someone to be directly responsible, at least in part, for *w*'s possession of the features in *C* is for the intentions of that someone to substantively figure in *w*'s possession of at least one of the features in *C*. (54–55)

So someone is the author of a comic if and only if her intentions substantively figure in at least one essential feature of its being a comic. But what count as "substantively" figuring and an "essential" feature?

Though Mag Uidhir's criterion is independent of any specific definition of comics, he applies McCloud's: "juxtaposed pictorial and other images in deliberate sequence intended to convey information and/or produce an aesthetic response in the reader" (9). As a result, letterers and colorists are not authors because comics require neither words nor colors. The application of McCloud also eliminates all conceptual writing because plot and story don't by themselves include juxtaposed images. Pablo Marcos is excluded as well because, though inks are an element of the juxtaposed images, authorial intentionality is limited to the deliberate sequencing of the images. Only Wenzel's,

Byrne's, or Pérez's penciled layouts create the sequence. If Shooter's script includes panel-by-panel descriptions, then Shooter may also be an author. But, by the Mag Uidhir–McCloud definition, Stan Lee wouldn't be an author of any comics. He contributed plot ideas and later words, but his intentionality didn't substantively figure in any feature essential to the comics' form.

Comic book scholar Arlen Schumer applies auteur film theory to draw similar conclusions: "By dint of the act of directing a film, and drawing a comic book story, the director and the artist are the true authors/auteurs of their respective final product" (477). This might please Kirby advocates, but, as Schumer acknowledges, the parallel collapses when a writer is the author "who does the visualizing of a comic book story" (478). Though Schumer designates not artist Dave Gibbons but writer Alan Moore as auteur of *Watchmen* due to Moore's notoriously detailed panel descriptions, the majority of comic book scripts include visualization and explicit directions for sequential layout, criteria that could give most writers auteur status. Grant Morrison seems especially deserving, yet his revered *Arkham Asylum* would be disqualified. Editor Karen Berger explains in an afterword: "Grant's script was not broken down like a traditional page-by-page comic book script, but more like a shooting script for a film, allowing Dave [McKean] the freedom to gauge the pacing and to bring his own interpretation to the story" (unpaginated). Though Morrison is credited as writer and McKean as illustrator, according to Mag Uidhir and Schumer, Morrison is no author at all.

There's a shared, major problem with Mag Uidhir's and Schumer's views. Because Mag Uidhir excludes all contributions except those essential to a work being a comic, while Schumer simply identifies drawing with authoring, each is too limiting. Applied to songwriting, Mag Uidhir and Schumer would have to conclude that no lyricist authors any song with a composer because songs don't require lyrics (Mag Uidhir) and because lyrics correlate with words rather than images in comics (Schumer). Applied to film, a screenwriter who contributes only dialog to a script doesn't function in any authorial role either because films don't require dialog (Mag Uidhir), or because writing dialog, since it's not like directing, doesn't function authorially itself (Schumer).

As far as potentially helping us understand the single voice of superhero comics, Mag Uidhir's and Schumer's views don't reduce the number of authors to one. In the case of *The Avengers*, each still leaves a plurality of authors. Yet there is something misleading about putting things that way. Though *The Avengers* would have some plurality of people counting in some manner as authors, those people speak in a singular voice. Each one's contribution is part of a unit. Each isn't a *co*-author but herself part of a group, or pluralistic, author, functioning as a unit.

Such group authorship isn't unique to comics. Most art falls somewhere on a range from one to many contributors functioning together. Novels typically have writers, editors, and book designers—and sometimes assistants, researchers, and uncredited ghostwriters. We generally identify only the credited writer as the author, but that's merely convention. Sculptures often have those who draft the design, quarry the raw material, divide that material into usable sizes, do the detailed chiseling, and smooth and polish—among other categories of artistic assistants. We generally take the overseeing chiseler as the creator, when the others sometimes had as much of a hand. Of course, some art forms are less pluralistic in authorship. But, though comics stand at the larger end of that range, their contributors function as a single unit—and in that sense a single author—just as much as other art forms do, producing a coherent whole.

Comic book readers don't usually treat comics as if they have multiple people counting as authors either. They treat the full cast of contributors as functioning as a single author. And well they should, since that's how the cast functions. Though the precise number of authors of any particular comic might be difficult to determine, together they speak univocally. Consider *Avengers* #174. The opening splash page is a unified whole: Iron Man, Hawkeye, Thor, and the Wasp stand before the supervillain The Collector, each shouting dialog appearing in talk balloons integrated into the full-page composition. Though Jim Shooter presumably communicated plot ideas to Bill Mantlo, who developed them into a typed script which Dave Wenzel sketched into layouts, none of their contributions is directly present. Whether Shooter communicated to Mantlo verbally or in writing, no document of his plot ideas remains. Mantlo's script is also unavailable, as are Wenzel's layouts, since Marcos literally inked over them, eventually erasing any of Wenzel's remaining pencil marks. Only two kinds of lines appear on the finalized pages: Marco's lines and Shelly Leferman's lettering. Even Phil Rachelson, whose color separations would have been executed by multiple freelance assistants, is only indirectly present, though his color design dominates the finalized pages too.

Each contribution to a comic combines interdependence and autonomy. Though inking requires pencils, inkers don't merely trace pencil marks. They create precise lines from vaguer markings, adding and eliminating details at will. Though pencilers work from scripts, pencilers don't merely obey script dictation. They actualize images based on inherently imprecise language, inventing details by necessity (as we demonstrated in chapter 7 when describing how Mark Buckingham drew Neil Gaiman's *Miracleman* script). Likewise, a scripter must shape into particular panel and page specifications the formless story ideas of a plot. Finally, though an editor oversees each step, each contributor acts within a range of freedom, with no single or even multiple contributors maintaining authorial control across the disparate roles. Yet the final, integrated product appears as if composed by a single author.

Given all this, the form in which superhero comics tells their stories encourages us to conclude that many who contribute to the creation of a particular comic book count collectively as a pluralistic author. Such an author functions as an individual, and so functionally *is* an individual, even though that author is composed of individual people as parts. This, however, presents a challenge.

Intentional Author

A pluralistic author of a comic book uses words and images to tell a story. With them, the pluralistic author desires to achieve certain goals. These are intentional activities. They involve expressing and possessing semantic content, so those performing these activities themselves have intentionality. Indeed, Mag Uidhir, in his criterion of minimal authorship, contends that someone is the author of a comic if and only if her intentions feature in at least one essential aspect of its being a comic. So he too recognizes the role of intentions and thus intentionality. Normally, though, individuals are thought of as having intentionality. Mag Uidhir likely had individuals in mind also. A pluralistic author, though acting as an individual, is ultimately a plurality. This leads us to refine our "What if?":

What if a plurality had intentionality?

We see two ways that this could work. One is that a pluralistic author has *plural* intentionality. Each member of that plurality has her own intentionality, and the plurality's intentionality is the total. The other way is that a pluralistic author somehow has *singular* intentionality. Though each member retains her own intentionality, the author, who happens to be pluralistic, also has intentionality as any individual author would. Such pluralistic intentionality is often called "collective," a phrase coined by philosopher John Searle in his 1990 "Collective Intentions and Actions."

Though the first way might seem intuitive, it faces problems. Since each individual member of a pluralistic author has her own intentionality, it's unclear how such individual intentionalities "total" into the plurality's intentionality. Besides having different functions, each member of a pluralistic author has different thoughts that might lead to different actions. Some of these might be complementary, but others could be contradictory, incommensurate, or irrelevant. Pencilers may disregard script directives. *Deathlok* writer Dwayne McDuffie reports that Denys Cowan "felt free to alter my panel breakdowns and shot descriptions whenever he had a better idea" (28). Inkers may ignore pencil lines that do not suit their own preferences. Eric Shanower routinely added details—to Curt Swan's penciled cover for *The Legend of Aquaman* #1 (1989), for example—while Vince Colletta was notorious for eliminating them. If "totaling" means something like aggregating, then all of these individual intentionalities, regardless of how they relate, would be added one on top of the other. But then no coherent intentionality would result. Since a comic book is coherent, this kind of "totaling" doesn't account for the impression of singular, authorial intention.

These are reasons to support the second way in which a plurality could have intentionality. The pluralistic author has singular intentionality. Comics still have writers, scripters, plotters, pencilers, inkers, and so on. But this decomposition is explanatorily second. When understanding a comic book as an art form, the starting point should be how it's intended to be read, which is how it normally is read: as a unified whole. So superhero comics foist on us the thought experiment of explaining how all members of a comic's pluralistic author can collectively contribute in one voice like one author.

How can a pluralistic author have singular intentionality? While Plato just assumes that a city and an individual can speak with a single voice, Dennett proposes his "intentional stance" to explain how any object can speak, write, depict, or otherwise express or possess meaning. Such an object would then have intentionality. In Plato's parlance, it would have a "soul," while, for Dennett, it would have a "mind." Dennett doesn't analyze literary authorship. He doesn't adopt the intentional stance to objects whose parts have their own intentionality, but his strategy still explains how anything—including a pluralistic author—can have singular intentionality. We apply it in the next section.

Predictable Author

Dennett has discussed the intentional stance in nearly every major work (at least) through his 2014 *Intuition Pumps and Other Tools for Thinking*. Perhaps its fullest description appears in his 1981 "True Believers"—the very phrase Stan Lee uses to address his readers. Dennett argues that there are three interpretive perspectives: (a) the physical stance interprets behavior in terms of the mechanistic laws of the physical sciences; (b) the design stance interprets behavior by assuming that the behavior results from some design, because the object was created (by a human being) or evolved (through natural selection) to perform particular functions; and (c) the intentional stance interprets behavior by assuming that the behavior results from rationality, because the object has intentional states like beliefs and desires. As Dennett explains in his 1973 "Intentional Systems": "Rationality is the mother of intention" (19).

To illustrate Dennett's perspectives, consider this thought experiment:

> A meteorite is headed toward Earth. Superman wants to predict where it will land so he can prevent anyone from being injured. Which perspective should he adopt?

If he used the intentional stance and assumed the meteorite has beliefs and desires, then his prediction would be both inefficient, because it would needlessly complicate matters, and probably also inaccurate, because it would ignore physical laws. Superman could instead adopt the design stance and assume the meteorite has an agent-given or natural-given purpose. This too would complicate matters and ignore physical laws, again sacrificing efficiency and accuracy. Finally, he could adopt the physical stance and so, using facts about the meteorite as an object obeying various laws of motion, compute where it will land. Because adopting the physical stance is the most efficient and accurate way to predict the meteorite's impact, Superman should adopt it.

Because the physical stance is not always the best choice, next consider another thought experiment:

> The Joker has rigged a bomb to explode in the heart of Gotham City. Batman finds it and wants to predict when it will explode so that he knows how much time he has to defuse it.

Adopting the intentional stance and saying that the bomb "desires" to detonate at a certain time wouldn't make Batman's prediction efficient or accurate.

He could instead adopt the physical stance, understanding the bomb as having gears that turn and wires that electrons flow through, but then he couldn't analyze how the bomb functions as a whole. Adopting the physical stance might make Batman's prediction more accurate than the intentional stance, but any increased accuracy would be offset by decreased efficiency. Batman should instead adopt the design stance and assume that the bomb is designed to detonate at a certain time and simply to read its display.

To understand when the intentional stance is best, consider a final thought experiment:

> The Vision is playing chess with the Scarlet Witch. To win, he needs to keep predicting her next moves.

He could adopt the physical stance and apply laws of the physical sciences to her. But thinking about her muscles, eyeballs, and central nervous system wouldn't help him much, since he'd have to understand all these mechanistically, without appealing to their functions. So he could adopt the design stance instead, perhaps seeing human beings as having overall function—to eat, grow, perceive, locomote, and reason—as Aristotle did in the *De Anima*. But even if the Vision could settle on a list of human functions, he would be treating the Scarlet Witch like Batman's bomb. Being designed to eat, grow, perceive, or locomote doesn't explain why a human being might want to eat at only certain times, let alone what the Scarlet Witch will do on her next chess move. It doesn't even understand her as a chess player—someone who is selecting moves for specific reasons. That requires seeing her as having beliefs and desires, which requires understanding her as rational. While doing so risks accuracy—people aren't always rational—the increase in efficiency is so tremendous, the Vision would be irrational not to adopt the intentional stance.

Dennett explains how:

> First you decide to treat the object whose behavior is to be predicted as a rational agent; then you figure out what beliefs that agent ought to have, given its place in the world and its purpose. Then you figure out what desires it ought to have, on the same considerations, and finally you predict that this rational agent will act to further its goals in the light of its beliefs. A little practical reasoning from the chosen set of beliefs and desires will in most instances yield a decision about what the agent ought to do; that is what you predict the agent will do. (17)

Dennett admits that you need to engage in "a little practical reasoning" to make it all work, but no other stance would work as well for the Vision.

Also, no other stance would work as well for the Scarlet Witch when predicting the Vision's moves—even though the Vision isn't a human being. He's an android, a machine only designed to be like a human being. But the design stance isn't specific enough to interpret something with intentionality, regardless of whether or not it's human. In his 1996 *Kinds of Minds*, Dennett explains:

> There are hundreds of different computer programs that can turn a computer [. . .] into a chess player. For all their differences at the physical level and the design level, these computers all succumb neatly to the same simple strategy of interpretation: just think of them as rational agents who *want* to win, and who *know* the rules and principles of chess and the positions of the pieces on the board. Instantly your problem of predicting and interpreting their behavior is made vastly easier than it would be if you tried to use the physical or the design stance. At any moment in the chess game, simply look at the chessboard and draw up a list of all the legal moves available to the computer when it is its turn to play. [. . .] Now rank the legal moves from best (wisest, most rational) to worst (stupidest, most self-defeating) and make your prediction: the computer will make the best move. You may well not be sure what the best move *is* (the computer may "appreciate" the situation better than you do!), but you can almost always eliminate all but four or five candidate moves, which still gives you tremendous predictive leverage. (30–31)

Adopting the intentional stance toward the chess-playing computer makes the most predictive sense because the trade-off between efficiency and accuracy is positive.

Adopting the intentional stance helps with explanation too. That's because prediction and explanation are related. Predictions make sense of behavior that hasn't yet occurred, by showing what behavior would fit a pattern. Explanations make sense of behavior that has already occurred, by showing that it does fit a pattern. We should interpret a pluralistic author of a comic book as having intentionality only if adopting the intentional stance increases our predictive *and* explanatory power without hurting accuracy.

Does it?

Recall *Avengers* #174. The narration, dialog, imagery, and layout combine

From *Avengers* #174.

into a unified narrative. It's as if each word and picture is drawn by a single hand controlled by a single mind wishing to tell a single story about a team of superhuman heroes battling a supervillain. We would explain, for example, that Hercules's posture is one of shock at the sudden death of the Collector by a powerful but unknown being known only as the "Enemy," a shock simultaneously communicated by the content of his expressively lettered talk balloon: "By the silver bow of Apollo!" (29). We would also understand his diction to reflect his Olympian upbringing. More basically, we would understand the figure to be Hercules because of its identifying shapes and colors, a highly predictable pattern of ink marks repeated from multiple previous appearances and one that we predict will be repeated multiple times more. Above all, we would understand everything as elements of a seamless whole.

Admittedly, a reader could still analyze *Avengers* #174 according to the individual roles of its contributors. We could understand pen lines according to the inker's intentionality in relation to the absent but implied pencil lines which we would interpolate to reflect the intentionality of the penciler. Did Marcos accentuate Hercules's shocked posture, selecting his personal preference from the range of available postures contained in Wenzel's more loosely defined penciling? Other inkers might have drawn Hercules's forearm slightly thinner or thicker, and his elbow joint rounder or more angular. But when we analyze the comic this way, the coherent whole vanishes. Instead of reading a story, we're dissecting the process of its creation. While such analysis has its virtues, adopting the intentional stance toward the pluralistic author makes the most explanatory sense of the comic book as a unified story told through words and images.

Real Author

So far, we've argued that collectively many contributors to a comic book should be understood as a singular author with singular intentionality. Maybe this isn't so surprising. From a legal point of view, a corporation too is a singular person with singular intentionality. Comic book contributors wouldn't necessarily be any different, especially given that both Marvel and DC are corporations.

But that's legally. We mean our claim literally. There really—literally—is a single author of *The Avengers* with beliefs and desires. For Dennett, that's analogous to there really being a single human mind in any one head, even though it's a "a huge, semi-designed, self-redesigning amalgam of smaller machines," including neurons, and a single chess-playing computer on any one desk, even though it's a complex, fully designed amalgam of smaller machines, including circuits. Though Dennett's examples include machines whose parts don't have intentionality, while a pluralistic author would be a machine (in Dennett's sense) whose parts do, they are all really singular with singular intentionality. And what allows the parts of a pluralistic author—that is, its individual contributors—to have intentionality (while the parts of a single human mind and single chess-playing computer don't) is what makes all these pluralities have singular intentionality. Balancing efficiency against accuracy, it makes the most sense to adopt the intentional stance to explain their behavior as a whole.

Dennett does argue that adopting the stance requires our *assuming* that the object whose behavior we're predicting is rational. That makes Dennett sound like he might believe that intentionality and rationally are both useful fictions that help us make predictions. But, as he explains in his 1991 "Real Patterns," adopting the intentional stance works because it detects patterns in behavior that are really there. These intentional patterns are not detectable *as* patterns from the physical or design stances, though their parts would be detectable as parts of mechanistically physical and designed objects. For Dennett, Superman's meteorite really doesn't have intentionality because there really isn't any intentional pattern that adopting the intentional stance reveals. Batman's bomb really doesn't have intentionality because in that case there really isn't any intentional pattern that adopting the intentional stance reveals. But the Scarlet Witch *and* an actual chess-playing computer really do have intentionality because there really are intentional patterns that adopting the intentional stance reveals.

Likewise, as readers of comic books, we identify patterns in their words and images. There really are individual intentions coming from multiple authors. As readers who are also subjects in our own thought experiment, we automatically take the plurality of authors of a comic as a single, pluralistic author with singular intentionality. In "True Believers," Dennett explains: "*What it is* to be a true believer is to be an *intentional system*, a system whose behavior is reliably and voluminously predictable via the intentional strategy" (15). An individual mind, a chess-playing computer, and a pluralistic author are each a "true believer." Each has the patterns of behavior to prove it. Applying Dennett to comics explains why we read their singular yet pluralistic authors, like the readers Stan Lee addressed in his monthly columns, as True Believers.

CONCLUSION

"COMICO, ERGO SUM!"

Like the characters that they feature, superhero comics are powerful. That's partly because they're culturally pervasive. DC and Marvel have each published over thirty thousand comic book issues in the last eight decades, some selling millions of copies. Recently the market has shrunk, so hits of the last decade reach only a quarter million. But superhero comics continue to exercise their power through TV and Hollywood franchises. *Wonder Woman* and the *Avengers* movies each have held top-ten film slots for biggest moneymakers, and we can expect more of the same.

But superhero comics aren't just financially and culturally powerful. They're philosophically powerful too. They are an especially immersive genre, able to communicate thought experiments often better than academic philosophy. When we're caught up in their stories, we're caught up with their ideas—and those ideas stay with us in ways that only narratives can. That's why they're so good at philosophy. Philosophy-trained comic book scholar James McLaughlin rhetorically asks, "Should comic books, especially the mainstream American superhero comic books that most people are familiar with, be taken seriously?" (364). To answer yes, he describes their philosophical content: "When other planets are explored, or when the hero travels back or forward in time, or when worlds upon worlds are invented, there is metaphysics and epistemology and logic. Comic books can't help but be philosophical" (365). Superhero comics also have an especially distinctive form. As a medium, they are their own philosophical thought experiments, posing puzzles that put philosophy on the spot. We look back now at the thought experiments in this book to draw further connections and determine what lessons superhero comics impart.

Content

As we've seen, philosophers, especially the analytic ones dominating the English-speaking academic world, analyze concepts and define terms. They often introduce thought experiments with these ends in mind. When it comes to describing those thought experiments, though, superhero comics have the upper hand.

Instead of abstractly pitting consequentialism against deontology, comics pit—or, in this case, invite *us* to pit—Superman against Batman. While academic philosophers speak obliquely about Moral Twin Earth, comics fill in the details of worlds like Bizarro's and Earths-1, -2, and -3. Though Descartes's skepticism is intellectually gripping, the comic book depiction of Captain America saying goodbye to a pocket-universe Bucky is emotionally fraught. Rather than simply comparing and contrasting eternalism and presentism about time, Marvel showcases the adventures involving Dr. Doom's time machine, vividly illustrating those views. We all change our minds and what we mean by our words, but when comics retcon, reboot, and multiverse their stories we can concretely experience what proper names mean—and why different views of those names matter. Though Donald Davidson can debate with other academic philosophers and even himself whether history or interpretability is more important when it comes to meaning, considering the adventures of various swampthings better illustrates what's at stake.

In each case the superhero comic book scenario moves us to imagine the content of what's being communicated. Rather than merely tracking lifeless principles or desiccated descriptions, we imagine flesh-and-blood characters interacting in fulsome landscapes, cityscapes, spacescapes, and beyond, then imaginatively experience those ourselves. The content of a superhero story becomes *our* content. We live it while we read it. Reading about Superman might persuade us that consequentialism is the superior moral code. Reading about Reed Richards might convince us that time is eternalist. These comics invite us *into* their worlds, experiencing them from the inside—interacting with superheroes as they perform their superdeeds. Academic philosophers, for all their analytic powers, don't.

Of course, as we explained in the introduction, there is a trade-off in switching from academic philosophy to comics when looking for thought experiments. Though their descriptions are less vivid, academic philosophical ones are more controlled. When Kant tests his deontological view against promising falsely, he tells us exactly what's relevant to note (one's intention) and blocks out what's not (its consequences). There are no other details—the color of Superman's cape, the height of the buildings he leaps, the implausibility of disguising himself with a pair of glasses—that matter. When Davidson asks whether the content of our thoughts depends on the history of our worldly interactions, he's explicit that when we read about Swampman's actions, that's what we're to watch for. We're not supposed to get distracted about how it's "entirely by coincidence" that the same lightning strike that produces Swampman just happens to kill Davidson too. While such a coincidence raises questions that comic book readers might ask, philosophers just accept it and move on.

Superhero comics therefore express philosophy powerfully in some ways but not as carefully in others. Philosophical views about proper names are as dry as academic philosophy can be. Comparing Marvel's retconning of Donald Blake with DC's rebooting of Wonder Woman contrasts referentialism and descriptivism better than standard academic examples do because they add more detail. But their ensuing multiverses muddy the waters with narratives whose lessons need working out. While it's clear that Gargunza is deceiving Miracleman by making him think that he's awake when really he's asleep, it's unclear from descriptions of Earth-o, Earth-1, and Earth-2 whether superhero morality is relative or absolute. Though philosophers such as Terence Horgan and Mark Timmons wouldn't want to leave a thought experiment that philosophically ambiguous, comic book creators such as Gardner Fox have other priorities.

Form

In the first six chapters of this book, we considered thought experiments concerning comic book content. There comic book characters were part of the thought experiment. In the last two, we considered thought experiments concerning their form. Here we found comic book readers to be active participants.

In the foreword to *The Art of Comics*, Warren Ellis writes: "Comics are a strange beast. [. . .] Comics take things from all other art-forms and sew them together into a weird hybrid animal" (xiii). Whether or not *all* other art forms are involved, it is striking how comics use both words and images sequentially to tell stories to its readers. That alone sets them apart from most forms of art and communication. We suggested that H. Paul Grice's analysis of implicature can be applied to both words and images. Context determines whether an image is depicting something conventionally or conversationally. Comic book artists, as much as writers, generally follow Grice's Cooperative Principle—respecting Quantity, Quality, Relation, and Manner (and ultimately the aesthetic norm of naturalism) when they depict things. Sometimes, however, their images flout the principle and its maxims altogether, and depict nothing at all.

That in turn raises the question of which writers and artists—and pencilers, inkers, colorists, and letterers—count as a comic book author. Superhero comics in particular are team products, with each producer's creative contribution not always clearly defined. Trying to make sense of authorship, we concluded that readers should regard the team as a whole that's responsible. Borrowing from Daniel Dennett's work on the intentional stance, we explained how a pluralistic author could also be singular. The team of comic book producers is like the individual elements of the human mind. Strange as it might sound, that plural yet singular author believes, desires, and intends things as much any individual human being does. Though comic book readers might not put things this way, it's the result that reading superhero comics as thought experiments suggests.

Form vs. Content

So far we've been assuming that using philosophy to study the content of superhero comics and using it to study the form are distinct. A lot of times they are—but not always. Some deny that form and content themselves neatly separate. Aristotle held that we could distinguish form from content only in thought but never in fact. Willard van Orman Quine argued that the formal aspects of language and the experiential aspects of content are always intermixed. Aristotle and Quine might not be right—the philosophical jury is still out—but their instinct to show how form and content interact is on the mark.

Adopting Dennett's intentional stance, we can say that *each* comic book that we've discussed is created by an individual author who happens to be composed of a plurality of different people. Each of these individual, even if pluralistic, authors has beliefs and desires as much any other individual author would. We *should* say that because it makes good predictive and explanatory sense—even if we should also treat the particular people who comprise the pluralistic author as particular human beings too.

Because individual yet pluralistic authors have beliefs and desires that are sometimes philosophical, we might also describe each individual yet pluralistic author as a philosopher creating her own thought experiment, whose content we examined (much as we could describe the individual yet pluralistic author of this book, "Gavaler-Goldberg," as one). Though the particular scripters and inkers and editors who contribute to each comic book may have no intention to grapple with philosophical issues, as a collective they do. Together they're a single philosopher because adopting the intentional stance toward their stories reveals philosophical beliefs and desires as well as intentions of communicating them. Since philosophers trade in thought experiments, and superhero comic book authors, understood as singular, intentional beings, are philosophers, they trade in thought experiments too. Since such author-philosophers produce only superhero comics, their philosophical positions are contained in them. That's why we can treat superhero comics as containing thought experiments in the first place.

Applying our notions of conventional and conversational depiction, based on Grice's notions of conventional and conversational implicature, we can then explain how superhero comics do depict things with their images. Images are typically the result of four human beings—a scripter, penciler, inker, and colorist—all of whom, along with other contributors to the comic, count collectively as a singular, pluralistic author. Each image is itself the product of such an author. It's individuals who express conventional and conversational implicatures, according to Grice. Likewise, it's individuals (who may be pluralistic) who express conventional and conversational depictions, according to us. So appealing to our Gricean understanding of comic book form allows us to explain how comics communicate the particular thought experiments that they do in their content. When they don't communicate anything—as when the initially bumpy-skinned Thing or Spider-Man's sometimes-purple costume or Superman's juvenile delinquents transform for no inferable reason—the intentional stance fails to explain the beliefs of a pluralistic author. There's then no thought experiment or anything else meaningful. But that's because the author doesn't have any clear beliefs to explain.

More often, however, superhero comics' pluralistic authors do communicate. To introduce worries about skepticism, the pluralistic author of *Miracleman* communicates the existence of two worlds, the real one and an induced dream, by rendering each in a different artistic style—just as the pluralistic author of *The Avengers* communicates the new god Michael's ability to destroy and reconstruct an identical Starhawk by drawing both versions of Starhawk in the same style. These pluralistic authors may also be understood as implicitly communicating a commitment to one philosophical view rather than another. The pluralistic author of *Wonder Woman* arguably does so with descriptivism by rendering the rebooted Diana character in a style different from the styles of the previous character of the same name, while the pluralistic author of *The Mighty Thor* arguably does the same with referentialism by communicating the consistency of the retconned Donald Blake through a single style.

We might even extend the intentional stance, and account of conventional and conversational depiction, to an entire publishing house. While we say that Marvel writers' philosophical understanding of time changes, we could instead say that Marvel's own understanding changes—adopting the intentional stance toward Marvel as a whole. When we explain this by describing how Marvel comic book images depict this change, we're applying our Grice-inspired analysis to the same. Marvel initially treats time as eternal by (among other things) depicting a time traveler standing in two time periods simultaneously. That's what the publishing house, as an individual, communicates.

Putting Grice aside, is adopting the intentional stance toward creative teams and publishing houses by treating them as individuals truly helpful in predicting and explaining their behavior? Maybe it's just accidental—the coincidental product of personal histories and interactions—that a comic communicates a particular thought experiment. Luck would have it that writers, artists, scripters, pencilers, and all the rest converge on a philosophical theme. In that case, maybe only when we have overt examples of philosophical influence—when, say, we know that Alan Moore read continental philosophy while writing about Swamp Thing—should we argue that a comic book is philosophical at all. But this would be like adopting the physical stance toward a ticking bomb. While the components of the bomb do follow physical laws, it's unlikely that we'll trace them all in time. Just assume that the bomb was designed to go off when its display says it will, and adjust accordingly as needed. It would also be like adopting the design stance toward a computer chess game. Knowing that the game was created by engineers isn't in itself enough for us to anticipate what moves the computer will make. We need to think that *it* will make them, and that requires trying to figure out (as any of us would do) which move is the best.

Even in the case of Moore, we can't be sure that he knew, let alone intended to express, issues about thought and meaning similar to those that Davidson explores in his own swamp creature thought experiment. But adopting the intentional stance toward the pluralistic author of *Saga of the Swamp Thing* is the best way to explain how the comic expresses a coherent story generally and even to predict pages ahead of time where that story might go. For Dennett, that's enough to make the pluralistic author not only a single author but also a philosopher.

Yet maybe this seems circular. Reading a comic book as if it were a thought experiment written by a philosopher apparently means that the comic book *is* a thought experiment written by a philosopher. That seems to give a reader extraordinary superpower. Like Wonder Woman's mother fashioning her from inanimate clay, or Odin conjuring the identity of Donald Blake from nothing, the reader calls the philosopher into being. But not from inanimate nothing. A reader adopts the intentional stance because the independent qualities of a comic book reward that stance with predictive and explanatory success. It picks up on patterns of behavior that are already there—patterns that can't be seen from the purely physical or design level. This is the same justification for adopting the intentional stance toward anyone. Like Descartes, we may each run the Cogito to determine that "I" exists. But everyone else's thoughts—including those of the pluralistic minded author of a comic book—must be inferred from their behavior. Since the behavior of a comic book author is the creation of a comic book, from the reader's perspective a singular, pluralistic author exists. It's as if that author is saying: "Comico, ergo sum!" And it's as if we're interacting with the thought experiment that is the author herself.

Philosophical and Superhero Comic Book Lessons

As we explained in the introduction, this is a book that uses superhero comics to illustrate philosophical thought experiments, and then uses philosophy to explain superhero comics. In closing we'd like to draw out seven philosophical and superhero comic book lessons.

First, philosophers of all kinds are more common than people realize. We've mentioned a couple of ancient Greek philosophers, Plato and Aristotle. We've talked about a few later historical philosophers, including seventeenth-century René Descartes, eighteenth-century Immanuel Kant, and nineteenth-century John Stuart Mill. We've also discussed several twentieth- and twenty-first-century philosophers, focusing on Terence Horgan and Mark Timmons,

Donald Davidson, H. Paul Grice, and Daniel Dennett. Besides the authors of individual comics and series, we now add to their ranks twentieth- and twenty-first-century philosophers DC and Marvel.

Second, academic philosophers in particular shouldn't hesitate to turn to superhero comics for thought experiments when working on academic philosophy. This runs against all but the most recent trends. Aaron Meskin writes:

> Comics have been among the most denigrated of the popular arts—a largely disposable art thought to appeal primarily to children and/or the so-called lowest common denominator. This, combined with philosophical aesthetics' tendency to concern itself with the fine or "high" arts, is surely part of the explanation for the neglect of comics. ("The Philosophy of Comics" 854–55)

Yet, Meskin continues, comics are not a low art—a category distinction increasingly dismissed by twenty-first-century critics. Meskin himself acknowledges the auteur excellence of Art Spiegelman's *Maus* and George Herriman's *Krazy Kat* ("The Art of Comics" xxiii). While the philosophers who are DC and Marvel champion the non-auteur works of the superhero subgenre, this is where some of the most absorbing thought experiments are found. Davidson describes the qualities of Swampman in a single prose paragraph, while Moore explores the myriad and evolving qualities of Swamp Thing in a multiyear comic book series. Admittedly, comic book authors don't treat their scenarios explicitly as thought experiments, examine the assumptions involved, or draw lessons from them. But academic philosophers might. Why shouldn't they focus their analytical skills on these more fully developed stories?

Third, we've merely skirted the edges of what the philosophy of comics itself looks like by imaging ourselves as subjects in one big comic book thought experiment. While others have done more work in the philosophy of comics, some topics haven't even been touched. How much time, if any, can pass in a static image? Do superheroes look like their drawings, and, if so, do they change when different artists draw them differently? If the words in caption boxes are spoken by third-person, omniscient narrators, are the images inside panels drawn by third-person, omniscient narrators too? We can start to address these by considering the reactions of readers to them. "The very idea of a philosophy of comics is sure to generate skepticism," wrote Meskin ("The Philosophy of Comics" 1), but that field now exists and should continue to grow. Sellars wrote: "The aim of philosophy, abstractly formulated, is to understand how things in the broadest possible sense of the term hang together in the broadest possible sense of the term," and comics, including the superhero kind, fall under "things in the broadest possible sense" (1).

Fourth, academic philosophers shouldn't just talk to other academic philosophers. They've got a role to play in explaining pop culture generally. Though superhero comic book scenarios are more vivid than academic thought experiments, they're also less worked out. Likewise, while the comic book medium itself embodies a thought experiment, comic book creators tend not to reflect on them. Not everyone should be a "pop" philosopher, but academic philosophers are trained to analyze things, and comic book content and form are worth analyzing—and not just for other academics, either.

Fifth, other scholars of popular culture should pay attention to the intersection between philosophy and comics too. Sometimes that intersection is intentional, as with Moore. Often it's not. Regardless, it's still worth investigating, especially since the intersection works in both ways. Davidson is not the first philosopher to use comic book tropes. Swampman was a response to Hilary Putnam's 1973 "Meaning and Reference," which included its own story about Putnam's identical counterpart on Twin Earth, a world which, as we discussed in chapter 2, is like the various alternate Earths popular at DC at that time. Likewise, in 1974, the year after Marvel premiered *Tales of the Zombie*, Robert Kirk infected philosophical debates with his own zombies, hypothetical creatures behaviorally indistinguishable from humans but lacking consciousness. Though we haven't found evidence of direct influence, these aren't historical coincidences either. Philosophers, like everyone else, absorb what's around them. Pop-culture ideas have a way of spreading across academic disciplines, including philosophy. That deserves further study.

Sixth, superhero comic book creators—the nonpluralistic, particular, human kind—might chat with academic philosophers. Moore did that, and others could too. There are so many concepts ripe for exploration in the fantastical universes of superheroes. In his 1952 "The Identity of Indiscernibles," philosopher Max Black asks whether two perfectly identical spheres—having the same height, weight, location, and every other property—can *be* two spheres rather than one. In his 1739–40 *A Treatise of Human Nature* and 1748 *An Enquiry concerning Human Understanding*, philosopher David Hume asks whether causes *have* to be followed by their effects, or whether there can be effects that aren't necessarily connected to their causes or even (Hume leaves us to ask) that move backward instead of forward in time. These are the sort of mind-bending abstractions that superhero comics are adept at making entertainingly concrete. Philosophers like asking these kinds of questions. Superhero comic book authors might answer them.

Finally, we offer the seventh lesson in the form of—what else?—a final superhero thought experiment:

> Let us tell you our own science fiction story—if that is what it is. Suppose a human being (you can imagine this to be yourself) has been subjected to a series of experiments in which her brain (your brain) has been forced to visualize worlds where fantastical beings—people who are stronger, smarter, more powerful than you—unmask morality, metaphysics, and meaning through extraordinary adventures. Imagine that these adventures, printed on real paper and held in your own hands, transport you to alternate realities where the hidden foundations of your own world are suddenly made manifest. The abstractions of consequence and duty take human form through tangible, cape-billowing action. You see for the first time deeper questions governing morality (superhero and otherwise) when the otherworldly mirror images of those now-tangible abstractions take bizarrely opposite actions. The principles of reality as a whole at first lull you into deceptive sleep until you declare, in your own voice, "I exist," only to worry that you might be the figment of someone else's dream. The principles of time in turn fly up and explain themselves to you in fantastic color. You watch heroes evolve and stories change, holding on for dear narrative life to their names, pondering what they mean. The swampy complexities of thought sprout new bodies, sometimes dependent on older ones, other times on things less strange and yet more radical.
>
> Then, as the pages in your hands continue to talk to you in the chatty voice of a friend, you focus on the medium itself. You ponder how words and images can both do the talking, and you wonder in what ways. Next you imagine all the hands that wrote those words and drew those images, so many that it's ridiculously complicated to count—until, ultimately, you see all those hands together collectively tightening in a grip as singular as your own. Finally you realize that that grip belongs to a True Believer like you. You've been the subject in a thought experiment.

WORKS CITED

If what we say in chapter 8 is right, then many contributors collectively constitute a single author. So each contributor should be listed either individually or collectively as author. Because that would make these citations confusing, we follow the common practice of citing the various kinds of writers as "writers," and then pencilers and inkers as "artists," and no one else. In cases where authors are both writers and artists, we cite them as "writer-artists." We list artists first if we discussed only them.

Abel, Jessica, and Matt Madden. *Drawing Words and Writing Pictures*. New York: First Second, 2008.

Alphona, Adrian, Jacob Wyatt (artists), and G. Willow Wilson (writer). *Ms. Marvel*. Vol. 2. New York: Marvel, 2015.

Aristotle. *De Anima: A New Aristotle Reader*. Ed. and trans. John L. Ackrill. Princeton, NJ: Princeton University Press, 1988.

———. *On Interpretation*. *Aristotle's Categories and De Interpretatione*. Clarendon Aristotle Series. Ed. and trans. John L. Ackrill. New York: Oxford University Press, 1961.

Backster, Cleve. "Evidence of a Primary Perception in Plant Life." *International Journal of Parapsychology* 10.4 (Winter 1968): 329–48.

Bendis, Brian Michael (writer), and Mark Bagley (artist). *The Mighty Avengers* #9 (April 2008), Marvel.

———. *The Mighty Avengers* #10 (May 2008), Marvel.

Berger, Karen. Afterword. *Batman: Arkham Asylum—the 25th Anniversary Edition*. New York: DC, 2014.

"Bizarro." DCComics.com. October 7, 2015.

Black, Max. "The Identity of Indiscernibles." *Mind* 61 (1952): 153–64.

Brennan, Joseph Payne. "Slime." *Nine Horrors and a Dream*. Sauk City, WI: Arkham House, 1958.

Brenner, George E. (writer-artist). "Murder by Proxy." *Supermen! The First Wave of Comic Book Heroes 1936–1941*. Ed. Greg Sadowski. Seattle: Fantagraphics Books, 2009.

Bright, M. D., Mike Gustovich (artists), and Dwayne McDuffie (writer). *Icon: A Hero's Welcome*. New York: DC, 1993.

Brown, Eliot (artist). Cover. *Amazing Spider-Man* #262 (March 1985), Marvel.

Byrne, John (writer-artist), and Mike Machlan (artist). *Avengers West Coast* #51 (November 1989), Marvel.

Byrne, John (writer-artist), Joe Sinnott (artist), and F. Mouly (colorist). *Marvel Two-in-One* #50 (April 1979), Marvel.

Byrne, John (writer), and Ron Wilson (artist). *Marvel Two-in-One* #100 (June 1983), Marvel.

Cameron, Ross P. "Improve Your Thought Experiments Overnight with Speculative Fiction!" *Midwest Studies in Philosophy* 39 (2015): 29–45.

Caplan, Ben. "Serial Fiction, Continued." *British Journal of Aesthetics* 54 (2014): 65–76.

Carney, James, Robin Dunbar, Anna Machin, Tamás Dávid-Barrett, and Mauro Silva Júnior. "Social Psychology and the Comic-Book Superhero: A Darwinian Approach." *Philosophy and Literature* 38 (2014): A195–A215.

Carrier, David. *The Aesthetics of Comics*. University Park: Penn State University Press, 2000.

Cawalti, John G. *Adventure, Mystery, and Romance: Formula Stories as Art and Popular Culture*. Chicago: University of Chicago Press, 1976.

Cohn, Neil. "The Limits of Time and Transitions: Challenges to Theories of Sequential Image Comprehension." *Studies in Comics* 1 (2010): 127–48.

———. *The Visual Language of Comics*. London: Bloomsbury, 2013.

Cohn, Neil, and Hannah Campbell. "Navigating Comics II: Constraints on the Reading Order of Page Layouts." *Applied Cognitive Psychology* 29 (2015): 193–99. visuallanguagelab.com. January 9, 2016.

Cole, Jack. "The Claw Battles Daredevil." *Supermen! The First Wave of Comic Book Heroes 1936–1941*. Ed. Greg Sadowski. Seattle: Fantagraphics Books, 2009.

"Comics Code Revision of 1971." CBLDF.org. Accessed February 16, 2019. http://cbldf.org/comics-code-revision-of-1971/.

Coogan, Peter. *Superhero: The Secret Origin of a Genre*. Austin, TX: Monkey Brain, 2006.

Cook, Roy T. "Drawings of Photographs in Comics." *Journal of Aesthetics and Art Criticism* 70 (Winter 2012): 129–38.

———. "Judging a Comic Book by Its Cover: Marvel Comics, Photo-covers, and the Objectivity of Photography." *Image and Narrative* 16.2 (2015): 14–27.

Cooke, Jon B., and George Khoury. "Born of the Bayou: Just What Makes a Swamp Creature?" *Swamp Things. Comic Book Creator* 6 (November 2014): 10–11.

Cottingham, John, ed. *Descartes' Conversations with Burman*. 1647. New York: Oxford University Press, 1976.

David, Peter (writer), Salvador Lorroca, and Scott Hanna (artists). *Heroes Reborn: The Return* #1 (1997), Marvel.

———. *Heroes Reborn: The Return* #2 (1997), Marvel.

———. *Heroes Reborn: The Return* #3 (1997), Marvel.

———. *Heroes Reborn: The Return* #4 (1997), Marvel.

Davidson, Donald. "Knowing One's Own Mind." 1987. *Subjective, Intersubjective, Objective.* New York: Oxford University Press, 2002. 15–38.

———. "Radical Interpretation." 1973. *Inquiries into Truth and Interpretation.* New York: Oxford University Press, 2001. 125–40.

De Smedt, Johan, and Helen De Cruz. "The Epistemic Value of Speculative Fiction." *Midwest Studies in Philosophy* 39 (2015): 58–77.

DeMatteis, J. M. (writer), Mike Zeck, and John Beatty. *Captain America* #287 (November 1983), Marvel.

Dennett, Daniel C. *Darwin's Dangerous Idea.* New York: Touchstone, 1995.

———. *Intuition Pumps and Other Tools for Thinking.* New York: Norton, 2014.

———. *Kinds of Minds.* New York: Basic Books, 1996.

———. "Real Patterns." 1991. *Brainchildren: Essays on Designing Minds.* Cambridge, MA: MIT Press, 1998. 95–120.

———. "True Believers." 1981. *The Intentional Stance.* Cambridge, MA: MIT Press, 1987. 37–42.

Descartes, René. *Meditations on First Philosophy.* 1641 Latin. 1647 French. 3rd ed. Trans. Donald A. Cress. Indianapolis: Hackett, 1993.

Ditko, Steve (artist), and Stan Lee (writer). *The Amazing Spider-Man* #23 (April 1965), Marvel.

———. *Marvel Masterworks: The Amazing Spider-Man.* New York: Marvel, 2009.

"Earth-3." DCComics.com. October 7, 2015.

Eco, Umberto. "The Myth of Superman." 1962. Trans. Natalie Chilton. *Diacritics* 2 (Spring 1972): 14–22.

Eisner, Will. *Comics and Sequential Art.* New York: Norton, 2008.

Ellis, Warren. Foreword. *The Art of Comics: A Philosophical Approach.* Ed. Aaron Meskin and Roy T. Cook. Malden, MA: Wiley-Blackwell, 2012. xii–xiii.

Englehart, Steve (writer), Richard Howell, and Jim Mooney (artists). *The Vision and the Scarlet Witch* #4 (January 1986), Marvel.

Erion, Gerald J., and Barry Smith. "Skepticism, Morality, and *The Matrix.*" *The Matrix and Philosophy: Welcome to the Desert of the Real.* Ed. William Irwin. Peru, IL: Open Court, 2002. 16–27.

Finger, Bill, Gardner Fox (writers), and Bob Kane (artist). *The Batman Chronicles.* Vol. 1. New York: DC, 2005.

Fingeroth, Danny. "Nobility of Purpose" *What Is a Superhero?* Ed. Robin S. Rosenberg and Peter Coogan. New York: Oxford University Press, 2013. 125–28.

Fox, Gardner (writer), and Mike Sekowsky (artist). *Justice League of America* #29 (August 1964), DC.

Frege, Friedrich Ludwig Gottlob. "On Sense and Reference." 1892. *The Philosophy of Language.* 6th ed. Ed. A. P. Martinich and David Sosa. New York: Oxford University Press, 2012. 35–47.

Frye, Northrop. "Comic Fictional Modes." *The Anatomy of Criticism*. Princeton, NJ: Princeton University Press, 1957. northropfrye-theanatomyofcriticism.blogspot .com. October 8, 2015.

Gaiman, Neil. "Miracle Man #17, Second Story." *Panel One: Comic Book Scripts by Top Writers*. Ed. Nat Gertler. Thousand Oaks, CA: About Comics, 2002.

Gaiman, Neil (writer), and Mark Buckingham (artist). *Miracleman* #17 (June 1990), Eclipse.

Gavaler, Chris. *On the Origin of Superheroes*. Iowa City: University of Iowa Press, 2015.

———. "Refining the Comics Form." *European Comic Art* 10.2 (2017): 1–23.

Gerber, Steve (writer). *Essential Defenders*. Vol. 2. New York: Marvel, 2006.

Gerber, Steve, Mary Skrenes (writers), and Jim Mooney (artist). *Omega: The Unknown Classic*. New York: Marvel, 2005.

Goldberg, Nathaniel. *Kantian Conceptual Geography*. New York: Oxford University Press, 2015.

Greenberger, Bob. "Of Ghostly Guardians and Resurrections." *The Spectre* #1 (April 1987), DC.

Grice, H. Paul. "Logic and Conversation." *Syntax and Semantics*. Vol. 3. Ed. Peter Cole and Jerry L. Morgan. New York: Academic Press, 1975. 41–58.

Groensteen, Thierry. *Comics and Narration*. Trans. Ann Miller. Jackson: University of Mississippi Press, 2011.

Groth, Gary. "Peer Pressure." *The Comics Journal Library*, vol. 1: *Jack Kirby*. Ed. Milo George. Seattle: Fantagraphics Books, 2002. 109–14.

Hart, Terry. "Marvel v. Kirby: Work for Hire and Copyright Termination." *Copyhype* August 3, 2011. Copyhype.com. December 7, 2015.

Hayman, Greg, and Henry John Pratt. "What Are Comics?" *A Reader in Philosophy of Arts*. Ed. David Goldblatt and Lee Brown. Upper Saddle River, NJ: Pearson Education, 2005. 419–24.

"hero." *Oxford English Dictionary Online*. Oxford University Press, June 2015. October 8, 2015.

Hopkins, Robert. "The Speaking Image: Visual Communication of the Nature of Depiction." *Contemporary Debates in Aesthetics and the Philosophy of Art*. Ed. Mathew Kieran. New York: Blackwell, 2005.

Horgan, Terence, and Mark Timmons. "Troubles for New Wave Moral Semantics: The 'Open Question Argument' Revived." *Philosophical Papers* 21 (1992): 153–75.

Howe, Sean. *Marvel Comics: The Untold Story*. New York: Harper, 2012.

Hume, David. *An Enquiry concerning Human Understanding*. 1748. Ed. Tom L. Beauchamp. New York: Oxford University Press, 1999.

———. *A Treatise of Human Nature*. 1739–40. Ed. David Fate Norton and Mary J. Norton. New York: Oxford University Press, 2000.

Ichikawa, Jonathan Jenkins, and Benjamin Jarvis. "Thought-Experiment Intuitions and Truth in Fiction." *Philosophical Studies* 142 (2009): 221–46.

James, William. "The Dilemma of Determinism." 1884. *The Will to Believe and Other Essays in Popular Philosophy*. Cambridge, MA: Harvard University Press, 1979.

Johnston, Rich. "Into the Unknown." *Comic Book Resources*. June 14, 2005. December 7, 2015.

———. "Secrets of the All-New All-Different Marvel Universe—Time Travel, Magic and Machines (Spoilers)." *Bleeding Cool*. January 7, 2016. bleedingcool.com. January 22, 2016.

Kant, Immanuel. *Groundwork of the Metaphysics of Morals*. 1785. Trans. Mary Gregory and Jens Timmermann. New York: Cambridge University Press, 2012.

Kelly, Stuart. "Alan Moore: 'Why shouldn't you have a bit of fun while dealing with the deepest issues of the mind?'" *Guardian*. November 22, 2012. January 9, 2016.

Kirby, Jack (artist). Cover. *Journey into Mystery* #83 (August 1962), Marvel.

Kirby, Jack, and Joe Simon (writer-artists). "Blue Bolt." *Supermen!* Ed. Greg Sadowski. Seattle: Fantagraphics Books, 2009.

Kripke, Saul. *Naming and Necessity*. 1970. Cambridge, MA: Harvard University Press, 2005.

———. *Reference and Existence*. 1973. New York: Oxford University Press, 2013.

Lee, Jim (writer-artist), Brandon Choi (writer), and Scott Williams (artist). *Fantastic Four 2*, #1 (November 1996), Marvel.

Lee, Stan. "More Than Normal, but Believable." *What Is a Superhero?* Ed. Robin S. Rosenberg and Peter Coogan. New York: Oxford University Press, 2013. 115–18.

———. "Synopsis: The Fantastic Four." *Marvel Firsts: The 1960s*. New York: Marvel, 2011.

Lee, Stan (writer), and Jack Kirby (artist). *Essential Fantastic Four*. Vol. 1. New York: Marvel, 2008.

———. "Thor the Mighty and the Stone Men from Saturn!" 1962. *Marvel Firsts: The 1960s*. New York: Marvel, 2011.

———. "Who Is the Real Don Blake? The Answer at Last!" 1968. *The Mighty Thor* #254 (December 1976), Marvel.

Lee, Stan, and Roy Thomas. "Stan the Man and Roy the Boy: A Conversation between Stan Lee and Roy Thomas." *Comic Book Artists* 2 (Summer 1998). TwoMorrows.com. December 7, 2015.

Lethem, Jonathan (writer), and Farel Dalrymple (artist). *Omega: The Unknown*. New York: Marvel, 2008.

Lewis, David. "The Paradoxes of Time Travel." *American Philosophical Quarterly* 13 (April 1976): 145–52.

Lobdell, Scott, and Mark Waid (writers), Adam Kubert, and Dan Green (artists). *Onslaught: Marvel* #1 (October 1996), Marvel.

Loeb, Jeph. "Making the World a Better Place." *What Is a Superhero?* Ed. Robin S. Rosenberg and Peter Coogan. New York: Oxford University Press, 2013. 119–24.

Mag Uidhir, Christy. "Comics and Collective Authorship." *The Art of Comics: A Philosophical Approach.* Ed. Aaron Meskin and Roy T. Cook. Malden, MA: Wiley-Blackwell, 2014. 47–67.

Mantlo, Bill (writer), Sal Buscema, and Mike Esposito (artists). *Marvel Team-Up #44* (April 1976), Marvel.

———. *Marvel Team-Up #45* (May 1976), Marvel.

Marston, William Moulton (writer), and Harry G. Peter (artist). "Wonder Woman Comes to America." 1941. *Wonder Woman: The Greatest Stories Ever Told.* New York: DC, 2001.

McCloud, Scott. *Understanding Comics: The Invisible Art.* New York: HarperCollins, 1993.

McDuffie, Dwayne. Foreword to "Deathlok #5 'Deus Ex Machina.' *Panel One: Comic Book Scripts by Top Writers.* Ed. Nat Gertler. Thousand Oaks, CA: About Comics, 2002.

McGonigal, Andrew. "Truth, Relativism, and Serial Fiction." *British Journal of Aesthetics* 53 (2013): 165–79.

McLaughlin, Jeff. "Comic Book Artists and Writers and Philosophers." *International Journal of Comic Art* 11 (2009): 364–71.

Meskin, Aaron. "The Art of Comics: An Introduction." *The Art of Comics: A Philosophical Approach.* Ed. Aaron Meskin and Roy T. Cook. Malden, MA: Wiley-Blackwell, 2014, xv–xlii.

———. "The Philosophy of Comics." *Philosophy Compass* 6 (2011): 854–64.

Michelinie, David (writer), and Bob Layton (writer-artist). *Iron Man #250* (December 1989), Marvel.

Michelinie, David (writer), Bob Layton (writer-artist), and John Romita Jr. (artist). *Iron Man #149* (August 1981), Marvel.

———. *Iron Man #150* (September 1981), Marvel.

Mill, John Stuart. *A System of Logic, Ratiocinative and Inductive: Being a Connected View of the Principles of Evidence and the Methods of Scientific Investigation.* 1843. New York: Cambridge University Press, 2001.

———. *Utilitarianism.* 1864. Indianapolis: Hackett, 2002.

Miller, Frank. *Batman: The Dark Knight Returns.* 1986. New York: DC, 1997.

"Miracleman Alias Marvelman." *Miracleman #1* (August 1985), Eclipse.

Moore, Alan. Interview by Jon B. Cooke and George Khoury. "The Saga of the Swamp God: The Tender, Unsettling Horrors of Alan Moore's Epic Tale of Swamp Thing and Abby." *Swamp Things. Comic Book Creator* 6 (November 2014): 132–49.

———. Interview by Heidi MacDonald. "A for Alan, Pt. 1: The Alan Moore Interview." *Beat.* March 16, 2006. January 10, 2016.

Moore, Alan (writer), Stephen Bissette, and John Totleben (artists). *Saga of the Swamp Thing*. New York: DC, 1987.

Moore, Alan (writer), and Alan Davis (artist). *Miracleman* #3 (November 1985), Eclipse.

———. *Miracleman* #4 (December 1985), Eclipse.

———. *Miracleman* #5 (January 1986), Eclipse.

Moore, Alan (writer), and Dave Gibbons (artist). *Watchmen*. New York: DC, 1987.

Moore, Alan (writer), and John Totleben (artist). *Miracleman* #12 (September 1987), Eclipse.

Moore, John Francis (writer), Anthony Castrillo, and Mark Pajahillo (artists). *X-Force* #64 (March 1997), Marvel.

Morris, Tom. "God, the Devil, and Matt Murdock." *Superheroes and Philosophy*. Ed. Tom Morris and Matt Morris. Peru, IL: Open Court, 2008. 45–61.

Morrison, Grant (writer), and Jim Lee (artist). *The Multiversity: Mastermen* #1 (April 2015), DC.

"Multiverse/Universe Listing." Marvel.wikia.com. January 22, 2016.

O'Neil, Dennis. *The DC Comics Guide to Writing Comics*. New York: Watson-Guptill, 2001.

Pérez, George (writer-artist), Len Wein (writer), and Bruce Patterson (artist). *Wonder Woman* #3 (April 1987), DC.

Plato. *Euthyphro*. *Plato: Complete Works*. Trans. G. M. A. Grube. Ed. John M. Cooper. Indianapolis: Hackett, 1997. 1–16.

———. *Republic*. *Plato: Complete Works*. Trans. G. M. A. Grube and C. D. C. Reeve. Ed. John M. Cooper. Indianapolis: Hackett, 1997. 971–1222.

Potter, Greg (writer), George Pérez (writer-artist), and Bruce Patterson (artist). *Wonder Woman* #1 (February 1987), DC.

Putnam, Hilary. "Meaning and Reference." 1973. *The Philosophy of Language*. 6th ed. Ed. A. P. Martinich and David Sosa. New York: Oxford University Press, 2012. 66–78.

———. *Reason, Truth, and History*. New York: Cambridge University Press, 1981.

"reboot." *Oxford English Dictionary Online*. Oxford University Press, June 2015. August 22, 2015.

"retcon." *Oxford English Dictionary Online*. Oxford University Press, June 2015. August 22, 2015.

"retroactive continuity." *Oxford English Dictionary Online*. Oxford University Press, June 2015. August 22, 2015.

Reynolds, Richard. *Super Heroes: A Modern Mythology*. Jackson: University Press of Mississippi, 1992.

Rice, Pierce. "The Origin of Thor." *Weird Comics* #1 (April 1940), Fox. Digital Comic Museum. digitalcomicsmuseum.com. August 21, 2015.

Richardson, Brian. *Unnatural Voices: Extreme Narration in Modern and Contemporary Fiction*. Columbus: Ohio State University Press, 2006.

Ross, William David. *The Right and the Good.* New York: Oxford University Press, 1930.

Russell, Bertrand. "Descriptions." 1919. *The Philosophy of Language.* 6th ed. Ed. A. P. Martinich and David Sosa. New York: Oxford University Press, 2012. 114–20.

———. "On Denoting." 1905. *The Philosophy of Language.* 6th ed. Ed. A. P. Martinich and David Sosa. New York: Oxford University Press, 2012. 105–13.

Schumer, Arlen. "The Auteur Theory of Comics." *Journal of International Comics Art* 14 (Spring 2012): 474–84.

Searle, John. "Collective Intentions and Actions." *Intentions in Communication.* Ed. Philip R. Cohen, Jerry Morgan, and Martha E. Pollack. Cambridge, MA: MIT Press, 1990. 90–105.

Sellars, Wilfrid. *Science, Perception and Reality.* Atascadero, CA: Ridgeview, 1991.

Shakespeare, William. *Hamlet: The Texts of 1603 and 1623.* Ed. Ann Thompson and Neil Taylor. London: Bloomsbury, 2014.

Shooter, Jim (writer), John Byrne, and Pablo Marcos (artists). *The Avengers* #165 (November 1977), Marvel.

———. *The Avengers* #166 (December 1977), Marvel.

Shooter, Jim, Roger Stern (writers), George Pérez, and Pablo Marcos (artists). *The Avengers* #167 (January 1978), Marvel.

Shooter, Jim (writer), George Pérez, and Pablo Marcos (artists). *The Avengers* #168 (February 1978), Marvel.

Shooter, Jim (writer), George Pérez (writer-artist), and Pablo Marcos (artists). *The Avengers* #170 (April 1978), Marvel.

Shooter, Jim (writer), Sal Buscema, and Klaus Janson (artists). *The Avengers* #171 (May 1978), Marvel.

Shooter, Jim (writer), Sal Buscema, and Klaus Janson (artists). *The Avengers* #172 (June 1978), Marvel.

Shooter, Jim, David D. Michelinie (writers), Sal Buscema, and D. Hands (artists). *The Avengers* #173 (July 1978), Marvel.

Shooter, Jim, Bill Mantlo (writers), David Wenzel, and Pablo Marcos (artists). *The Avengers* #174 (August 1978), Marvel.

Shooter, Jim, David Michelinie (writers), David Wenzel, and Pablo Marcos (artists). *The Avengers* #175 (September 1978), Marvel.

———. *The Avengers* #176 (October 1978), Marvel.

Shooter, Jim (writer), David Wenzel, Pablo Marcos, and Ricardo Villamonte (artists). *The Avengers* #177 (November 1978), Marvel.

Siegel, Jerry (writer). *Tales of the Bizarro World.* New York: DC, 2000.

Siegel, Jerry (writer), and Joe Shuster (artist). *The Superman Chronicles.* Vol. 1. New York: DC, 2006.

———. *The Superman Chronicles.* Vol. 2. New York: DC, 2006.

Steibel, Robert. "I'm Gonna Open Sealed Door to Negative Zone!" *Comics Journal.* September 30, 2013. Tcj.com. December 7, 2015.

Steranko, Jim (artist-writer). *Captain America* #111 (March 1969), Marvel.

Sturgeon, Theodore. *The Complete Stories of Theodore Sturgeon.* Vol. 1. Ed. Paul Williams. Berkeley, CA: North Atlantic Books, 1994.

"superhero." *Oxford English Dictionary Online.* Oxford University Press, June 2015. October 8, 2015.

Swan, Curt, and Eric Shanower (artists). Cover. *The Legend of Aquaman* #1 (May 1989), DC Comics.

Tallon, Philip, and Jerry L. Walls. "Why Not Live in the Holodeck?" *Star Trek and Philosophy: The Wrath of Kant.* Ed. Jason T. Eberl and Kevin S. Dicker. Peru, IL: Open Court, 2008. 161–72.

Thomas, Roy. "The Thing about *Man-Thing.*" *Alter Ego* 81 (October 2008): 20–28.

Thomas, Roy, ed. *The Heap.* Vol. 1. Kingston-upon-Hull: PS Artbooks, 2012.

Thomas, Roy (writer), John Buscema, and George Klein (artists). *The Avengers* #56 (September 1968), Marvel.

Thomas, Roy (writer), John Buscema, and Chic Stone (artists). *Fantastic Four* #160 (July 1975), Marvel.

Thomas, Roy (writer), John Buscema, and Sam Grainger (artists). *Fantastic Four Annual* #11 (1976), Marvel.

Thomas, Roy (writer), and Sal Buscema (artist). *Marvel Two-in-One* #20 (October 1976), Marvel.

Thomas, Roy, Gerry Conway (writers), and Gray Morrow (artist). "Man-Thing!" *Marvel Firsts: The 1970s.* Vol. 1. New York: Marvel, 2012.

Thomas, Roy (writer), Jim Craig, and Pablo Marcos (artists). "What if Spider-Man Had Joined the Fantastic Four?" 1977. *What If? Classic.* Vol. 1. New York: Marvel, 2004.

Thomas, Roy, Dann Thomas (writers), and Tom Mandrake (artist). *Shazam: The New Beginning* #1 (April 1987), DC.

Thomas, Roy, Dann Thomas (writers), Paul Ryan, and Danny Bullandi (artists). *Avengers West Coast* #61 (August 1990), Marvel.

Tittle, Peg. *What If . . . Collected Thought Experiments in Philosophy.* New York: Routledge, 2005.

Tupper, E. Frank. *The Theology of Wolfhart Pannenberg.* Philadelphia: Westminster, 1973.

US District Court Southern District of New York. "Marvel v. Kirby." July 28, 2011. *Hand of Fire: The Comics Art of Jack Kirby.* December 7, 2015.

Wein, Len, Chris Claremont, Steve Gerber, Bill Martio, Mary Skrenes, Tony Isabella, Tim Starlin, and Don McGregor (writers). *Essential Defenders.* Vol. 2. New York: Marvel, 2006.

Wein, Len (writer), Jim Starlin, and Joe Sinnott (artists). *Marvel Feature* #11. *Marvel Firsts: The 1970s.* Vol. 2. New York: Marvel, 2012.

Wein, Len (writer), and Bernie Wrightson (artist). *Roots of the Swamp Thing.* New York: DC, 2009.

Whitehead, Alfred North. *Process and Reality: An Essay in Cosmology.* 1929. Ed. David Ray Griffin and Donald W. Sherburne. New York: Free Press, 1978.

Williams, Bernard. *Moral Luck.* New York: Cambridge University Press, 1981.

———. "Postscript." *Moral Luck.* Ed. Daniel Statman. Albany: State University of New York Press, 1993.

Witek, Joseph. "Comics Modes: Caricature and Illustration in the Crumb Family's *Dirty Laundry.*" *Critical Approaches to Comics.* Ed. Matthew J. Smith and Randy Duncan. New York: Routledge, 2012. 27–42.

Wittgenstein, Ludwig. *Philosophical Investigations.* 1958. Trans. G. E. M. Anscombe. New York: Basil Blackwell, 1986.

Wolf, Mark J. P. *Building Imaginary Worlds: The Theory and History of Subcreation.* Hoboken, NJ: Taylor and Francis, 2014.

Wolfman, Marv (writer), Sal Buscema, and Dave Hunt (artists). *The Avengers* #169 (March 1978), Marvel.

Wolfman, Marv (writer), and George Pérez (artist). *History of the DC Universe: Book One* (1986), DC.

Zub, Jim (writer), and Steve Cummings (artist). *Wayward*, vol. 1: *String Theory.* Berkeley, CA: Image, 2015.

INDEX